RELICS OF DEATH IN VICTORIAN LITERATURE AND CULTURE

Nineteenth-century Britons treasured objects of daily life that had once belonged to their dead. The love of these keepsakes, which included hair, teeth, and other remains, speaks of an intimacy with the body and death, a way of understanding absence through its materials, which is less widely felt today. Deborah Lutz analyzes relic culture as an affirmation that objects held memories and told stories. These practices show a belief in keeping death vitally intertwined with life – not as memento mori but rather as respecting the singularity of unique beings. In a consumer culture in full swing by the 1850s, keepsakes of loved ones stood out as nonreproducible, authentic things whose value was purely personal. Through close reading of the works of Charles Dickens, Emily Brontë, Alfred Lord Tennyson, Thomas Hardy, and others, this study illuminates the treasuring of objects that had belonged to or touched the dead.

DEBORAH LUTZ is Associate Professor of Victorian Literature and Culture at Long Island University, C. W. Post Campus. She is the author of *Pleasure Bound: Victorian Sex Rebels and the New Eroticism* (2011) and *The Dangerous Lover: Gothic Villains, Byronism, and the Nineteenth-Century Seduction Narrative* (2006).

CAMBRIDGE STUDIES IN NINETEENTH-CENTURY
LITERATURE AND CULTURE

GENERAL EDITOR
Gillian Beer, *University of Cambridge*

Editorial board
Isobel Armstrong, *Birkbeck, University of London*
Kate Flint, *Rutgers University*
Catherine Gallagher, *University of California, Berkeley*
D. A. Miller, *University of California, Berkeley*
J. Hillis Miller, *University of California, Irvine*
Daniel Pick, *Birkbeck, University of London*
Mary Poovey, *New York University*
Sally Shuttleworth, *University of Oxford*
Herbert Tucker, *University of Virginia*

Nineteenth-century British literature and culture have been rich fields for interdisciplinary studies. Since the turn of the twentieth century, scholars and critics have tracked the intersections and tensions between Victorian literature and the visual arts, politics, social organization, economic life, technical innovations, scientific thought – in short, culture in its broadest sense. In recent years, theoretical challenges and historiographical shifts have unsettled the assumptions of previous scholarly synthesis and called into question the terms of older debates. Whereas the tendency in much past literary critical interpretation was to use the metaphor of culture as "background," feminist, Foucauldian, and other analyses have employed more dynamic models that raise questions of power and of circulation. Such developments have reanimated the field. This series aims to accommodate and promote the most interesting work being undertaken on the frontiers of the field of nineteenth-century literary studies: work that intersects fruitfully with other fields of study such as history, or literary theory, or the history of science. Comparative as well as interdisciplinary approaches are welcomed.

A complete list of titles published will be found at the end of the book.

RELICS OF DEATH IN VICTORIAN LITERATURE AND CULTURE

DEBORAH LUTZ

CAMBRIDGE
UNIVERSITY PRESS

CAMBRIDGE
UNIVERSITY PRESS

University Printing House, Cambridge CB2 8BS, United Kingdom

One Liberty Plaza, 20th Floor, New York, NY 10006, USA

477 Williamstown Road, Port Melbourne, VIC 3207, Australia

4843/24, 2nd Floor, Ansari Road, Daryaganj, Delhi - 110002, India

79 Anson Road, #06-04/06, Singapore 079906

Cambridge University Press is part of the University of Cambridge.

It furthers the University's mission by disseminating knowledge in the pursuit of
education, learning and research at the highest international levels of excellence.

www.cambridge.org
Information on this title: www.cambridge.org/9781107434394

© Deborah Lutz 2015

First published 2015
Reprinted 2016
First paperback edition 2017

A catalogue record for this publication is available from the British Library

Library of Congress Cataloging in Publication data
Lutz, Deborah.
Relics of Death in Victorian Literature and Culture / Deborah Lutz.
pages cm
Includes bibliographical references and index.
ISBN 978-1-107-07744-7 (Hardback) – ISBN 978-1-107-43439-4 (Paperback)
1. English literature–19th century–History and criticism. 2. Death in literature.
3. Relics in literature. 4. Literature and society–Great Britain–History–19th century.
I. Title.
PR468.D42L88 2014
820.9'3548–dc23
2014032221

ISBN 978-1-107-07744-7 Hardback
ISBN 978-1-107-43439-4 Paperback

For Mindy Duncan Lutz
April 20, 1971 – March 12, 2007
and
Stella Lutz
February 1996 – May 25, 2007

But such a tide as moving seems asleep,
Too full for sound and foam,
When that which drew from out the boundless deep
Turns again home.

—Tennyson

Contents

Illustrations

Acknowledgments

This book emerged over many years, and numerous individuals helped it finally come into fit form. To Talia Schaffer and Elaine Freedgood I owe a deep debt for their generous support of this book in its many stages and incarnations. Their ideas helped shape the project from early on, and their feedback on chapters was brilliant and in every way essential. I am blessed to be a member of a writing group of Victorianists who tirelessly and enthusiastically read much of this book: my gratitude to Carolyn Berman, Caroline Reitz, Tanya Agathocleous, Adrienne Munich, and, as always, to Talia. I am grateful to Robert Douglas-Fairhurst for his unfailing kindness and for believing in this project. Thanks for welcoming me to Oxford, for those many meals, and for arranging for me to speak at Magdalen about relics. Many in the English faculty shared their ideas and gave of their time – especially Stefano Evangelista and Sally Shuttleworth – and thanks to the Victorian Research Seminar for letting me try out my Brontë chapter on them.

Many friends and colleagues read proposals and drafts. Thanks to Benjamin Friedman, for his deft editing; James Bednarz, for his many kinds of support; Eve Kosofsky Sedgwick (always missed), who provided the seeds for the project in conversation and whose shadow lurks at the back of all of these words; Jeff Dolven, for the notion of "representational removes"; Greg Maertz, for fellowship advice; Duc Dau; Herb Sussman; John Maynard; Melissa Dunn; Sean O'Toole; Martha Stoddard Holmes; Tom Fahy; Kristofer Widholm; Francesca Simkin; Gerhard Joseph; and Pam Thurschwell. The Victorian Seminar at the CUNY Graduate Center provided essential feedback on an early incarnation of this project, especially Anne Humpherys, and part of the Dickens chapter got an airing and comments at the yearly Victorian Conference. I have been lucky to have the encouragement and assistance of John Kucich, Will Fisher, and Maggie Nelson.

This book would not have been possible without the kindness I have received from curators, librarians, and staff at libraries, archives, and museums. Tim Moreton at the National Portrait Gallery, London, brought out of storage many death masks and spent an afternoon with me looking at them and talking them over. His great generosity and largeness of spirit were foundational for this project, as was his vast knowledge of British portraiture and its place in nineteenth-century literature. Thanks to the charming Elizabeth C. Denlinger at the Carl H. Pforzheimer Collection of Shelley and His Circle, The New York Public Library, for sharing her interest in objects and for showing me many relics of the Romantic poets. Across the hall at the Henry W. and Albert A. Berg Collection, Isaac Gewirtz, Joshua McKeon, and Lyndsi Barnes set out many personal effects for me to turn over, sniff, shift about. Sarah Laycock and Ann Dinsdale at the Brontë Parsonage Museum, Haworth, West Yorkshire, brought hundreds (literally) of objects out of store and let me handle them in their quiet library. Heather Millard at the Manor House Museum and Art Gallery, Castle Yard, Ilkley, went out of her way to be informative and welcoming. She pored over things in the Bradford archive with me, sent me photographs, and was as generous as can be with her time and expertise. Kathryn Jones at the Royal Collection and Alexandra Barbour at Windsor Castle unearthed teeth jewelry from Frogmore for me. Bruce Barker-Benfield of the Bodleian Library helped with Shelley relics and books bound in human skin, and he gave me a warm welcome to Oxford and its collections. Thanks to John Vincler and Maria Isabel Molestina at the Morgan Library and to Susan Halpert and Leslie Morris and other staff who welcomed me at the Houghton, Harvard. Suzanne Canally, Librarian at the Senate House Library, University of London, told me about many relics in London. Thanks also to Lisa Darms and Charlotte Priddle at the Fales Collection, New York University.

To the staff and curators at the following collections I give my thanks for hosting me and fulfilling requests. In the UK: the British Library, especially Rachel Stockdale; the Victoria and Albert Museum, in particular Esther Ketskemety; the British Museum, especially Virginia Smithson; the Wellcome Collection; the National Maritime Museum; the Keats House Museum; the Hunterian Museum; the Foundling Museum; the Freud Museum; the Charles Dickens Museum; the Sir John Soane Museum; the Museum of London; the Florence Nightingale Museum; Westminster Abbey; Apsley House; Highgate Cemetery; and the Pitt Rivers Museum. In the United States the New York Public Library's Rose Main Reading

Room, the General Research Division, the Art and Architecture Library, and the Photography Collection; Butler Library, Columbia University; Bobst Library, New York University; the Thomas J. Watson Library, the Metropolitan Museum of Art; and the Mütter Museum, Philadelphia. Other places: the Keats-Shelley House, Rome; the Sigmund Freud Museum, Vienna; the Kunstgewerbemuseum, Berlin; and the Treasury in St. Mark's Basilica, Venice.

For ideas discussed over drinks, coffee, dinner, and e-mail I am grateful to Marcia Pointon, especially for sending me lists of books about death, for conversations about death masks, and for her gorgeous writing about hair jewelry; David McAllister, for his invitation to speak about death masks at Birkbeck; Sharon Marcus, for her thoughts about hair, scrapbooks, and albums; Wayne Koestenbaum; Domenick Ammirati; Jean Mills; Rachel Szekely; Cara Murray; Sina Najafi at *Cabinet*; Roland Albrecht and Marianne Karbe, of the Museum der Unerhörten Dinge, Berlin; and Tony Sebok, for being sure this book would make it. To Deborah Rubin, my gratitude for shaping profoundly my writing life. I am grateful for the affection of my family: Pamela, Sandy, Doug, Veronica, and Leroy.

At Long Island University, thanks to John Lutz, Dean Katherine Hill-Miller, and Robin Marshall. At the library, I thank the ILL staff, especially Claudette Allegrezza, and the periodicals staff, in particular Barbara Parascandolo. A grant from the LIU Post Faculty Research Committee provided funds for the illustrations.

Parts of Chapters 2 and 4 were first published in *Victorian Literature and Culture* 39.1 (2011), 127–142. A section of Chapter 2 appeared originally in *NOVEL: A Forum on Fiction* 45.3 (2012), 389–408 and is reprinted by permission of Duke University Press. In addition, an article in *Cabinet Magazine* 12 (2003), 12–15, was worked into Chapter 5.

A grant from the ACLS Fellowship Program of the American Council of Learned Societies gave me leave time to write this book.

Introduction: lyrical matter

> For love is never without its shadow of anxiety.
> We have this treasure in earthen vessels.
>
> —George Eliot[1]

As Esther is dying, in Elizabeth Gaskell's *Mary Barton*, she grasps a locket containing her daughter's hair. She has worn it around her neck since the girl's death many years ago, and now she touches it to her lips once or twice just before she dies. A series of gestures can be traced here. The first is the cutting of the tress, possibly postmortem. Wearing the encased fragment against her body, hidden by her clothing and tucked into her "bosom," Esther doubly conceals the relic but also carries it into the public thoroughfare of her days. The dying kiss, a third gesture, regenerates links to the dead, bringing forth the specter of reunion in the afterlife. The tender action might have the opposite meaning: perhaps the kiss is an affirmation of the final parting. Although Gaskell presents a dramatic picture of such performances, what she describes was a commonplace series of rituals used to remember the dead during the Victorian period.

The dead body's materiality held a certain enchantment for Victorians, a charmed ability to originate narrative. Bodies left behind traces of themselves, shreds that could then become material for memories. Such vestiges might be found in objects the body had touched as it advanced through existence: clothing worn, letters written, utensils handled. The hands may have formed matter into a work of art, or a more ordinary possession, depositing some mark of its maker. More concretely, the body itself or its parts functioned for the Victorians as mementos: the snippet of hair made into jewelry or even a bone or desiccated organ kept in a special container. Less tangibly, the body – its presence, then absence – could be felt in spaces it had inhabited, such as rooms, houses, or spots in nature. Although these "substances" fall in disparate registers – a room and a portion of skin, for example, have widely different legal, ethical, and

I

religious statuses – they all share the capacity to be marked by or *to be* the physical presence of a beloved or revered individual. Central to this study is the body as a material thing that affects other material things. Corporeality, for many Victorians, lent the resonance of subjectivity to objects, laded them with leavings of the self. Part of this understanding of the body-as-thing was informed by the desire to find in and through these keepsakes an active, revivified love for that individual now dead.

Integral to the exploration of the "thingness" of the body is the influence on corporeality (and on "things" of all sorts) of Victorian death culture. The cultural forces that played a part in the various, and changing, attitudes toward death in the era range from philosophical to aesthetic to religious. Romantic individualism and sentimentalism, carried into the later nineteenth century, gave artifacts a more personal character; they leant to death-inflected mementos a quality of transmitting selfhood. The Evangelical revivals of the 1830s and 1840s, which were heavily influenced by Romanticism's focus on emotionalism, popularized the idea of the "good death," a set of beliefs that gave the corpse and its offshoots an illumination, a vitality, reflected from that shining afterlife where the individual was believed to have gone. Spiritualists, in a movement beginning in the 1850s, felt that the dead still lingered among the living and that the materiality of these spirits – and their imprint on matter, substance, and space – proved it. Even Victorian atheists, especially in the late nineteenth century, located in the mortal passage and its embodiment a conviction that our objecthood defined our selfhood at all stages of existence. Death culture therefore shaped the Victorian understanding of the body as a revered object.

The Victorian representation of the cadaver as a special type of information- and emotion-laden artifact also influenced – and was influenced by – the literary. The body and the book intersected. This sometimes happened with a palpable literalness: a lock of hair, a pinch of cremation ash, or even a mummified organ was kept between the covers of a book. A volume was bound in the skin of an individual. Yet, more commonly, this intersection happened figuratively. Personal effects could act as "repositories" for stories about the past, or for lyrical memories. Matter stood in for lived presence, for the narrative of a body. As such, these mementos are the material objects that beg to be "read" more than, arguably, any other objects. They sometimes wore their use on their very surface – like a wooden toy smoothed by handling, chipped with incident – and thus they became texts to be deciphered. Postmortem art, such as death masks, saved a moment in the chronicle of being. The literariness of remains was often enhanced by their aestheticization. They were usually framed within jewelry or cases – sometimes inscribed – as if they were bound books or formally structured poems. From mortality and its residue sparked narrative, and thus did stories emerge from mementos, just as moving life fossilized into these final representations, these objects that had once been subjects.

Death keepsakes could be literary, but literature of the period also often featured such mementos, as subjects for poetry or as tropes in plots. Moreover, some of the texts discussed in these pages had a direct influence on Victorian death culture and its relationship to the body, such as the novels of Dickens and Tennyson's *In Memoriam*. Other writers subtly developed commonplace ideas about mortality and materiality found in the larger culture of the nineteenth century, such as John Keats, Emily Brontë, Dante Gabriel Rossetti, and Thomas Hardy, thus giving us a more complex understanding of the use of physical memorials. In the following pages novels and poetry are read as a means to understand the relic culture they elucidate, just as relics are "read" to theorize their begetting of signs, tales, and lyricism. The former method borrows from the well-established practice of material culture criticism. Elaine Freedgood has described the task of the material culturist in reading "nonsymbolic objects" in Victorian novels. Such interpretation "involves taking a novelistic thing materially or literally and then following it beyond the covers of the text through a mode of research that proceeds according to the many dictates of a strong form of metonymic reading."[2] Thing theory also tells us that poems and novels themselves can be understood as relic-like; this is part of the project of thinking about how and why relics were treated by Victorians like poems and novels.[3] Corpses, texts, stories, and poems interknit; they inform us of Victorian practices of making meaning in the face of – and *with the face of* – death.

Although the following chapters continue an exploration of what James Curl has called "the Victorian celebration of death," but with a more material inflection, they also ask what thing theory has to tell us about attitudes toward the body, and particularly the corpse, during the period. In other words, how can thing theory help us develop a better understanding of death culture in the era? Furthermore, how might the study of material culture itself be transformed when it is brought to bear on relic culture? As one of our most important proponents for theories of material culture, Bill Brown makes the case that "granting the physical world its alterity is the very basis for accepting otherness as such."[4] Granting the corpse and its oddments a place in living narrative is a means to recognize the singularity and irreplaceability of all individuals, their incommensurable otherness. Approaching this idea from another direction, we see that such objects shift our understanding of all objects during the period. As commodities became ever more symbolic by the middle of the nineteenth century, as the object lost its quality as the "thing itself" and became increasingly mediated by its role as a market "good," the death memento held onto its immediacy. Corporeal keepsakes, having no "use value," kept the thing as thing enchanted. A lively memento culture respects the object's magic.

Although this book is about nineteenth-century British death culture, Chapter 1 begins an argument that weaves through all the chapters: the materiality of this culture has a steady and broad historical connectedness to the relics of the Catholic cult of saints. This continuity is signaled by using the term "secular relics" to refer to the objects that are at the center of this study. The word _relic_ derives from the Latin plural "reliquiae," which means "remains."[5] The remnant of a body and its movements, relics of the sacred or secular kind gain their meaning from physical intimacy. What makes a relic a relic is its closeness not only to a once-alive human body, but also to a still-alive body that venerates its tactility. A relic, as the Catholic faith defines it, can be primary (also called first class), meaning an actual organic part of the body, such as a finger bone or hair. A secondary or second-class relic has been in contact with a body and might contain residue of it, such as blood, sweat, or tears. Things that prove embodiment, that have the texture of a life lived: these are relics. The Catholic worship of dead corporeality had its secular counterpart in a highly personal "religion" that became increasingly prevalent by the end of the eighteenth century. Unlike the saints' relics, however, which are venerated by many, the mementos under discussion held their significance because a handful of people, or even just one, loved the individual donor of them. Although this study brings religion into its reading of these objects, it privileges what might be called a "lyrical" reading of them. For secularists, Catholic relics can have a certain poetry about them. Gazing on an ancient vial filled with what is said to be Jesus's tears can have a deep poignancy. With what longing and hope have the faithful over centuries imbued this little historical residue? Without believing in the authenticity of the object, let alone the miraculous abilities ascribed to it, we can still feel the dialectics of imagination and enchantment that enriched this passion for corporeal tokens. These lumps of matter, set in their whimsical or nightmarish narratives, have dreamlike qualities. If one were to dream of objects, one might imagine they could levitate, fill a room with perfume, begin to bleed or cry, or suddenly become as heavy as a boulder in a desire not to be moved. With their magic, saints' relics are some of the earliest and most powerful Western fetishes – devitalized substance that seems to yet house a soul or an animating spark. Matter, for medieval Catholics, was fertile, "maternal, labile, percolating, forever tossing up grass, wood, horses, bees, sand, or metal," according to Caroline Walker Bynum.[6] No other objects are, arguably, more infused with the special "thingness" the material culturalist studies: with ideas, with interiority, with the metaphysical. "Thing theory" should always start here.

Connecting nineteenth-century British death culture to the distant past is, however, only one project of this book. Pointing to another historical continuity, one that looks forward to twentieth-century attitudes toward death and its materiality, the afterword argues that most aspects of Victorian relic culture disappeared after the Great War. As belief in an afterlife became less and less common, as death became increasingly a medical problem, to be dealt with by science and hospitals, and as the fear of death became so overwhelming that death was something to be denied, the dead body was often treated as an object of loathing. With the rise of secularism, privatization, and medicalization in the late nineteenth century, the slide toward what Diana Fuss has called the death of death had begun.[7] No longer was it common practice to hold onto the remains of the dead. Rarely would a lock of hair be kept, to be worn as jewelry, nor did one dwell on the deathbed scene, linger on the lips of the dying to mark and revere those last words, record the minutiae of slipping away in memorials, diaries, and letters. Rooms of houses were increasingly less likely to hold remains; no one had died in the beds in which the living slept.

The dematerialization and disembodiment of death's mementos – of secular relics of all sorts – occurred also because of changes in technology. In the Victorian era, and for many centuries before it, the written words of a loved or revered one, for example, were still usually holographic. The telegraph, the telephone, the typewriter: these would, starting in the late nineteenth century, largely replace holography. The manuscript references in its very etymology the hand that wrote it. Handwritten texts – such as correspondence, journals or diaries, or professional writing of whatever sort (such as a novel) – become relics of a special kind. The paper may have been chosen by the author of the text. The writer, especially of letters, would often record not only when the text was written, but also from whence, giving not only town or city, but sometimes the name of the abode or inn. Thus steeped in the details of time and place, these artifacts embody specificity – a kind of singular localism. Moreover, the ink that scored the page might be unique, and handwriting has come to be connected inextricably with the character of the "hand" and the identity of the writer. Many of these documents contain a signature – an incommensurable trace of legal selfhood. Their franking and traveling through the postal system further establishes letters as recorders of individual experience in a historical place and time. Added to these elements that make these documents authentic, irreplaceable artifacts is the status of the pages as contact relics. The actual skin swept the paper, handled it, inscribed it, possibly folded it (not to mention, to return for a moment to saints' relics, wet it with tears, sweat, or, to be dramatic, blood). Letters could contain other types of mementos; they might be relics with further relics inside them. To give a literary example, in Thomas Hardy's 1892 serialized version of *The Well-Beloved* (then called "The Pursuit of the Well-Beloved"), he begins with a chapter called "Relics." The main character sits in front of his fire at midnight, in his London rooms. He is burning personal papers, among them "several packets of love-letters, in sundry hands."[8] When he throws one on the fire, the flames illuminate the handwriting, "which sufficiently recalled to his knowledge her from whom that batch had come" (216). As the room teems with the ghostly presence of the lover who is long gone, represented by her recognizable "hand" on the pages, "suddenly there arose a little fizzle in the dull flicker: something other than paper was burning. It was hair – *her* hair" (217). He had forgotten that he had placed her curl in the envelope with her letter. "'Good heavens!' said the budding sculptor to himself. 'How can I be such a brute? I am burning *her* – part of her form . . . I cannot do it'" (217). A first-class relic nested in a second-class one, her tress evokes her body; her handwritten letter calls up her character. Both can represent her so completely to him that to destroy the packet can feel like annihilating her. A simple way for us to contrast the different understanding the Victorians had of death's ability to infuse materiality is to compare the artifact Hardy's character burns to the majority of the correspondence written from the late twentieth century onward. Letters became increasingly delocalized and stripped of corporeal connection. For instance, e-mails can't contain a tress of hair, a fragment of cloth, a pressed flower; they have no interiority. By the end of the twentieth century, postmortem written remains rarely were touched by disappeared flesh.

As these examples clarify, this history of secular relic love – which reached its height of popularity in the Victorian period and then its decline by World War I – intertwines with a history of the technology of memory or recording devices. Written descriptions are only one means to hold onto the physicality of the dead. Speaking more materially, the remembrance of the countenance, appearance, and feel of a person was often preserved through drawings, miniatures, paintings, and life or death masks, for the few who could afford such things. Little everyday items had an especially poignant weightiness in the many centuries before more modern recording devices. Clothing, hair, teeth, and characteristic possessions such as a favorite drinking cup became indexical reminders of the body, which had no other concrete means of being carried on into future eras. Rather paradoxically, it was when the most important technology for such recording – photography – came into common use that the popularity of traditional material technologies reached their height. Eventually, photography would come to largely replace relic culture. Just as it was leaving and would soon be mostly obsolete, relic cherishing had its decadence. For a time, photography existed alongside and in conjunction with the older forms, as is taken up more fully in the afterword. It is precisely this transitional nature of the period that makes it the most compelling and consequential era in which to study material memorialization.

This distancing of death and its "thingness" that begins around the first decades of the twentieth century has been taken up by many twentieth- and twenty-first-century theorists and historians. Walter Benjamin is one such thinker who wrote often about what was lost as the nineteenth century became the twentieth. His influential theory of the aura has relevance to a history of death culture despite the fact that it emerges from a discussion of the nature of the "work of art." The aura of an artwork such as a painting consists of its "presence in time and space, its unique existence at the place where it happens to be."[9] As with the relic, the authenticity of the artwork resides primarily in its "testimony to the history which it has experienced."[10] Benjamin is referring to a more general type of history, one that involves larger units of people, whereas the keepsakes under discussion here testify to personal history. Nevertheless, there is nothing more "auratic," arguably, than death mementos; indeed, relics serve to define precisely what the concept of the aura means. When the mechanical reproduction of the work of art became available in the nineteenth century with, first, lithography, and then, more important, photography, the aura began to be fully appreciated just as it became ever rarer. Benjamin's central argument in the essay – the sense of heightened awareness and relishing of what is just slipping away – works equally well for the history of relic culture. The understanding and subsequent reverence for the aura of art and of death keepsakes came most pervasively only when it was endangered, in decay.[11]

Benjamin believed that turning away from death has led to the disappearance of the art of storytelling. Writing in the early 1930s, he called his contemporaries "dry dwellers of eternity" because "today people live in rooms that have never been touched by death."[12] Avoiding the sight of the dying, one misses the moment when life becomes narrative, when the meaning of life is completed and illuminated in its ending. Benjamin privileges the shared moment of death, when relatives, and even the public, gather around the dying to glean final words of wisdom, to know perhaps, in the end, the whole story. The historian Philippe Ariès describes a Christian account of the final ordeal of the deathbed when in the moment of death the salvation or damnation of the dying is determined, thus changing or freezing, for good, the meaning of the whole life.[13] Similarly, Victorian relic culture sees death, and the body itself, as the beginning of stories rather than their end.[14] Rather than denying death, the relic could help make apparent the terrible poignancy of the body becoming object; it could reenact that moment, again and again. Relic culture expressed a willingness to dwell with loss itself, to linger over the evidence of death's presence woven into the texture of life, giving that life one of its essential meanings.[15]

The past manifest

The story of Victorian relic culture, which includes in its plot the stirrings of widespread agnosticism and atheism, the rise of mechanical mementos in photography, and the fading of material embodiment with the growing commodity culture, can only be selectively told between the covers of one monograph. Death keepsakes had varied meanings to varied individuals and groups; a single relic might shift in significance depending on its viewer or possessor. Even to the individuals who most cherished it, the memento's expressiveness could be blunted or heightened over the years. Sometimes corpses and their leftovers appeared fearful or loathsome to Victorians; other times they were treated with indifference. Although these pages will touch on this larger range of emotions toward the physicality of the dead, they privilege the conventional reverencing – religious and secular – of remains. Texts, acts, and individuals who create excessive performances of such appreciation are also brought to the fore to understand the broader practice (Rossetti and the Pre-Raphaelites, for instance, and Brontë's representation in *Wuthering Heights*). Chapters are necessarily based on exemplary texts and objects; they represent a vast pool of instances and depictions of relic love. The depth and breadth of the relish for death's material markers can only be limned here.

One organizing principle of these chapters, and a concern behind the choice of texts and objects, is the shifting terrain of representation in the nineteenth century and the changing relations between language, image, and object. Eschatology played its part in these changes. In certain cases, it even transformed common acts of representation. In forming theories about relics and their texts, representational removes work as essential building blocks. "The thing itself," or the actual corpse and its parts, requires no removes. Body-part stories serve to situate attitudes toward remains and the meanings that seemed to be engrafted onto these fleshly fragments. Contact relics require stepping back one remove. Materials like clothing, paper, and wood represent "the thing itself" because they touched it, therefore also gaining a carapace of personhood. Postmortem art provides an explicit representation of the dying and the dead. Death masks, effigies, and other types of aestheticization picture and sometimes touch the thing itself. Expanding out from the corpse by several removes leads to the consideration of spaces that seemed, to Victorians, to be infused with corporeality, even when the cadaver and its remnants were no longer located there or even locatable. Yet caught up in the very notion of representation are questions of authenticity. A growing complication that can be seen most clearly with hair jewelry, but that affected death culture more broadly, the commodification that came with hairwork's popularity endangered its authenticity. When not infused with the aura of singularity, death keepsakes could become unmoored from their close relationship with one unique body, becoming unstable signs with a representational promiscuity. Just another replaceable, disposable thing among many such things, hair had a meaning that might be easily transferable. The afterword takes up the increasing devaluation of this "thing itself," as death lost much of its embodiment in the first decades of the twentieth century. Threaded throughout all these chapters is the literary representation of relics, with language located at a distant remove from pure objecthood. Words' association with eschatology and the function of narrative and poetry in embodied death are central concerns of this book. An inquiry made repeatedly throughout these pages: has the object, the story, the poem been enlivened by embodied tactility? And another: does representation remain tethered to the body and its materials?

A further subject that has such a deep momentousness to Victorian relic culture that it serves as a means to organize the following chapters is the distinction between religious and secular "readings" of materiality.

Romantic and Gothic constructions of the "beautiful death," a notion steeped in secular individualism, fomented a belief in the importance of the memory of the individual and the faith that their possessions could serve to keep some part of them enlivened, even if only in memory. However, intermingled with this need to hold onto the memory of the beloved was an anxiety that this matter might finally signify nothing and that death was simply meaningless annihilation. Unfolding this dialectic of doubt and its function in Victorian death culture leads to the evangelical "good death," which located in remains an afterlife that kept them enlivened, vigorous, and hence sources of consolation. With the Spiritualists, who took materiality as evidence of a Christian afterlife, the excessive need to replay repeatedly sensational manifestations of spirits' material substance exposed the instability of faith's hold over death culture (and Victorian culture more generally). This shadow of doubt marked already is found fully in atheistic views of perishing, which find in remains the possibly of representing pure loss rather than consolation. The seeping away of the faith that once played over relics could reduce remains to bald, blank things with the comfortless significance that beloved subjectivity turned into rotting matter.

Implicated in these arguments about representational layers and religion is the nature of subjectivity and its relationship to the other. Although the through-line analysis of this book centers on mementos of the dead and the why and how of their collecting, framing, and treasuring by those predeath, a subset of this larger argument includes the self imagining her own thingification in death. In other words, imaginatively locating some aspect of the beloved dead in matter can also involve being able to see oneself as becoming or being material. Envisioning one's own demise, one's self as a cadaver, and even seeing prefigurations of this state of becoming-object in the sequence of daily life are ways of thinking found in the texts of Victorian writers. Throwing oneself out into the object is not far from merging with another. The boundaries between self and other slip; discovering the other in materiality can be a means to both find and lose oneself. All selves disappear into mass imbued with temporality.

The following chapters are arranged along roughly chronological lines, an itinerary that maps historical changes in attitudes toward death, the body, and materiality. Ranging from the Romantics to the start of the twentieth century, the book's focus falls midcentury, the transitional time that most fully brought relic issues into popular discourse. Because the primary ideas of this book have their roots in eras before the Victorian period, some reaching back to more ancient practices of corpse veneration and deathways are necessary. Each chapter has its small loops back to earlier eras – particularly to the medieval cult of saints – just as each one flickers along a continuum of representations of death, from the cadaver to the literary. Although a literary-historical methodology is brought to bear on relic culture, such boundaries are, at times, set aside, an approach useful in locating small acts of intimacy that manage to burst out of neat categorizing. The secular version of these gestures became particularly legible during the Romantic era, the starting point for Chapter 1, when the personal effects and remains of nonreligious individuals began, in a broad fashion, to be treated as glowing with fetishistic value. Some of this secular relic love grew out of the celebrity or hero cult of the time, which contributed to, and emerged from, the radical individualism of Romanticism. One section of Chapter 1 thus examines the relic collecting of famous people and events, such as the craze for historical artifacts, like the soldiers' bones and pieces of clothing gathered after the Battle of Waterloo. This type of souvenir culture had the potential, though, to be at odds with the more private rites under discussion here. One aim of this book is to attempt, as much as possible, to recover what was essentially an intimate act – a communing with a dead loved one. Therefore, although celebrity souvenirs are scrutinized because they were the most visible form of material commemoration, more average rites of remembrance remain this study's primary interest. Because the longer history of relics is taken up in Chapter 1, its priority is corpse parts – the "things themselves": hearts, penises, hair. A gothic attraction to fragments, decay, and ruins has its place here. Readings of the poetry of John Keats and the Victorian Romantic Dante Gabriel Rossetti, two writers especially caught up in locating memories of the posthumous, are the fulcrum of this chapter. The "beautiful death" and other theorizations of last things are investigated through these poets and their contexts.

Another Victorian Romantic provides the focal point of Chapter 2: Emily Brontë and *Wuthering Heights*. Moving forward to the 1830s, 1840s, and early 1850s, Chapter 2 considers the sweeping influence of Evangelicalism on the Victorians. Brontë represents a certain extreme of Evangelical death culture in *Wuthering Heights*, which she entwines with a Romantic religion of love. Contact relics are central to this chapter, and a general shift is made from the relics of the famous to commonplace objects suffused with meaning by their closeness with the body and habits of a more unexceptional loved one. These keepsakes from any ordinary body had value only to a few people; their narratives trace histories of intimacy. Chapter 3 elucidates another aspect of Victorian death culture, one attentive to how living bodies can become thing-like or corpse-like when death is viewed as the natural backdrop to life's stories. Postmortem art is a key trope in the chapter, working as a means to think about representations of the posthumous both after death and before. This complex acceptance of death's ability to sway the living, to influence respect for the body as matter, is localized and analyzed in Dickens's novels, especially *Great Expectations*. Although Dickens promoted the evangelical "good death," he also found pleasure in thinking of bodies of all sorts – corpses and animated, talking flesh – as things, not so different from other mid-Victorian things. Thinking of the body as an object also points to more mundane types of death that happen every day, such as the potential for selves to become ossified in the midst of animation. All moments tend toward death, which is both the comedy and the tragedy of being.

Lingering still in the middle of the nineteenth century, Chapter 4 brings Tennyson's *In Memoriam* into the discussion. Elegies functioned in similar ways to shrines, as structures used to lament loss and to remember the absence of the body. Tennyson's desire to provide a "place" – the elegy – for Hallam to continue to dwell is linked with the practice of literary pilgrimages, especially popular during the mid-Victorian era. The play of faith and doubt integral to this entire study appears again with Tennyson's *In Memoriam*, which was used by many contemporaries as either consolation literature or as a means to think about religious uncertainty and its effect on mourning practices and their material nature. Chapter 5 extends the notion of religious doubt to the 1870s, 1880s, and 1890s with Hardy and the industry in hairwork. The most common type of secular relic during the Victorian period, hair snippets from the dead radiated with multiple meanings, but as the century came to a close, they increasingly became reminders of death's more bleak meaning, representing the vanished individual as lost and thus irreplaceable. Such specificity and singularity resisted efforts to subsume the relic and its referent into a general religious belief. Yet the worry that hair jewelry might be fraudulent – made of someone else's hair rather than that of the loved one – thus destroying its ability to provide proof of the singularity of individuality, became a fresh concern. Hair relics in Thomas Hardy's works, in particular *Far From the Madding Crowd*, are symbolic of the simple acceptance of the mortal passage as the fate of all objects. The afterword takes the story of relics to the end of the nineteenth century and the first few decades of the twentieth. New technologies of recording memories of the dead supplanted relics; remembrance no longer needed the body to be reenacted.

Putting aside the historical and literary for a moment, this book gives pride of place to these fragments of matter themselves. Poignant, humorous, and even absurd, these objects still glimmer with meaning after the many years that have passed; they teem with a past still profoundly relevant, thus attesting to the ability of materiality to stay animated and consequential. One of the central fears of death is, of course, to become a thing and nothing more, with no spirit, no personality, no afterlife. And then to have no one care that one has died. Yet this book revives stories in which matter can itself inspirit, can lead to further care and remembrance. This study gives them their due through description and narrative; these things bustle on these pages, turning this book into a speaking thing itself, a compendium of death's souvenirs. Relics can be disruptive of argument, narrative, and convention, but they can also knit them together, express them in their materiality. The following chapters perform this, functioning as a book of death and an object bristling with material liveliness.

CHAPTER I

Infinite materiality: Keats, D. G. Rossetti, and the Romantics

> In all shapes
> He found a secret and mysterious soul,
> A fragrance and a spirit of strange meaning.
>
> —William Wordsworth

The heart that wanders and speaks

Residing mutely among the manuscripts, books, and letters of the Pforz-heimer Collection at the New York Public Library, fragments of Percy Bysshe Shelley's skull appear like sections of veined, dried leaves, with a russet color and shaved so thin they are almost transparent (see Fig. 1).[1] To pore over them is to be filled with questions: is this truly bone from that historical body? If so, what meaning comes embedded in this corporeal trace? Why would such a grisly reminder of annihilation, of a body lost forever, be cherished, kept, shown about? Curls of hair from the heads of Byron's mistress Teresa Guiccioli, Leigh Hunt's granddaughter, and Mary Shelley retain the softness and shine of living, tucked away in little envelopes with accompanying letters. When the pages of Shelley's red leather diary are rifled, a circle of seemingly just-cut hair (anonymous) slips out, sealed with black wax and a kind of crest with an esoteric code.[2] Little pieces of the bodies of the Romantic poets and their friends and lovers can be found, today, scattered about the world in archives, libraries, and museums (see Fig. 2). At the Keats-Shelley Memorial House in Rome, for instance, one can gaze on parts of Shelley's jaw, locks of Keats's hair, and a square, cut out by a servant, of the bed curtains that surrounded Byron's unhappy honeymoon bed. Keats's hair also gleams out of a ring in the Bodleian, Oxford, and so many people plucked violets and daisies from his grave in Rome, dried them, and placed them in books and envelopes that the gesture became a kind of tourist tradition.[3] More of what are reputedly Shelley's ashes are set behind glass (along with a lock of his hair

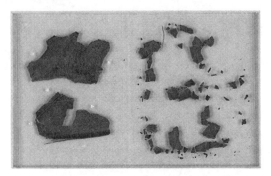

Figure 1. Shelley's skull fragments, reputedly collected by Trelawny after the cremation on the beach at Viareggio, 1822.

Figure 2. Gold brooch with the hair of John Keats made in Rome to Joseph Severn's design. This replica of the lyre on Keats's headstone is strung with his hair. K/AR/01/002, ca. 1822.

and one of Mary Shelley's) inside the front and back covers of a manuscript entitled *The Last Days of Percy Bysshe Shelley*, now at the British Library (see Fig. 3).[4] Yet the Romantics weren't the only group of "celebrities" that generated a relic culture: every substantial library or archive has a body part, a book bound in human skin, or fragments of hair stored away. In the shadow of the more carefully studied items whose meaning comes from words (manuscripts, letters, first editions) sit little objects that speak only through their presence, texture, and metonymic aura. Almost entirely overlooked by researchers as subjects of inquiry in their own right, these secular relics appear, if at all, only at the very end of lists of a collection's holdings, or recent acquisitions, catalogued under such vague terms as "realia," "personal effects," "ephemera," or "3-D objects."[5] This attests to the fact – which, perhaps, needs no such evidence – that such artifacts have lost much of the fetishistic magic they once had for the Romantics and Victorians. But it also begins to open a door – one that I want to step through in this book – into the shared space of body parts and the literary. Their profound relationship will be a central theme throughout these chapters.

The tale of Shelley's wandering heart calls up some of this old enchantment – an ancient intimacy with death – and the way that such fleshly things begot narrative (called, by Hermione Lee, "body-part stories").[6] The self-dramatizing and unreliable Edward Trelawny – a friend of Byron, the Shelleys, and the Leigh Hunts – told the story of Percy Bysshe's death and cremation many times over, changing the details with each retelling, shrouding the events with layers of embellishment and high romance.[7] With his friend Edward Williams and a young hired hand, Shelley set out on the *Don Juan*, on July 8, 1822, to cross the Gulf of Spezia. The boat went down in a storm, and their bodies were not found until ten days had passed, washed up on the shore and in badly decomposed states. Due to the requirements of the Italian quarantine authorities, the corpses were buried on the coast where they were found. Realizing that the only means to move them would be to cremate them, Mary Shelley, the widow, agreed to their destruction a few weeks after their first burial. Trelawny, Lord Byron, and Leigh Hunt arranged for a furnace to be constructed, and aided by Italian health officials, they attended the cremation, on the beach at Viareggio. Trelawny, the only one of the three who had the stomach to watch the burning, made of himself the key protagonist and hero of the scene. Hunt sat in Byron's carriage for much of the ordeal, and Byron swam off into the Gulf. In the version published in his *Records of Shelley, Byron, and the Author* (1878), Trelawny claims that, despite the fire being "so fierce as to produce a white heat on the iron, and to reduce its contents to gray ashes," Shelley's heart "remained entire." "In snatching this relic," Trelawny goes on, "from the fiery furnace, my hand was severely burnt."[8] An unpleasant disagreement ensued between Mary Shelley and Leigh Hunt over the possession of the organ, with Mary finally claiming ownership. Although most of Shelley's ashes were buried in Rome's Protestant cemetery, where Keats was interred, Mary carried the heart (or a small pile of ashes, according to some sources) back to England.[9] She kept whatever was left of the heart in a large-format, paper-bound copy of Shelley's *Adonais*, now at the Bodleian, in a page torn off and folded in four (some accounts note it was wrapped in silk).[10] (It is difficult to imagine the organ able to fit inside what is essentially a pamphlet – especially given that, as Trelawny claimed, Shelley's was an unusually large heart. It must have either become sufficiently withered and small by this time or was ashes from the start.) After Mary died, the heart was retained by their son, Percy Florence, and buried with him upon his death in 1889. Many of the activities and fantasies that developed around Shelley's remains call to mind the kind of reverence to be found in the Catholic cult of saints. His body parts were treated as miraculous (the heart so heavy with the fullness of meaning even flames couldn't destroy it), and legends arose about the materiality of his death (not only his body, but also the books and other items he carried on him on that last voyage). Those who adored him felt the need to have the power of possession, a power most potent in the act of giving (Trelawny, for example, gave bits of Shelley's bone and ash to friends and family members he particularly cherished).[11] The remains of the Romantic poets and the things they touched – and the bodies of so many famous and unknown individuals of the late eighteenth and nineteenth centuries – were, in a sense, sacralized, imbued with a passionate longing that gave them a strange sort of animation. Not only did death bring the tragedy of turning people into things – of subject into object – but it might also start inanimate objects to life, cause them to travel, move about, generate meaning.

In this chapter, I begin to address why the secular relic came to hold so much significance and to lead to so much action, thought, and writing. To open this discussion, I explore the shared history of the relics of saints and those of secular figures. The veneration of saints' leavings and the Romantic attentiveness to death's physical nature both involved finding in mortal remains an access to the eternal, the infinite. The Romantic idea of the "beautiful death" and the gothic fascination with death and corpses developed out of a long and varied history of ideas about the meaning and place of dying. Aestheticizing and eroticizing death happened through keeping and framing remains, such as Mary Shelley's storing her husband's heart in his elegy, but also through excavating the meaning of the end through words. The poem was another means to structure the chaos that death might bring. Relics in their "settings" and poetry in its tight arrangement of parts (words) shared formal qualities. Although this chapter examines Romantic poetry and ideas more broadly, its focus narrows to

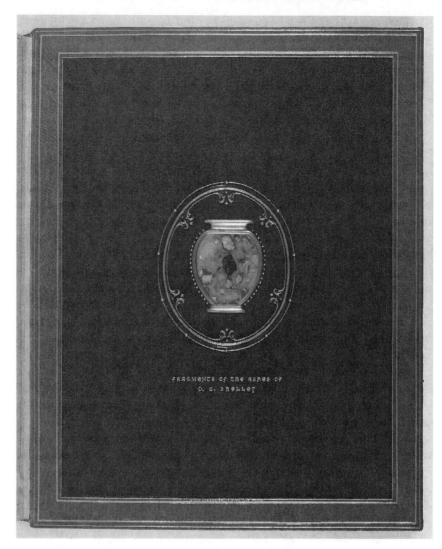

Figure 3. Shelley's ashes set in the back inside cover of *Percy Bysshe Shelley, His Last Days Told By His Wife, With Locks of Hair and Some of the Poet's Ashes.*

a few poems by Keats and their embodiment of the death of the self. These ideas are carried into the Victorian period by considering the poetry and, briefly, the art, of the late Romantic Dante Gabriel Rossetti, who with his fellow Pre-Raphaelites, was instrumental in spreading Keats's ideas and poetry (not to mention his relics) to a wide Victorian audience. Keats had a strong interest in relics and gothic notions about death, as did Rossetti after him. They engaged with the death culture of their time more than most, I will argue, and their ideas, writings, and art influenced Victorian views of death and its materiality.

The endless time of the body-as-thing

The wandering and dispersed nature of the corpse fragments of the famous men and women (and the possessions closely associated with them) of this Romantic circle is a continuation of such bodily meanderings that stretch back at least to early Christianity. In a practice well established by 400 AD, the saints' bodies and their precise locations (areas deemed "ad santos," or "near the tombs of the martyrs") became material sites where God intervened in human lives, according to believers, by a miraculous infusion into earthbound matter.[12] What would appear to be lifeless remains – dead meat, essentially – maintained a kind of numinous vitality. Not only were these talismans thought to be incorrupt, and thus not subject to the decay, rot, and earthly dissolution of all that is human, but also the saint was believed to be actually present at her tomb.[13] The fourth-century saint Gregory of Nyssa described the luminous aliveness of relics: "Those who behold them embrace, as it were, the living body in full flower."[14] A sixth-century tomb inscription speaks also of this: "Here lies Martin the bishop . . . whose soul is in the hands of God; but he is fully here, present and made plain in miracles of every kind."[15] Rather than the full stop of death, expressive like nothing else of temporal finality, the relic is "linked by a bond to the whole stretch of eternity," according to Victricius, the fourth-century Bishop of Rouen.[16] These little objects or shriveled corpses, suffused with limitless time, were thought to work miracles of healing on any humble soul who came in contact with them, like the dead man who comes to life, in II Kings 13:21, when he touches Elisha's bones. Joan Carroll Cruz recounts numerous "blood miracles," such as those reputedly arising from contact with St. Patricia's bleeding corpse, after her "translation" (the term used when saints' relics were moved) to Naples in 1549. A Roman knight in terrible pain opened her glass reliquary and drew a tooth from its socket. As red blood poured forth from her mouth, the story goes, the knight became cured of his bodily ills. When Saint Januarius's ancient, dried blood is brought close to a bust reliquary containing his head, believers claim that the blood turns back into liquid. When displayed by the Cardinal of Naples on feast days, the revivified liquid binds the witnesses to the divine, blessing them with an immortality they can share in, if only for a moment.[17] Relic worship has always been a deeply localizing practice, defined as a need to be close to, or touch, a set of precise material objects. *Hic locus est*: "here is the place." To spread the practice of Christianity, the saints' body parts were dispersed, fragmented into ever-smaller pieces, sometimes through open theft (the most celebrated example being the body of St. Mark, purloined from Alexandria to increase the prestige of a still-fledgling Venice).[18] Tales of wandering hearts – not so different from Shelley's – abound, as the organs have always symbolized the center of emotional power.[19] Hearts often had their own reliquary boxes, sometimes themselves shaped like hearts (vessels shaped like what they contain – such as leg, foot, arm, or rib reliquaries – are called "speaking reliquaries").[20] Some small reliquaries were made to be worn on the body, as jewelry or portable talismans (called *enkolpion* or *phylacteries*), to aid or protect the wearer with divine power.[21] Thus could the deanimated flesh still walk about, still be a part of a perambulatory narrative.

These receptacles remind us of the representational removes, mentioned in the introduction, always at work in body-part stories. The heart is *the thing itself*. Its box is often a jeweled representation of this immanent original, frequently inscribed with text authenticating the contents. A shrine or religious space such as a cathedral becomes a further encasement or representation. Poetry or other writing about such artifacts then draw us to an even further remove from the material object. Another way to think about this: the center of meaning resided in stuff and substance, in these historical fragments around which elaborate stories were spun. A contraction of this representational layering on (of) the dead body, one that will have important implications for Romantic and Victorian writing about death, can be found in certain medieval tales of miracles involving the branding or inscription of flesh itself. Caroline Walker Bynum recounts stories of stigmata appearing on the bodies of the faithful, from the twelfth to the sixteenth centuries, which were understood as types of inscription or carving done by the crucifix (seen as a writing instrument).[22] The legend of St. Francis of Assisi as told by St. Bonaventure details how the wounds of the crucifixion were "not imprinted on tablets of stone or wood by the hands of a craftsman, but marked on the members of his body by the finger of the living God."[23] Bynum describes late medieval devotional texts that depict Christ's body as a manuscript and the pen as a flail or a nail, with his blood as ink. The manuscripts that contained these images were themselves made of parchment – also skin.[24]

The material of the body became a text, and texts became representations of body parts. The miracle can reside in the intimacy of flesh with writing or in the way that inscription can make the body a thing not subject to the decay of substances, but rather "eternal."

To return now to the history of saintly and secular relics, which includes inscription on and about the body, the relic collecting of nonsaints that became common by the end of the eighteenth century was not, in the main, a religious practice. Although some forms of religious belief bolstered the cherishing of remains – such as Victorian evangelicalism, which will be explored in Chapter 2, and spiritualism, discussed in Chapter 4 – the ritual had largely pagan motives, especially for the Romantics. Nevertheless, the desire for secular body parts and other materials of death had its roots in the longings for the relics of the saints. One point of connection between these different historical practices comes from their shared genesis in a type of polytheism. Historians of early Christianity observe that the worship of saints in late antiquity was a continuation of the pagan desire to have a personal "god."[25] A walk through cities important to the cult, such as Rome or Venice, makes this notion perfectly clear – these churches are shrines to the lives and body parts of these historical figures; their link to the one Christian God is, arguably, tenuous. Such material "paganism" was a principal complaint that led Martin Luther to affix his text to the wooden door; relics being, to him, "all dead things."[26] Reformation and Enlightenment iconoclasm shifted much of the worship of the corpses of religious figures to secular ones. Another way to think about the larger history of relic culture is to understand it as a development away from an insubstantial, abstract godhead and toward the human, the local, and the material. Peter Brown argues that the roots of the late-antique and early medieval belief in the personal "patron saints" can be located in an earlier faith in having an "invisible friend" such as a *genius* or guardian angel. The close-knit chain that linked three elements in the past – the human, the nonhuman mediators, and the divine – began to change with the patron saint. Brown sees this as a transfer "to a dead human being [of] all the sense of intimate involvement with an invisible companion that men in previous generations had looked for in a relationship with the nonhuman figures of god ... or angels."[27] Although some form of secular relic veneration can be found from antiquity onward – coexisting with the cult of saints – it became more widespread and legible with the gradual decline in faith in the saints, most markedly in Britain with the Henrician Reformation, which started in 1533. The Enlightenment continued to dim this faith, and the healthy culture of secular relics in the eighteenth and nineteenth centuries was a further movement toward a belief in human intimacy and in the idea that love for one body might be sacralized: ideas we will find as structural notions in the poetry of Romantics and Victorians, especially Keats and Rossetti.

In late medieval Britain, a tradition of devotion to sacred relics and images thrived. Saints were "friends and helpers," Eamon Duffy notes, or, in the words of a contemporary, "kynd neyghbours, and of our kno-wyng."[28] Various saints moved in and out of fashion, and a town's own local saints and those connected to an individual's trade or guild especially flourished. A reliquary in Tavistock parish church, for instance, which contained the hair of the Blessed Virgin and of St. Mary Magdalene, gained more strands of hair from St. Katherine of Alexandria, who had risen in prominence, by the early sixteenth century.[29] When Henry VIII finally broke with Rome in 1533, he didn't at first see this as a step away from traditional religion. In fact, those who preached against the worship of relics, whether they be Lollards or the newer Lutherans, were still aggressively pursued as heretics in the late 1520s.

But the iconoclasm that had been growing throughout the 1520s gained ground with the support of sympathetic authorities after 1533, and when Thomas More, a great advocate of the cult of saints, was imprisoned in the tower in 1534, Thomas Cromwell had a wider field for his reforms. The royal visitations of the monasteries that began in July 1535 to root out the use of saints' cults and miracles to make money became a means to carry off relics and send them to Cromwell. From Bury St. Edmunds, for instance, came the saint's nail parings, St. Thomas Becket's penknife and boots, and the coals that roasted St. Laurence. From Bath Abbey was dispatched the combs of Mary Magdalen, St. Dorothy, and St. Margaret, along with a ligament of St. Petri, which women had carried to them and placed on their bellies when giving birth. The finger of St. Stephen, also coveted by women in childbirth, was stripped from Kelham.[30] The Pilgrimage of Grace in Yorkshire, along with other rebellions and general unrest, were punished severely, often by death. Cromwell's Injunctions of 1536 strongly prohibited the display and worship of relics. The dissolution of the monasteries and the dismantling of shrines continued throughout 1537 and 1538, bringing with them rebellions. A second set of injunctions issued by Cromwell in 1538 contained language more contemptuous of relics. Duffy explains that the reform varied greatly from region to region, from Nicholas Shaxton of Salisbury, who demanded that all relics be sent to him, "namely of stinking boots, mucky combs, ragged rochets, rotten girdles, pyld purses, great bullocks' horns, locks of hair, and filthy rags" to conservative dioceses where enforcement hardly existed.[31] Authorities destroyed many of the saints' relics in Britain by 1538, but some still existed, although their cults had been mostly annihilated.[32]

After Cromwell's fall in 1540 and King Henry's partial reversals of reform, the reign of Edward VI brought more radical measures, with the 1547 Injunctions ordering that any relics still existing be removed and destroyed. In 1552, the King's commissioners stripped churches of their treasures, especially objects made of precious metal such as reliquaries, many of which were melted down. Churches saved some by selling them to private individuals, who often kept them hidden and in the family, in anticipation of the royal visitations. Many of these found their way into museum collections in the nineteenth century.[33] Local people hid images and relics under church floors, walled them into niches or other parts of the church, or buried them on church grounds, in cemeteries, or in gardens. When churches and their grounds underwent restoration or renovation, or fell to ruin over time, such artifacts often came to light. The five years of Mary's reign starting in 1553 saw Catholicism restored in part, and in a few cases relics and their cults were reinstated, such as those of St. Wulfran in Grantham, Lincolnshire. Less than a year after Queen Elizabeth's accession in 1558, she issued a set of injunctions that abolished all devotion to saints, and the wardens in Grantham had to sell the silver and copper shrine for St. Wulfran's relics.[34] The visitations and suppressions during Elizabeth's reign, and the rise of the puritans, were broadly effective in stamping out the traditional cult of saints by the 1570s.[35]

Relic worship continued, however, with the body parts and personal effects of kings and queens, an ancient practice dating back to the Saxons and earlier. On occasion royals became full-fledged saints, with their own thriving cult, such as Henry VI, whose worn hat was put on by pilgrims to Windsor to heal their headaches. Thought to be connected to the divine, the flesh of kings and queens had a certain holiness about it and had the capability, it was widely believed, to cure illness with touch.[36] Yet much of the collecting of royal remains had secular motivations, specifically political ones (although the saints' relics were also manipulated for political power throughout their history). Mary Stuart wore red to her execution in 1587 to indicate her martyrdom, and her executioners cleaned away her blood for fear that supporters would collect some on fabric, to form relics.[37] When Charles I was beheaded in 1649 – martyred, many of his supporters thought – witnesses did succeed in soaking their handkerchiefs in his blood, and fragments of the scaffolding were sold.[38] Although some collectors of such talismans believed that these materials might bring them closer to God, as saints' relics could, and might even spark miracles, they didn't form around them shrines and pilgrimages after the cult of saints disappeared. Yet, like religious artifacts, they had a localizing quality: it is precisely these *things*, just *here*, that work as evidence. In these objects might be accessed, if only fleetingly, a kind of immortality, one linked to profound historical occurrences that would, people felt, never be forgotten.

Close kin to royal relics were what we might call "celebrity" personal effects. Moving further away from the sacred and toward the humanistic, the collecting of the body parts and personal possessions of famous statesmen, criminals, writers, artists, and historical figures increased when the saints' shrines, reliquaries and relics disappeared.[39] In a practice well established in Britain by the 1650s, the famous became the new patron, or personal, "saints."[40] Lorna Clymer explains how Oliver Cromwell's head, after having been exhumed in 1661 with the rest of his body and speared on poles set on top of Westminster Hall as a kind of symbolic punishment, became a "family relic" for a period, later traveling around Britain, displayed and exhibited, throughout the eighteenth, nineteenth, and twentieth centuries.[41] "Celebrity" relic collecting became an increasingly popular practice beginning in the late eighteenth century and continuing throughout the nineteenth century.[42] Péter Dávidházi traces the historical connections between the cult of saints and those of literary figures, using Shakespeare as his test case. He observes that "studying literary cults one can . . . find examples of barely secularized prayers . . . pilgrimages to sacred places, relic worship, the celebration of sacred times."[43] He finds numerous instances of Shakespeare being treated as a Christ-like figure beginning in the late eighteenth century. Pilgrims wanted to touch what Shakespeare had touched, and a system of authenticating Shakespeare relics was set up in the mid-nineteenth century by the trustees of the historical sites, much like the policing by the Church of the authenticity of saints' relics.[44] When Milton's body was exhumed in 1790, his teeth, a hand, parts of his jaw, and morsels of hair were snatched up and treated like relics. "While the prominence of his literary corpus was certainly increasing," Clymer explains, "Milton settled through synecdoche into many private collections where his dismembered body parts were, in the words of one nineteenth-century viewer of a rib supposedly Milton's, 'religiously preserved [as] precious relic[s].'"[45] Collectors wanted to own historical relics, such as soldiers' bones taken from the field after the Battle of Waterloo (Byron gathered some of these and had them shipped back to England), to give them the sense that they had played some role in these events, now vividly brought back to life in the souvenir. The collector could also feel that he or she authenticated the history or the existence of the celebrity, could affirm, "here is proof that it truly did happen or that she did exist." These relics show us the "capacity of objects to serve as traces of authentic experience," as Susan Stewart explains in her remarks on the poetics of souvenirs. The souvenir is "an object arising out of the necessarily insatiable demands of nostalgia."[46] Walter Scott's love of the things of the past followed this pattern, and his use of historical relics as a means to feel that past again was an important influence on others during this time. His collections at Abbotsford (amassed from 1812 until his death in 1832), which included such keepsakes as the crucifix carried by Mary Stuart to her execution, a portion of her gown, and James VI's hunting bottle (dating from 1600–1615), provided a model for reexperiencing history through materiality.[47] (Scott's immensely popular novels were also "collections" of a sort, and his readers felt touched by the historical past when reading of the old myths, ancient structures, and aged manuscripts incorporated into his stories.) As Susan Pearce remarks in her history of European collecting, historical objects and relics were "used as material witness to the truth of historical narratives."[48]

The increase in relic love that began in the late eighteenth century was due in part to a growing cult of personality, an emphasis on the heroic individual endemic to Romanticism and carried into the 1830s and '40s with the worship of such figures as the Duke of Wellington and Byron, whose death in 1824 did not end the fervent admiration for him by many young Victorian writers.[49] Mid-eighteenth-century Enlightenment thought that stretched into the nineteenth century also brought about a shift from allegiance to religious figures to national ones. One instance of a relic that represented the nationalism of the Enlightenment – an oddment that is difficult not to mention because of its symbolism of national potency and its popularity as a traveling display – was a long scrap of gristle claimed to be Napoleon's penis lopped off by the abbé who administered last rites.[50] (This wandering penis could be fruitfully compared to the half dozen or so fragments of flesh claimed to be Jesus' foreskin, also called the Holy Prepuce.) The Romantic poets themselves worshipped the relics of their heroes. Byron in particular felt his life intertwined with Napoleon and his virility (and his fame and notoriety); he made a replica of Napoleon's famous carriage to travel around Europe. Many of the Romantic poets recognized that they themselves, as national heroes, might become collectors' items. They believed in the centrality of the individual, and this led them to fix their eyes on posthumous fame, spurring them to carry the theme into their writing.[51]

Romantics such as Wordsworth, Shelley, and Keats imagined their own bodies becoming relics, and they set figurations for the death of their speakers (which were, in certain cases, themselves) within the unfolding of their poems. Andrew Bennett remarks that "one of the key motivations of the literary as it was conceived and defined in the Romantic period is the possibility of future, posthumous recognition or canonization."[52] He argues that, for the Romantics, "the function of writing is to achieve – in the sublime and impossible moment of inscription – immortality, posthumous life, life after death."[53] Wordsworth, for example, spent many years writing *The Prelude*, knowing that it wouldn't be published until after his death, as literary "remains." In "Tintern Abbey," Wordsworth works on the problem of how a poet could "remain in his remains . . . after his death."[54] Shelley, whose corpse parts (as we have seen) would come to be fragmented and to voyage abroad, much like the dispersed relics of saints, was interested in imagining poetic inspiration as a fragmentation of the poet's body. In "Ode to the West Wind," the speaker pictures his body martyred like Christ's: "I fall upon the thorns of life! I bleed!"[55] But through this martyrdom, the speaker's ideas, his words arranged in these stanzas, might be spread around the world, as the wild wind strews the leaves about, as its breath plays the lyre. "Oh! Lift me as a wave, a leaf, a cloud!" (line 53). The death of the body could lead to the miracle of a vaster inspiriting.

> Drive my dead thoughts over the universe
> Like withered leaves to quicken a new birth!
> And, by the incantation of this verse,
>
> Scatter, as from an extinguished hearth
> Ashes and sparks, my words among mankind! (lines 63–67)

The dissemination of remains are equated here with the posthumous scattering of poetic verse – one's words, one's formed and framed fragments. Somewhat like a reliquary, the stanzas arrange these fragments of sentiment into a glorifying receptacle, one that becomes easily portable, that can travel about like an organ. As we will see later, Keats also considered, in many of his poems, the inspiration of self-death as a beautiful moment linking the body – and materials touched by bodies – with infinity. And these poems become monuments to this enlivening principle of death: little objects themselves that spark an endlessness.

For these reasons (and others that will be explored in the following pages), holding onto parts of the corpses of literary figures became increasingly common, as if those wonderful texts they wrote might be reconstituted through their material selves, just as the miraculous and infinite might be felt through saints' corporality. Samantha Matthews examines the way that famous poets' bodies during the Romantic and Victorian periods seemed to "confirm the poet's uniqueness," and admirers even imagined "the material body's miraculous transformation into a textual body."[56] She argues that the cadavers of these poets acted, for believers, as "a direct physical link to genius, something remaining of the complex, irreplaceable life and personality now beyond recall."[57] One of her examples, that of Robert Burns, foregrounds the touch of sacralization surrounding the remains of such celebrated figures. When his body was exhumed in September 1815, in order to move him to a more illustrious site, the discourse surrounding his corpse – "the sacred deposit," as one witness named it – calls to mind the magic involved in the disinterring and translation of saints. One observer described the corpse as if it were the body of an incorrupt saint: "the remains of the great poet, to all appearance nearly entire, and retaining various traces of vitality, or rather exhibiting the features of one who had newly sunk into the sleep of death." The soil on his grave gained a precious status, because of its "more than priestly consecration."[58] Such an attractive cadaver couldn't be resisted for relic plundering, and when his wife died in 1834 and the tomb was reopened to bury her with him, his skull was removed for a casting (and phrenological studies), and various dark tresses made their way into collections.[59]

    With the relics of the famous arise the possibility – indeed, the probability – that they lack authenticity. The history of the religious belief in the miraculous remains of saints, Jesus, and the substances associated with them is shot through with anxieties about the manufacture, dispersal, and sale of fraudulent materiality. False miracles and counterfeit matter might (and often did) cast into doubt the provenance of any thorn or bit of wood claimed to be part of the Crown of Thorns or the True Cross. Even with secular relics such questions arise, such as those bits of Shelley's skull at the Pforzheimer. Historical souvenirs were also sold, hence leading to further possibilities for corruption. Visitors to the site of the Battle of Waterloo, for instance, could buy relics of all sorts; much of what Byron collected there he purchased from souvenir hawkers. The taint of commerce that could cause relics to fail to do their work – to revivify the historical event, person, or saintly body – will be explored in Chapter 5. But I want to introduce the idea here that, without belief to back them, remains could become matter merely, material no different from any other material. With the remains of the famous, letters of authentication, notes from curators and librarians, labels, frames, and displays all became essential metonymic appendages to the fragments of matter, similar to the way that the saints' reliquaries affirmed the value of the brown, often invisible fragments, through finely wrought gold and thick encrustations of gems.

Yet the relics that will be the focus of this book were personal, and hence their authenticity was more likely to be secure. They are not of the first type – saints' relics – nor of the second type – "celebrity" ones – but rather of a third. They came not from a saint, a great historical event, or the famous, but from any ordinary body. Of worth to a small number of people, these relics became unmarked graves, of value to no one, when those few who knew their meaning died. They told a story, highly personal and intimate, sacred to few, alive only in a specific locale and set of years. For those who didn't know the narrative of the donor, the relic became a materialized secret, a kind of dead letter of the object world.[60] These are the material objects that, to return to the remarks about archives made at the start of this chapter, lead us to see most fully the loss, by the early twentieth century, of the fetishistic magic of first-class relics (actual body parts). The very need to attach chronicles and records to these objects shows us that these scraps of bone and hair are mere waste without a narrative accretion. Indeed, the things that tell us the most about this historical practice are the ones that, because they needed *no* story to be of profound value, have now been destroyed. There was a time when such artifacts, steeped as they were in time and place, needed a mere glance from someone who had loved that body to bring forth an entire edifice of intimate memory. While the studies mentioned earlier by Samantha Matthews, Lorna Clymer, and Susan Pearce trace histories of fame, prestige, and wealth, in the following chapters I want to recover, as much as possible, a history of more ordinary examples of death's materiality.[61] Such things seem to keep their stories embedded internally – a secret to those not already on "speaking" terms with them. In a manner akin to the magical liquefaction of blood relics when the right material was brought next to them, the aliveness of these objects "happens" when precisely the right person, or set of people, come close, with memories. The anthropologists Elizabeth Hallam and Jenny Hockey call this "reactivation," when "dormant" materials become rejuvenated with meaning.[62]

The preservation of the fragments of one's loved ones has an ancient – if difficult to trace – history, but the practice of making such relics into jewelry and wearing them on the body became especially visible by the 1630s (for example, bracelets woven entirely of human hair, like those described in John Donne's poems, "The Funerall" and "The Relique," published in 1633).[63] Hallam and Hockey see the shift from the veneration of religious relics to the remains of ordinary people as a change in "venue" or context: "where once relics had accumulated in churches as mediators of collective memory, by the nineteenth century, material remains fashioned as mementoes sustaining family memories were located in the home."[64] Collecting and sharing such relics became increasingly common by the 1780s. In addition to curls of hair, teeth and other body parts that were thought to be especially imbued with the personhood and singularity of the donor, such as a caul, were cherished and sometimes worn (for instance, Queen Victoria had her children's teeth made into a number of jewels, see Fig. 4).[65] Emerging philosophies of the self and other – some

Figure 4.   Matching earrings and a pendant made of gold-mounted enamel in the shape of fuchsia flowers, symbolizing humble love. Their stamens are represented by the baby teeth of Princess Beatrice. Written in gold on the pendant: "our baby's first tooth," RCIN 52540, 52541.1 and.2.

quite radical and others part of a longer tradition of sentimental fashion – led to this development and will be explored later. The writing and ideas of the Romantic poets helped to make secular relic collecting the pursuit of any sensitive individual with time and leisure. For Keats especially the death-inflected personal object became a rich repository for feeling and self-revelation. Keats's writing and thought, influenced by a gothic approach to the body and mortality, found in the flesh of the self and the beloved a means to understand the fragility of existence as a rich joy.

The secret life of objects and the beautiful death

Alongside rising individualism and nationalism, a shift in thinking about objects also helped foment Romantic and Victorian relic culture. Judith Pascoe sees the emergence of the practice of collecting everyday objects (such as ceramics, playing cards, monogrammed handkerchiefs) during the Romantic period as reflecting "a culture's new understanding of the past as an idealized lost world, partly salvageable through the recovery and preservation of old objects and documents."[66] Although new emotions for material objects developed during this period, to be explored further later, Pascoe elides some historical continuities in this particular passage of her otherwise perceptive and important study. One of the uses of bringing the history of relic culture into histories of collecting and of "thing theory" is to ground secular materialism in the long history of the sacred object. This lost world the Romantics so wanted to recover through "thingness" was not so different from the communion with divine things – imbued with the enchanted past of a human who had touched God as well as the earth – desired ardently by the faithful. Like religious relics, secular things could have the quality of being that *one true object*: an actual piece of history, a real fragment of the body of a great person. To touch or own such a relic was to feel that the literary genius or other "sacred" body might be personally connected to one, might work as a kind of "patron saint" or "invisible friend." As one's saints became increasingly personal, finally narrowing down to a religion of one, with the saint being one's lover, family member, or best friend, so too did relations with the things around one.

With the Enlightenment came a strong belief in the capability of knowledge to bring order to the chaotic world. Systematizing and classifying the material environment could be a means to both control it and bring it closer. Such a closeness, along with myriad other factors, started a shift in thinking about things.[67] Collecting became an increasingly popular activity, a means to arrange one's habitat, to know and own it. Historically important objects, such as art and antiquities, which had been amassed by the wealthy for centuries, were more frequently displayed publicly. The founding of the great British museums can be dated to this time, an activity of grouping, cataloguing, and studying objects that would reach its climax in the nineteenth century. (The British Museum opened to the public in 1759, for instance; the National Gallery in 1824; the Victoria and Albert Museum – called the South Kensington Museum at first – in 1852; the National Portrait Gallery in 1856; the Natural History Museum in 1881; and the National Gallery of British Art, later renamed the Tate, then Tate Britain, in 1897.) Aristocratic country homes first opened to tourists during the last quarter of the eighteenth century. The wealthy could invent or reinvent themselves through the semipublic display of their property and their collections of things, and complex personal taste could be expressed through the interiors.[68] Horace Walpole built the fantastic gothic property Strawberry Hill in part to add a sense of sublime mystery to his character and story. William Beckford forged a rich identity by transforming Font-hill House into a gothic abbey, full of the ancient and exotic. Sir John Soane turned his house into a museum of the self. Elizabeth Fay studies the Romantic era emergence of such house museums, which she under-stands as a movement of the self identifying with its objects. "Objects yoke together sign and symbol, cross-functioning as metonyms of the collector's life and metaphors of his personality and spirit."[69] She describes Walpole's house as a "stand in for his body."[70] Not only did the collecting of valuable items become common practice, but, more important for this study, the collecting of personal bric-a-brac that had little outward value but was more clearly linked to the body and to intimacy – pebbles from a favorite beach, ribbons that belonged to friends, and locks of hair – became more and more fashionable throughout the Romantic period, peaking during the mid-Victorian era.

   In addition to the influence of Enlightenment thinking, another explan-ation for the shift in attitudes toward possessions was the Romantic fashion for the sentimental, for a sophisticated cultivation of wrought-up and drawn-out feelings, which was often expressed in an emotional closeness with one's immediate environment, possessions, one's own body, and those of others.[71] The multifarious stuff and substance around one could be suffused with individual desire, the longings and nostalgia of the singular self. Materiality came to be ever more threaded with one's self-hood, and thus also with the loved other. Objects gained a new rich texture, became a special meeting point between interiority and the external world. Judith Pascoe eloquently calls the Romantic period a "time when the notion that objects are imbued with a lasting sediment of their owners" gained new traction.[72] The entanglement of one's material surroundings with one's body and personality meant that when a loved one died, those objects and that very body could seem to contain lingerings of the lost self. William Godwin was one of many who expressed this increasingly pervasive attachment to "the physical aspects of a dead friend" in his 1809 *Essay on Sepulchres*:

> I cannot love my friend, without loving his person. It is in this way that everything which practically has been associated with my friend, acquires a value from that consideration; his ring, his watch, his books, and his habitation. The value of these as having been his, is not merely fictitious; they have an empire over my mind; they can make me happy or unhappy; they can torture, and they can tranquilize; they can purify my sentiments, and make me similar to the man I love.[73]

Romantic emotionalism thus bled into the objects of daily life. Moving through the world came to mean leaving a bit of oneself in the things around one, or finding a fragment of the self in those things. Relationships with others, the rich experience of individual history, found a nesting place in materiality. Creating one's interiority through the external, finding memories in the secret life of objects, came to be a new way of understanding experience.

For many Romantic writers, poetry was the medium through which matter – even dead matter – could be enlivened, reinvigorated, and connected to the personal body (one's own and that of the loved one). Sacralizing the common materiality of the external sphere could be done through verse, which might then lead to a kind of infinity found through ordinary objects and the body. Shelley proposes in his *Defense of Poetry* that poetry defamiliarizes things, lending them a fresh patina of wonder: "Poetry lifts the veil from the hidden beauty of the world, and makes familiar objects be as if they were not familiar; it reproduces all that it represents, and the impersonations clothed in its Elysian light stand thenceforth in the minds of those who have once contemplated them."[74] Andrew Bennett reads this passage as Shelley's statement that poetry casts the light of the "blessed dead" – the Elysian light – on objects around us, giving them thus a boundlessness and an intimacy with self and other.[75] Wordsworth's writing and thought were likewise crucial in redefining this interplay between self and things that would help vitalize a secular relic culture. In its simplest form, Wordsworth had a reverence for the immediate materials of living – those things others take for granted, such as the home. Of the cottage at Grasmere he wrote, "May not a man have a salutary pleasure in doing something gratuitously for the sake of his house, as for an individual to which he owes so much."[76] He had a local piety, a love for that dear place, his dwelling grounds. Both places and objects were needed to "fix" yearning and imaginative activity, similar to the shrines and remains of the saints as precise locations where blessing were "fixed." The nature of Wordsworth's object love was, of course, more personal – humanist – than that of traditional relic cults.[77] In the immanent, the homely, was to be found most potently the absence of loved ones. In Wordsworth's words: "How a thought of the presence of living friends brightens particular spots, and what a shade falls over them when those friends have passed away."[78] Wordsworth's preface to the third edition of *Lyrical Ballads* was an influential statement about the power of poetry to find what Thomas Carlyle would call, in the early 1830s, "natural supernaturalism": the sacred (or what passed for the sacred for atheists like Shelley, such as the infinite or sublime) in the everyday materials of life. Any unremarkable self might be able to discover a kind of access to divinity – a touch of the eternal, the infinite – but not through reaching, or by activating, some ethereal space, some generalized, abstract thought or imagining. Rather, the sights, sounds, and textures of the familiar, the unregarded – the host of golden daffodils, "the thousand blended notes" of the birds, the glow-worm, and the feeding cattle – could work as points of access.[79] Wordsworth puts it succinctly in the last lines of "Ode: Intimations of Immortality": "To me the meanest flower that blows can give / Thoughts that do often lie too deep for tears" (XI, lines 15–16). In many of his poems, Wordsworth expresses a broader Romantic idea: that the self – and the other – can be contained, and rediscovered, in the commonplace materials of life. Thingness is what makes being legible. And the poem makes legible thingness.

Poetry, for many Romantics, had this power of opening up the potentially infinite. The objects worth limning in verse were usually common ones that managed to both foreground mortality and to point to limitless temporality, somewhat like a square of a saints' tunic, a reminder of death yet a means to access the eternal realms of paradise. Stated differently: their interest turned often to the type of substance that would spark two opposing emotions – a sense of sad finality and a hope for the eternal.[80] The objects' temporal status was matched by their spatial one: they were eminently local, but they also pointed to the vast, just as Wordsworth used a specific place – or a poem – to evoke an everywhere.[81] The loss that death brought moored people, in Wordsworth's philosophy, in the material and natural world. Of a cherished place, he writes: "What happy fortune were it here to live! / And if I thought of dying, if a thought / Of mortal separation could come in / With paradise before me, here to die!" (*The Recluse*, I, lines 11–14). Death is folded into what could be won through the substance around one, just as the parish church, for instance, is a center of community for both the living and the dead, "a point to which are habitually referred the nearest concerns of both" ("Essay upon Epitaphs," 813). In "We are Seven," the child believes her two dead siblings are not lost because their graves can be seen from her house and because she often knits, hems, sings, and eats on their grassy tomb. Because they are located and can be dwelled with, they cannot be unrecoverable.[82] Materiality – including the grave – had the potential to call up a recognition of both death and continuity: and death as a kind of continuity. The body of the departed, becoming an object at death, worked as another means to recover memory, indeed, perhaps the most important and radical. To return to an earlier example: Mary Shelley found, in the shriveled heart of her husband, a whole life of meaning.[83] To the uninitiated, this thing had the status of a pinch of dust. Said differently: death could have gift-like qualities, especially when rooted deeply in the thingness of being.

Another way of thinking about Wordsworth's attentiveness to death and graves is to connect him to a movement with intimate ties to Romanticism: the gothic. Even before Walpole published *The Castle of Otranto* in 1764, which started the fad for gothic novels, a cult of melancholy emerged from the Graveyard School of poetry in the 1740s and '50s.[84] In poems by Edward Young, Thomas Gray, Thomas Parnell, and others and the novels of Walpole, Radcliffe, and Maturin, a love of the types of longing and sadness sparked by graves, ruins, decay, and fragments of the human corpse was developed. This "cult of tombs," as Ian Ousby calls it, signaled a stance toward death as an event or theme that brought sublime, aestheticized feelings, as did other types of objects and poetry itself.[85] The extreme emotionalism of the gothic and romantic aesthetic cast the frenzy that could be caused by the death of a lover in a subtly erotic light (especially in many gothic novels).[86] In addition to Coleridge and Byron (with poems such as "The Rime of the Ancient Mariner," "Christabel," *The Giaour*, and "The Prisoner of Chillon"), Keats especially steeped his poetry in gothicism.

Keats's attachment to the gothic appeared in his development of the idea of the "beautiful death" in his writings. The historian Philippe Ariès argues that the Romantic understanding of death as beautiful was more than a literary phenomenon. In his history of cultural ideas about death, Ariès explores how this way of thinking emerged out of a varied and long set of traditions. In the first stage of this history, which Ariès calls "the tame death" and dates to the early Middle Ages, the dead were always present among the living. Death, announced beforehand, could be faced without fear, with only a mild sadness. Accepted stoically, death appeared as the simple, natural progression of every living thing. "Thus, regret for life goes hand in hand with a simple acceptance of imminent death," Ariès explains. "It bespeaks a familiarity with death."[87] One needn't think about death because it was so close, so much a part of daily life. He locates a shift to a different view during the late medieval period, what he calls "the death of the self." At the moment of death, the dying individual might be saved or damned. During this "last ordeal," the dying called on the saints to help her fight against the demons who tempted her toward damnation. The outcome of this tussle would determine the meaning of her whole life. Before death, "the biography is not complete and is still subject to retroactive revisions."[88] Macabre imagery, such as statues of decomposed corpses – called transis – became common during this time because of a new passionate love for life. A difficulty in succumbing to death, which continued into the Renaissance and beyond, grew out of a newfound sense that what could be possessed on this earth had enough value to lead to terrible regrets about leaving it behind. Gradual cultural changes during the Renaissance led to what Ariès calls the "remote and imminent death." The hour of death became less important because thoughts of mortality spread over the whole span of a lifetime. Living and dying well became braided, and a careful Christian should be ready to die at any moment. Stretched as it was across the larger fabric of a life, death itself became, somewhat paradoxically, distanced, diluted rather than tame and always present as it was during the Middle Ages. "Death is now an intrinsic part of the fragile and empty existence of things, whereas in the Middle Ages death came from outside," Ariès explains.[89] The vigorous simplicity of earlier periods when mortality wasn't intellectualized or mulled over obsessively was lost with death's remoteness. Beginning in the eighteenth century, Ariès finds the start of what he calls the "great fear of death." "For until now," he argues,

> incredible as it may seem, human beings as we are able to perceive them in the pages of history have never really known the fear of death. Of course, they were afraid to die; they felt sad about it, and they said so calmly. But this is precisely the point: their anxiety never crossed the threshold into the unspeakable, the inexpressible.[90]

Ariès describes the end of the eighteenth century and the nineteenth century as the time of the "death of the other." The new focus on the passions wrought by the death of a loved one emerged in part because the number of people one might love dwindled down from a large social pool to members of the immediate family. Love for this small and close-knit group began to outweigh considerations of self-interest starting in the nineteenth century. These few, or even just one, became ever more exceptional and irreplaceable. This attachment and its emotions, Ariès argues, was cultivated, glorified even, making the separation of death more lacerating and inviting "the bereaved person to compensate for his loss through memory."[91] Memory came to inhere in material markers of the lost self and body. Thus celebrating the singularity of those few beloved meant relishing the traces they left behind.[92]

Death, now a mysterious and profound concept that could hardly be grasped, became oddly gorgeous, even in certain cases desirable. Ariès quotes a woman from the early nineteenth century who had literary leanings: "Oh! Death is always mingled with poetry and love, because it leads to the realization of both."[93] This romanticization of death is seen clearly in perceptions of the young dying of tuberculosis during the late eighteenth and the nineteenth centuries. In her history of the idealization of such deaths, Patricia Jalland quotes Edgar Allan Poe: "I would wish all I love to perish of that disease. How glorious! To depart in the heyday of the young life, the heart full of passion, the imagination all fire."[94] Andrew Motion points out that many in the early nineteenth century thought that artists were especially susceptible to an illness that seemed to bring – perhaps even developed from, some at the time thought – a heightened sensitivity and intensity. Robert Douglas-Fairhurst explores a popular assumption in the nineteenth century that tuberculosis was "a slow and decorative wasting away of the flesh, and so one peculiarly suited to writers, those creatures of refined sensibility who are forever thought to be trying to escape the limitations of the bodies through the reach and endurance of print."[95] Some believed that falling in love increased the chances of catching and dying from the disease and that consumptives were excessively sexual: this might be a result of the disease or even a cause of it, the speculation went. Byron commented when studying himself in a mirror, "I look pale ... I should like to die of a consumption... all the ladies would say 'Look at that poor Byron, how interesting he looks in dying.' "[96] Motion observes that the tragic death of Keats, who was thought by many throughout the nineteenth century to be a sensualist who died for love, furthered these confusions.[97] Shelley tried to console Keats: "this consumption is a disease particularly fond of people who write such good verses as you have done."[98] Keats himself couldn't escape the idea that his obsessive love for Fanny Brawne may have hastened his disease, a belief that he felt the strongest when caught up in the dark bitterness of dying so young. He entwined his love and death in letters to her, his phrases conventional and somewhat light-hearted, yet deeply felt: "You cannot conceive how I ache to be with you: how I would die for one hour." And: "I have two luxuries to brood over in my walks, your Loveliness and the hour of my death."[99] Yet even before he knew he was fatally ill, his thinking about the death of oneself and the other in his poetry and personal writings had an aestheticized richness. When death is figured as beautiful, the detritus of that end becomes beautiful, too – objects to be pined over, stored away, treasured.

Keats, like Wordsworth and other relic collectors, found in artifacts that signify the ruins of time the crystallization of the eternal moment. Objects in many of Keats's poems, especially those that represent "art" as an abstract concept, have a kind of stillness and grandeur that complicates temporality. But more than this, they embody the speaker's mortality (and, perhaps, the author's) and gesture toward the poems being treasured, posthumously, as themselves remains, or "artifacts" that point to the eternal. With "Ode on a Grecian Urn," the poem is an inscription *on* an object originally meant to contain remains. Paul H. Fry sees it as "a poem that supplements a thing."[100] He goes on to remark that "in the first line the urn is most intimately related to the circumference or framework of time, which is death."[101] The Grecian urn starts to life in the speaker a vision of the movements of living – the lover about to kiss his beloved, the heifer being led to the sacrifice – which are inevitably fleeting gestures. Yet because they are frozen, sculpted forms that have persevered over such vast tracts of time, they also partake of eternity: "Ah, happy, happy boughs! that cannot shed / Your leaves, nor ever bid the spring adieu."[102] The form of the poem seeks to mimic the rounded form of the urn and, as Elizabeth Fay explains, it shapes itself around a core that once held a corpse.[103] The poem has the quality of an epitaph, inscribing as it does the tomb and limning "silence and slow time" (line 2).

The nightingale, in Keats's ode, although not the same type of "object" as an urn, is also an external "thing" that embodies the complicated weave of time, death, and a sense of the forever. Like Wordsworth's response to nature and matter in his writing, the speaker of "Ode to a Nightingale" finds himself profoundly stirred by the sight and sound of a bird that, when thought of as one individual in a long line of brethren, he views as an "immortal Bird" (line 61). He pictures the bird's song echoing down through the ages: "The voice I hear this passing night was heard / In ancient days by emperor and clown" (62–64). An aural trace of other sorrowful people thinking about death – such as the biblical Ruth and those looking out "magic casements" with forlorn longing – the song links the speaker's moment of mortality with that of all others. When he hears the call of this bird "not born for death" (line 61) he thinks, in the Keatsian way in which opposites mesh, immediately of his own dissolution and disappearance. Although this ecstatic, beautiful death denies the ugly death from "the weariness, the fever, and the fret / ... where men sit and hear each other groan / ... Where youth grows pale, and spectre-thin, and dies" (lines 23–26), the two are different faces of the same coin, sharing a common substance and even value. It is when the speaker wants most to die the Romantic death that leads to the sublime that he feels fully the ache of being yet alive, this very "fever and fret." Such a tangle of contradictions is found in the famous stanza about the beautiful death:

> Darkling I listen; and, for many a time
>   I have been half in love with easeful Death,
> Call'd him soft names in many a mused rhyme,
>   To take into the air my quiet breath;
> Now more than ever seems it rich to die,
>   To cease upon the midnight with no pain,
>   While thou art pouring forth thy soul abroad
>   In such an ecstasy!
> Still wouldst thou sing, and I have ears in vain—
> To thy high requiem become a sod. (lines 51–60)

To become such quotidian stuff as "a sod," or a chunk of dirt, is to no longer quiver with existence. But to not contemplate the sod – that is, to not fully realize that one (and the beloved other) will someday be an object – is also to not quiver with existence. Stuart A. Ende comments that Keats surrenders a portion of his self to "otherness" in these lines, "but he does so in a humanizing gesture that makes death not an object of terror but something 'easeful.'"[104] He also points out that "the poet, who is so powerfully drawn to pathetic representations, forgives their transience as well as his own, and by this gives the darkness its various perfumes."[105] Within Keats's philosophy of the "chameleon poet," and part of his complex idea of "negative capability," can be discovered the Wordsworthian understanding that the self can be encountered in external objects. In summarizing a conversation with Keats, his friend Richard Woodhouse wrote that a poet, Keats felt, should be able to "throw his soul into any object ... so as to see, feel, be sensible of, and express, all that the object itself would."[106] To "be" in an object involves an attempt to suspend time, or step outside of it. And finding being in an object is not so different from finding it in a poem, an idea that will be explored further later. As in so many of Keats's poems, meaning comes from balancing on the edge of the grave (or imagining doing so). To be half in love with easeful death is to know through and through what it means to be more than half in love with the daily breath of aliveness. Ende constructs this in a slightly different way: "In the encounter with the nightingale, the poet's acceptance of necessary death paradoxically makes him the spokesman for life."[107] Realizing the "thingness" of one's self (and of the loved one) leads, in Keats, to an erotic relationship to existence. It is in the fragility of this mortal frame that the full range of living is to be found: it is in the fact that at any moment "death" will ravage one by taking into its "air" one's quiet breath that one fully realizes the joy of being an animated body. Death can be viewed, Keats seems to be saying, as a tender lover when it makes us feel the throbbing of our hearts.

Keats's attention in his poetry to the mortal body takes us back to the gothic. Keats returns repeatedly to an attraction to the body caught up in its eventual death and even its day-to-day decay. Isabella, when she discovers that her lover has been murdered by her greedy brothers, in "Isabella; or, The Pot of Basil," finds his sylvan grave. Unearthing his corpse, she cuts off the head to take home and succor.

> She calm'd its wild hair with a golden comb,
>   And all around each eye's sepulchral cell
> Pointed each fringed lash; the smeared loam
>   With tears, as chilly as a dripping well,
> She drench'd away:—and still she comb'd, and kept
> Sighing all day—and still she kiss'd, and wept. (LI, lines 3–8)

She lends this wandering head her cool, purifying tears. Tending the fragmented corpse as if it were his sick body, as if he lingered, saint-like, in this detachable part, she sacralizes it (in a religion of one), revivifies it. She has the thing itself, the one true relic of her personal saint, and can practice her erotic, intimate gestures over it. Rooted in the *just* here and *just* now, she attempts to keep it "speaking" – tries to give it unending narrative – by placing it in a special reliquary, a "garden-pot," "its tomb." (This gesture also makes it more secret, more fully her own.) The enclosed relic at the heart of the poem has a silent gravity to it, similar to the formal qualities of the poem itself, which also make it "a very still poem," in John Barnard's estimation. Barnard believes that the stillness comes from Keats's choice of ottava rima, which has a limited number of rhyme words (ABABABCC) and, with the ending couplet, "creates a self-enclosed stanza ... each stanza is complete in itself" or is surrounded by a silence.[108]

Isabella tries to locate herself in the object, to find in it a vehicle for transcendence. She plants basil over it, which absorbs the nutrients of the decaying cadaver as well as the passion she bestows on it, carried by the tears that water it.

> And so she ever fed it with thin tears,
>   Whence thick, and green, and beautiful it grew,
> So that it smelt more balmy than its peers
>   Of basil-tufts in Florence; for it drew
> Nurture besides, and life, from human fears,
>   From the fast mouldering head there shut from view:
> So that the jewel, safely casketed,
> Came forth, and in perfumed leafits spread. (LIV, lines 1–8)

The basil transforms into a miraculous thing, a transfiguration of the relic. The corpse head is a "jewel, safely casketed" in a new coffin, which then lets it "come forth" into "perfumed leafits spread." Transferring all her love into the relic becomes a way to transform it into something that can be nurtured to grow and move about with new vigor. The basil becomes an odd kind of reliquary, carrying some morsels of the artifact that Isabella venerates. His body and her reverence for it become legible, and even edible, in the plant. Here "the holiness of the Heart's affection" – an idea that would infuse Keats's later work – makes love like a god and the body parts of the loved one as valuable as those of saints.[109] When her brothers take the reliquary plant away, the objects around her become "dead and senseless things" (LXII, line 1). Her selfhood no longer vivifies the object world; things no longer have a place in her inward self.

Similar to "Isabella; or, The Pot of Basil" the lover in "Bright Star" fixates on the passions embodied and mortalized. The speaker of "Bright Star" wants most to feel his lover's breathing – that sign of the delicate nature of the body's continued animation – against his cheek just as he thinks about their own brief span, contrasted with the eternal forms of the stars, the sea, the mountains and the moors. He wants to live forever, as the famous and poignant end couplet states, only if he can also continue to feel the texture and warmth of her mortality: "Still, still to hear her tender-taken breath, / And so live ever – or else swoon to death" (lines 13–14). This "sweet unrest" is the moment, still pulsing, caught in amber. The speaker finds in a singular temporal event enmeshed in material existence – being "Pillow'd upon my fair love's ripening breast" (line 10) – the possibility (or the desire) of never dying. Extreme love and desire might bring the beautiful death (swooning to death could be an orgasm, the "petite mort"), a will to die into life. Such a contradiction always resides in time – gone as soon as it arrives, yet also sometimes leaving a permanent residue – just as it can inhabit the body and other objects. And it might be found through poetry, as John Barnard argues (in a reading of the nightingale ode): "poetry, since it recreates that other order of time for each subsequent reader, also defies chronological time."[110] The moment fossilized – caught in materiality, perhaps – is also "caught" in the tight encasing of the sonnet. This fleeting now of love and the mortal is made permanent in iambic pentameter, similar to a heart enclosed in a golden, inscribed reliquary. Both the poem and the heart reliquary "speak," akin to Shelley's heart carried inside his elegy to Keats.

For Keats, most everything eventually led back to the body. Bodies are always steeped in time: this is what makes them alive, then dead, and immensely desirable. As he famously remarked: "axioms in philosophy" must be "proved upon the pulses."[111] The self's body could become inextricably entwined with the other's body, in death and in life. Keats had faith that "men who live together have a silent moulding, and influencing power over each other. They interassimilate."[112] Such a believer in the meshing of bodies found a great deal of meaning in a lock of hair. Discovered in, for example, a tress from the long-dead Milton – a relic addressed as "thy simplest vassal of thy Power" – is the "spirit" that "never slumbers, / But rolls about our ears / For ever and for ever" ("Lines on Seeing a Lock of Milton's Hair," lines 3–5). Andrew Bennett locates the Keatsian body in many of his poems: "The poet's body, his corpus or corpse – is repeatedly inscribed in the poetry in terms of the characterological body dissolving and disempowered, as weak, wasted, or failing."[113] If the body is in the poem, then the poem has the status of a speaking reliquary.

A wonderful little fragment of a poem Keats jotted down when he was close to his own demise is suffused with this auratic sense of the physical self. Here is the poem in its entirety:

> This living hand, now warm and capable
> Of earnest grasping, would, if it were cold
> And in the icy silence of the tomb,
> So haunt thy days and chill thy dreaming nights
> That thou would wish thine own heart dry of blood
> So in my veins red life might stream again,
> And thou be conscience-calm'd—see here it is—
> I hold it towards you— (lines 1–8)

The speaker imagines first "this living hand, now warm and capable" and then, almost simultaneously, he pictures it dead, as it will inevitably be. An inanimate thing, it will be silent, no longer able to "speak" through writing and through "earnest grasping." The addressee of the poem will be so haunted by this hand – and, more, by what it writes, which makes it legible – she will want to transfer her life force so that the stilled hand will stir once again. As itself a fragment scribbled on a manuscript of a play Keats was working on, the poem's form mirrors the hand that seems to be separated from its body. The poem has a startling feel for the materiality of both the flesh and of writing: the honest, sincere hand moving across the page, "warm and capable." Handwriting is itself a secondary relic – the hand touched the page. But it can also function as the "remains" of a personality, the shape of the handwriting mirroring the writer's character. (This image appears in *Hyperion*, when pondering the survival of poems after the poet's death: "When this warm scribe my hand is in the grave" [Canto I, line 18].) Strong memory and/or strong writing might reanimate the cold corpse, vampire-like. This is what writing always has the potential to do: to figuratively stream blood back into the deanimated author (blood from, if we follow this logic to its conclusion, the reader). To read this poem written by the hand of the long-dead poet is to reanimate him, the poem seems to say, especially to reinvigorate those writing fingers, to bring back to him his "voice," his warmth. The flesh takes on a visceral vigor in the last two lines of the poem. In a sudden move from the subjunctive to the indicative, the speaker exclaims: "see here it is – / I hold it towards you—" (lines 7–8). The reader finds herself confronted with a strange gesture. It seems almost as if the impossible could occur: Keats himself reaches his hand up through the book, down through the years (out of the grave, even), to affirm the immediacy – the blood-pulsing warmth – of his text (and his body configured textually). Or, said differently, Keats (or the speaker) finds in the very mortality of the hand (or body) that writes, its near-immortal ability to be reanimated when the text is read again, by a breathing stranger, any time, any place. The poem and the life-drained flesh are things that can be inhabited by the animate, but also made inward and thus revivified. The relic (or, its representation in words) in this case dwells in both the posthumous and the permanent predeath. A desire so strong that it might revitalize a dead body part has gothic touches (related to what occurs in Mary Shelley's *Frankenstein* with those corpse parts), but it also shares ideas with the ancient relic culture discussed in the first section of this chapter. The hand has an odd kind of incorruption, preserved within the formaldehyde of poetic language, waiting for the fresh blood of a new reader. As with blood relics, it "liquefies" when a new reader comes to it. An object that possibly brings access to endless time, this bit of flesh traced in words has a miraculous quality. The saint is supposed to linger around her relics, as the author seems to be revivable with this relic embedded in words. He is present at this "tomb": the poem, the hand. The poem works as a "speaking reliquary," being a representation of the *thing itself*, as if it "contained" the hand. Brooke Hopkins remarks that "the hand itself in question seems to be detached or cut off from the rest of the body in the act of writing itself into the poem which represents or embodies it."[114] In a gesture common among critics of this poem, he equates the poem with the poet's body, seeing it as "the body's grave."[115] Bennett reads many of Keats's poems in this light: "And it is death, I am saying, that is indelibly marked in Keats's poetry, inscribed in or on that corpus that we know as 'Keats.' The literal and figurative body of Keats is both present and prescient in the writing."[116] Here again we find the representational removes of relics – the hand is "set" in the poem, the reliquary. The words "represent" the hand. Furthermore, the poem is a reliquary that can wander and move, like Shelley's heart contained in an elegy. As saints' bodies were miraculously inscribed, so does Keats's flesh seem to have carved on it this poem. To die into a poem is exactly what a beautiful death is – death permanently aestheticized. When the hand seems to reach out of the page (and "when" works here, as this poem has an especially pronounced temporality to it) the poem localizes, feels rooted to that book, to the place and time of the reading act. The hand appears to be, like actual relics, a trace of authentic experience – a "proof" that this poem really was written by someone who once had blood running through his veins. The author might be seen, if you will, to almost climb into this poem, this hand, just as the poem shines with his vitality. Poetry – what was, to Keats, the most important art – conserves loss, congeals the everlasting truth in the subject made object.

Rossetti and the Victorian beautiful death

Although his name was not "writ in water," as his epitaph states, Keats's reputation was far from secure when he died. Even though Shelley worked to spread his poetry and name – writing *Adonais*, among other things – it fell to the set of late Romantics that gathered around Dante Gabriel Rossetti to carry his ideas to a larger audience. Richard Monckton Milnes, who would later become part of the Rossetti circle, developed a great relish for Keats, along with his fellow Cambridge Apostles, in the early 1820s.

(Tennyson and Arthur Hallam were Apostles who loved Keats, too, a point developed in Chapter 4). Milnes wrote the first biography of Keats, published in 1848 and widely read, and in 1854 he shepherded an important edition of Keats's poems, with a biographical introduction, into print.[117] He carried this love to the Pre-Raphaelites, who came together in part because of their shared appreciation for Keats's poetry and life, which they knew from Milnes's biography.[118] It was when he saw William Holman Hunt's 1848 painting of *The Eve of St Agnes* that Rossetti invited him to join the group; meanwhile, Rossetti was himself sketching a *La Belle Dame sans Merci*. One early task the group set itself was to limn *Isabella*; John Everett Millais would take this as a pushing off point for his famous painting *Lorenzo and Isabella*. Rossetti's brother William Michael took over the editing of Keats's poems from Milnes in the 1870s, and his sister Christina would write a sonnet, "On Keats," about his grave (which included the famous daisies and the epitaph). It was this circle that placed Keats in the public eye, making him posthumously famous. Out of his poetry they fashioned their own aesthetics of death and its materiality.

Rossetti pondered Keats's own death, an occupation many Victorian lovers of Keats undertook. According to Andrew Bennett, "to talk about Keats's character or his genius, and thus to talk about his poetry," was, in the Victorian period, "to talk about his sickness and ultimately his bodily dissolution."[119] To be influenced by Keats, then, was to be influenced by his dying – his corpse even – and its coloring of his poetry. When Rossetti wrote a sonnet on Keats, entitled "John Keats," it was about Keats's death, his remains, and the love that many had for his grave and relics.

> Thou whom the daisies glory in growing o'er—
> Their fragrance clings around thy name, not writ
> But rumor'd in water, while the fame of it
> Along Time's flood goes echoing evermore. (lines 11–14)[120]

The corpse is linked directly to the corpus. The "name" or reputation has the fragrance of the grave and seems, through the figure of the daisies, to grow "out of" the very corpse, somewhat like Isabella's basil plant. The words of the sonnet also grow out of the corpse, themselves flowering plants. This was one of a number of "relic poems" that Rossetti wrote about (on) his beloved predecessors. A sonnet about William Blake's "workroom and death room" begins "Here is the place" (line 1) and names the room the "Holy of Holies" (line 9). His sonnet "Percy Bysshe Shelley" has the subtitle "Inscription for the Couch, Still Preserved, On Which, He Passed the Last Night of his Life." Rossetti sacralized these literary figures, creating intimate epigraph poems that embody death, hold or inscribe remains.

In a strange mirroring of life and art, some of Rossetti's poems actually did travel through a grave and were even, to be rather gruesome about it, soaked in decomposing flesh. When his wife, the artist Lizzie Siddal, drank a fatal dose of laudanum on February 10, 1862, Rossetti placed in her coffin an unusual instance of grave goods.[121] In a gesture of remorse mingled with ardent grief, he wrapped in her famous hair his only copy of a manuscript of his poems. "I have often been writing at these poems when Lizzie was ill and suffering, and I might have been attending her, and now they shall go," Rossetti explained to Ford Madox Brown.[122] Such a sacrifice would prove his love for her, he felt, and his will to never forget. Yet this was not the usual gesture of adding something to the coffin, which might be of some use, mourners imagined, to the dead (Rossetti doesn't picture her doing any postmortem reading, for instance). Rather, Rossetti wanted something of himself to sit next to her stilled flesh, down in that dark coffin (especially if we think of a manuscript as itself a secondary relic, touched by Rossetti's own hands). In some sense, what he wants is a means to continue caressing her, beyond death.[123] Rossetti pulls a mournful eroticism out of death, an ache that comes from wanting something more just as it pulls away. Settling his words – those pages he warmed with writing – in the nest of his wife's hair moves the corpse into an aesthetic realm.

To draw that manuscript out of the grave would be, figuratively speaking, to uncorpse it, to bring it back into a predeath realm, to layer its relic status. Seven-and-a-half years after his wife's interment, Rossetti decided to do just that – to detach the calfskin manuscript from the buried remains. He sent an unscrupulous friend to dig up the text. "I feel disposed, if practicable," he wrote to Charles Augustus Howell, "by your friendly aid, to go in for the recovery of my poems if possible, as you proposed some time ago. Only I should have to beg *absolute* secrecy to *every one*, as the matter ought really not to be talked about."[124] When her coffin was unearthed in Highgate Cemetery, with Howell, some gravediggers, a lawyer, and a doctor looking on, it was pried open, and the manuscript was carefully pulled away from the long-buried corpse. The book emerged "soaked through and through," with the scent of decomposition clinging to it.[125] The poem Rossetti most desired to recover had "a great wormhole right through every page of it."[126] Howell's description of what he saw when the coffin lid was wrenched open became legendary: "All in the coffin was found quite perfect."[127] His words were taken to mean that

Lizzie's body was preserved, some surmised, by all the opium she took. One friend even reported that her hair had continued to grow after her death, crowding the box with its shining softness.[128] The image speedily moved from rumor into durable "truth": the pale visage, surrounded by her shimmering red hair, as enthralling in death as she was in life. She continued to hold, in the mind's eye, the position of the beautiful corpse. When her postmortem body was imagined, the image was not of an actual dead body, but of Siddal's "representations" before her death. Painted as a dead or dying woman well before her demise, she could be easily imagined looking the same after she really had perished, similar to the photos Sarah Bernhard had taken of herself in her coffin when she was still a young woman, which have remained as a posthumous (postmortem) vision of her death. Like a saint, Siddal's cadaver remained incorrupt, but not through divine intervention but rather through a kind of aesthetic faith and, perhaps, the power of desire.

Figuring death as beautiful became especially prevalent among the two sets that Rossetti led: the Pre-Raphaelites (a movement of the late 1840s and '50s) and their later grouping, the Aesthetic Pre-Raphaelites (of the 1860s to the '80s). Although the members of these two overlapping circles struggled with religious doubt in their own ways, as a whole they swayed toward agnosticism and atheism. In their attempts to fashion their own forms of spirituality, they represented only a minority in the 1850s and '60s, but by the late 1870s their religious quaverings or full unbelief could be found in ever-larger swaths of the population.[129] Rossetti, for example, held onto some vestiges of his High Church Anglicanism, whereas his brother William Michael was an open atheist as were their friends Algernon Charles Swinburne and William Morris. John Everett Millais, William Holman Hunt, and Rossetti began their careers making unconventional religious art, in an "early Christian" style, that had touches of radicalism, such as Millais's *Christ in the House of his Parents*, Rossetti's *Ecce Ancilla Domini!*, and Hunt's *The Hireling Shepherd*. Later they developed other means of representing their religious avant-gardism in their art and writing, one example being a Keatsian eroticization of death. The evangelical "good death," with its firm belief in an afterlife, could be shifted and transformed into the more radical beautiful death that contained a dash of doubt in the surety of a forever.

The Pre-Raphaelites often pictured death as a thing of grace, as either a dissolving into the natural world or a painless passing into a sublime realm. Their early Aesthetic theories celebrated the loveliness of a scene or person *because* it (or she) can, and does, eventually die. In their different ways, these artists kept their faith in some higher meaning, some transcendent truth even when they lost their faith in God, through their belief in Art – with a fervent capital "A" – as able to plumb the mysteries of existence. Art, which could replace religion, might be able to speak of death and what came after. The love of art for its own sake showed a willingness to revel in the charms of ephemerality, in vibrancy, in a flicker of light. According to this Aesthetic philosophy, even though art itself holds a stake in immortality, it draws out what becomes gorgeous because it can't last by virtue of its very nature. This type of experience of the world, of the process of making or loving, is what Pater would later call "burning with a hard gemlike flame ... on this short day of frost and sun." He goes on: "we are all under sentence of death but with a sort of indefinite reprieve ... For our one chance lies in expanding that interval, in getting as many pulsations as possible into the given time."[130] It is this passionate interval that Rossetti and his clan call forth when they grasp after the loveliness of what must fall away, and it is this "eternal" moment that they found in Keats's poetry. The backdrop of death, always hovering darkly, gives being its poignancy and richness. If one believes firmly in an afterlife, then art loses its power to expand the *only* interval, to pack in pulsations. In this vein, it is as the drowning, singing Ophelia that Millais's painting of 1852 envisions Siddal, an ecstatic death by melting into the liquid green of the flower-strewn stream. Representations of the aestheticized dying or dead (to be distinguished from postmortem paintings, which were representations of actual corpses, real individuals) proliferated during the nineteenth century.[131] The minor Pre-Raphaelite painter Henry Wallis made a stir at the Royal Academy in 1856 with his *The Death of Chatterton*, which shows the gorgeous poet after he swallowed arsenic and expired in his squalid artist's garret. *Fading Away*, a composite photograph of 1858 by Henry Peach Robinson, depicts a pretty young woman dying (quite peacefully, it seems) of tuberculosis, two female family members looking on, and a male one (a lover or husband?) turned away toward the window in despair.[132] In a different register is George F. Watts's painting *Found Drowned* of 1848. The pale body of a prostitute – she has probably committed suicide by throwing herself in the river – just emerges from the nighttime Thames, a marble statue still moved by the rushing water.

Rossetti's painting of aestheticized death was oddly prophetic because he began it by taking pencil sketches of Siddal just a few months before her death. Started before Christmas in 1861, *Beata Beatrix* pictures Siddal as Beatrice – the beloved muse of Dante, who died young, becoming early an inaccessible object for which to be aesthetically pined. Intricately interwoven with grieving, the work on this portrait went on for years after her death and functioned, perhaps, as a means to continue a tactile relationship with his wife, posthumously.[133] In *Beata Beatrix* such haunted thoughts permeate its moody, luminous figures. Beatrice in the center of the composition, modeled by Lizzie, has a gray heaviness about her face, eyes shut and head turned up. Spectral beings move past in the background. What Rossetti attempts to do here is catch the precise moment when Beatrice is translated. In other words, he depicts a divine death, as if his wife were a saint, when her spirit is "suddenly rapt from Earth to Heaven," as Rossetti described it.[134] This makes it a blessed death indeed, perhaps without dying even, a direct movement from a kind of ecstasy to transcendence. The painting holds Siddal frozen in a moment of always dying, always blessed, perpetually to be pined for but also somehow never truly having died. Rossetti represents here a version of the Victorian beautiful death, which varied in important ways from the Keatsian one. In Keats's poems, the death is of the self, and in the Victorian version the focus is usually the death of the other. Yet there is also something darker and more doubting here than what we find in Keats. Victorian Romanticism is less sublime, less exultant and triumphant. This beautiful death tries to (without ever really succeeding) obliterate death by materializing it, by making of the moment something permanent. But the moment never truly lasts, and aestheticizing it fossilizes the impossibility of having it.

Art, according to Rossetti's Aestheticism, is to be worshipped because it might be able to draw beauty and permanence out of fragility and mortality. Yet Rossetti added to his multifaceted and capacious spirituality the notion that love was another key element that might redeem a fallen world or might keep present the deceased lover. The troubling brought on by the absence of the lover and this absence pressing itself into materiality: these are driving forces of much of Rossetti's work. In the sonnet "Without Her" from the sequence *The House of Life*, the speaker asks, "What of her glass without her?"[135] Loss is palpable in the empty space not only of her mirror, but also of her dress. What of "her paths without her?" (line 5). Or her "pillowed place" (line 6) no longer hollowed by her cheek? Because of these tactile lacks, his heart becomes "a wayfarer" and finds that all "sheds doubled darkness up the labouring hill" (line 14). In the sonnets of "Willowwood," also part of *The House of Life*, grief for the drowned beloved creates "one lifelong night" (III, line 4). The speaker attempts to caress her again by drinking of the waters that killed her; he envisions the play of waves as her "passionate voice," the "dark ripple" as her "waving hair" and the surface "her own lips rising there / Bubbled with brimming kisses at my mouth" (I, lines 12–14). Only by feeling "Love's" face "pressed on my neck with moan of pity and grace" can he find "both our heads . . . in his aureole" (IV, lines 12–14). This process continues to be agitated into being, holding up some hope of reunion, but also lacerating with its tangible reminder of distance. "The Portrait" is a poem that limns the mystery of having a "life-like" representation of one who is dead, or has "the earth . . . over her" (line 9). His painting of her is all that is left.

> Yet only this, of love's whole prize,
> Remains; save what in mournful guise
>   Takes counsel with my soul alone, —
>   Save what is secret and unknown,
> Below the earth, above the skies. (lines 14–18)

Can this paint and canvas bring back that dead loved one, that "heart that never beats nor heaves / In that one darkness lying still?" (lines 69–70). The poem seems to say that it both can and can't revivify that stilled body. It calls up and pulls away, teasing out consolation and making the wound of death permanent. True presence seems almost to sit "with her [painted] face" (line 100). *She is there*, and "hopes and aims long lost with her / Stand round her image side by side" (lines 105–106). Yet the flavor of death can't be banished, these "hopes and aims" are "like tombs of pilgrims that have died / About the Holy Sepulchre" (lines 107–108). Her painted image entombs hope: there but buried. But the speaker (painter/poet) might also become entombed there, next to her, his saint. This takes us back not only to the Catholic notion of being buried "ad santos" and the belief that the saint hovered about her tomb, but also to the idea of Keats's body "written" into his poems.

All of these poems find in materiality – mirrors, clothing, and paint – metonymic relationships with the lover's buried remains. They stand in for her absent body, as does the "art" that is the poem itself. The material embalms her, and then the poem embalms the material, lending both a possible permanence. These poems, like so much of Rossetti's work, glorify both love and art to express the truth of death. He gives all three a kind of divine quality. Jerome McGann comments that "The Portrait" conveys "Rossetti's programmatic treatment of art as a kind of sacramental action."[136] This is the action that can abolish death (art replaces religion) but also reinstates it, seeing its sorrows as giving depth to the colors of being. When allied with art and love, death might open a hidden universe of form and feeling. Its secret eroticism was unfolded for Rossetti not only through art, but also through the body itself, especially hair. In many of the sonnets in *The House of Life*, adoration nestles in the recesses of the body of the loved one; the best of life's feelings are exteriorized and reside in the material of the lover, the body as vessel. Rossetti carries Keats's idea of the "interassimilation" of bodies into a more erotic and death-inflected realm. Thus in "Life-in-Love": "Not in thy body is thy life at all / But in this lady's lips and hands and eyes; / Through these she yields thee life that vivifies / What else were sorrow's servant and death's thrall" (lines 1–4). The speaker's "life" doesn't inhabit his own body, but rather gathers in her most expressive, mortal parts – her lips, hands, and eyes. His vitalism is thus lent to him by her, by her body, where it resides. The speaker goes on,

> Even so much hath the poor tress of hair
>   Which, stored apart, is all love hath to show
>   For heart-beats and for fire-heats long ago;
> Even so much life endures unknown, even where,
>   'Mid change the changeless night environeth,
>   Lies all that golden hair undimmed in death. (lines 9–14)

In her tress can be found not only her animation, but also his own. Their past can be located in the hair – to touch and view it is the means to reinvigorate memory. In the rich backdrop of sorrow and death, the lock of hair, now a relic, shines out with meaning and love, perhaps the only there is for the speaker.[137] The moving and breathing warmth of life – the heart-beats and fire-heats – can be found only in the object, one surrounded by, held by, the changeless night. Thus all meaning, unbidden, narrows to this point of arrested life. The memento seals in amber this night, it draws its gloom into it.[138] Rossetti finds in the everyday matter of the curl a sparking of the inanimate into dark animation, an infusion kindred to the Romantics' natural supernaturalism. It is these things that make the magical qualities of death – the mysteries of the coffin – legible. And the thingliness of the sonnet, its little box of words, encoffins the hair, as the grave does. Thus the speaker is also encoffined because the hair represents his own body, as does the poem.

The hair shines with meaning because it is leant the light of the beautiful death. With this attitude toward death, love is sacralized: the holiness of the heart's affections, as Keats calls it. Seeing the life-drained flesh as a sensual object as Rossetti does, vital because it foregrounds the ardor that can be found in all that is fleeting, is also to cherish it as a unique thing of art, just as is the poem, the relic. To see death as beautiful could work as a consolation – as art, death partakes of its immortality. Yet aesthetic faith tipped easily into a willingness to find a means to hold onto loss (rather than deny it) through its materiality. Rossetti needed to continue to reimagine, through poetry, painting, and relics, his wife's dying and postlife state. Two movements agitated him and kept him creating: the consolation of picturing her continued existence, somewhere, somehow, and the painful repetition of the sting of separation. Within this last repetition we can see a need to reassert her unique, material singularity as something (someone) that cannot be repeated. The power of love (allied always with art) – that all-reigning deity for Rossetti – might seem to dissolve the separation between life and death, but it could also draw that boundary line thickly again and again. What we find in this late Romanticism is a need to preserve loss. This later beautiful death could represent death as really death – aestheticized but still stark.

As can be seen in the case of Rossetti and the Pre-Raphaelites, the Romantic attraction to remnants and wreckage, brought into conjunction with the belief that the self can be contained in the material (and in the poem), provided a basic foundation for the love of relics that would grow stronger as the Victorian era began. As Romantic thinking about material culture and death developed in part from the worship of the saints' corpses, so, too, would the Victorians hold onto the belief in the magical vigor that might remain in death-infused things. The Victorians continued the movement of modernity toward privatization, humanism, and individualism, with relics of noncelebrities treated as shrines at which only a few might worship. Objects continued to hold a kind of enchantment: they could glimmer with the emotional life of the possessor or the one who gazed on them with strong desire. The materiality of death became, in the Romantic philosophy continued into the mid and late nineteenth century, not a full stop but rather a genesis for continued passion and vigor, as any material might be. Relics sparked memories; experiences seemed to suffuse the bodily fragments of the beloved dead. The nostalgic possessor felt that the scrap of a once-breathing body acted as a kind of doorway to the whole of a past life; it made it material, tangible, able to be held and represented. The remains of the loved one's body represented the endless meaning of a being in motion.

CHAPTER 2

The miracle of ordinary things: Brontë and Wuthering Heights

Glad comforter! will I not brave,
Unawed, the darkness of the grave?
Nay, smile to hear Death's billows rave –
    Sustained, my guide, by thee?

—Emily Brontë

Secondary Relics

It seems fitting, given Emily Brontë's preoccupation in her writing with death's ability to linger materially, that many objects that belonged to her and her family (including their house and the cemetery just in front of it) are treated now as precious because they were touched, handled, or dwelled in by the family (see Fig. 5). The Brontë Parsonage Museum in Haworth, West Yorkshire, guards such secondary relics (not a part of the body but treasured because they were touched by it) as the cabinet piano Emily played, the "Faith and Charity" cups and saucers the family drank from, Emily's writing desk and its miscellaneous contents, and her dog Keeper's metal collar.[1] Even pencil marks on a wall that used to be the children's bedroom and that "might have been" sketched by them are carefully framed, glassed in, and preserved.[2] The Parsonage's association with death would have developed even without Elizabeth Gaskell's description, in her 1857 biography of Charlotte, of the graveyard next to the house as "terribly full of upright tombstones" and the moors that stretch out behind it as "wild, bleak," evocative of solitude and loneliness.[3] As Wuthering Heights gained disciples throughout the latter half of the nineteenth century, its characters' dramatic demises caused a natural conflation of the atmosphere of the novel and the Brontë home. (After mostly hostile reviews, fellow late Romantics such as D. G. Rossetti, who called it "the best [novel] – as regards power and style – for two ages," sang its praises.)[4] Even today, the visitor to the Museum and its environs is

Figure 5.   The horse-hair-stuffed sofa on which Emily is thought to have died.

struck by the close-packed grave markers that rise, when seen from certain vantages, just under the house windows. Later Victorians who began to flock in increasing numbers to the house as a kind of shrine wrote of the death-imbued sadness of the scene, and elegies resulted, most famously Matthew Arnold's "Haworth Churchyard" of 1855.[5]

The Brontës and their followers were part of a larger Victorian movement that gave meaning to things touched by absence. When someone is lost – through death, distance, or estrangement – the everyday objects that formed part of the person's habitual round take on an extra layer of meaning. A sort of numinous quality can give the material of these things – the cloth, paint, wood, metal, or glass – a glowing patina of memory (see Fig. 6). The possessions of one gone for good can seem to be embedded with little histories of intimacy, with the touch of the dead one's hands or body. They can appear smoothed or rubbed by contact with the lost one; they seem to act as mute witnesses to the movements of days now stopped and all in the past. Absence comes to feel material, to be magically contained just here, in this little item washed up on the shores of time.

Figure 6.   Small wooden stool that Emily Brontë sat on to write.
She drew a sketch of herself on her diary paper of 1845 sitting on this stool writing.

Their link to a lost referent brings these commonplace utensils – a twisted glove, a monogrammed handkerchief, a child's spinning top, a sleek letter opener – out of the category of useful items that are largely ignored because of their familiarity and into that of inanimate matter with a mysterious liveliness, and thus approached with a sometimes painful reverence. In writing about the clothing of the dead, Peter Stallybrass muses on how a jacket "receives" the body of the living; hence when that loved one dies, "the clothes in their closets still hang there, holding their gestures."[6] It is as if the death of their owners transfers animation to the things themselves. As Bill Brown eloquently queries: "Why ... does death have the capacity both to turn people into things and to bring inanimate objects to life?"[7]

Of course the term *secondary* (or second class or contact) relics comes from the Catholic reverence for the saints and the objects that had close contact with a "divine" body.[8] A little strip of green ribbon with buttons in the shape of olives held in a crystal and gold reliquary at the Cathedral of Prato, Italy, is believed to have been the belt worn by Mary, the mother of Jesus. The rosary, white cape, and shoes of Saint Bernadette Soubirous draw pilgrims to Lourdes, and to Nevers they come for her traveling bag, purse, and umbrella. The abbot's staff, resembling a shepherd's crook, that Saint Bernard grasped for many years has been encased in silver and gold and is displayed at the abbey of Saints Peter and Paul at Dendermonde. Like primary relics, such artifacts, sanctified by contact with the flesh or bodily fluids – blood, sweat, tears – of a sacred human, reportedly work miracles, healing the sick or causing "evil spirits" to depart (qualities given, for instance, to the fabric that touched the Apostle Paul's skin).[9] As explored in Chapter 1, a mixture of the sacred and secular gave the personal effects of kings and queens a related value, such as Henry VIII's stirrups or a pair of gloves presented to Elizabeth I. In a gradual transfer of worship when the cult of saints largely disappeared from Britain, feelings of awe were directed toward the belongings of secular figures. Trees associated with Shakespeare's last home and birthplace were cut down and made into souvenirs, presumably because they were thought to have been touched by him at some point in his life, or, at the very least, they "witnessed" his living days.[10] Owning a bit of Napoleon or Nelson memorabilia was an exciting gesture, as was collecting a secondary "relic" (in addition to the primary ones mentioned in Chapter 1) from the Battle of Waterloo – such as dirt, branches from the trees that grew there, or bits of the clothing from the soldiers dead on the ground.[11] With the Romantic focus on radical individualism and the belief that the vivid personality could seep into the things surrounding one came a more powerful sense that onto the furniture of one's daily life might be rubbed a bit of that vital selfhood. The materials of life work as containers for the adoration of the dead friend or lover; in some sense, the passion for the beloved has been transferred from her self to these objects that are all that is left of her.

Carried into the Victorian period, the treasuring of the possessions of both the famous and the ordinary dead reflected, in many ways, the attention given to those fabric remnants, those parings of wood, marble (such as the "Holy Stairs," reputedly the 28 steps in Pilate's palace that Jesus climbed on the night of his crucifixion), and sponge (the "Holy Sponge," which, the story goes, was saturated with vinegar and offered to Jesus on the cross) of the divine. After her husband's death, Queen Victoria kept his bedroom exactly as it was when he died, transforming the chamber and its contents into personal relics and forming her own religion of one. She slept every night holding one of his nightshirts (a practice many Catholic believers would envy, as they so rarely can grasp the relics of the saint they adore, but rather must visit a church and can only, at most, kiss the reliquary) and kept a cast of his hand within touching distance.[12] Always alive to the capability of objects to soak up and hold experiences and memories, Victoria and Albert adored souvenirs, such as the trinkets set with pebbles gathered on trips to their favorite spots around England.[13] According to Lytton Strachey, "mementoes of the past surrounded her [Queen Victoria] in serried accumulations."[14] The collecting of the cast-off items of famous people flourished throughout the period among those who had leisure and money. William Michael Rossetti visited Claire Clairmont's Florence home in 1874, Judith Pascoe notes, to ask the half-sister of Mary Shelley for Shelley memorabilia. He was thrilled to take home "the last couch Shelley ever slept on."[15] When Livingstone's body was brought back from Africa in 1873, it and its effects were treated as a saint's remains might be.[16] Upon Gladstone's death in 1898, his wife received letters asking for the hat he was wearing in a famous photo, or some of his collars.[17] A lively interest in such artifacts can be found scattered throughout the London *Times*, as in an October 25, 1837, article about a man in Bath who claimed to possess a handkerchief used by Charles I at the time of his execution.[18] An exchange of letters in June of 1844 about the musket ball that killed Nelson, with a part of the braid from his epaulette adhered to it, resulted in the surgeon who had extracted it and placed it in a locket – William Beatty – presenting it to the Queen.[19] Prince Albert bought, according to another article, the Trafalgar coat and waistcoat that Nelson wore when he died, and he donated it to Greenwich Hospital.[20] Although these effects might not call up the kind of devotional fervor saints' relics did, they became cherished and displayed because they attested to historical events or persons whose existence changed the identity of a people. Seemingly infused in their very grain is proof that these events happened, and the seminal nature of their referents – a certain august air – still seems to cling to their matter.

But everyday people also stored up the beloved detritus of their commonplace dead. Wills – especially women's informal ones – list many such items, handed down as souvenirs of a life and as a way to leave a little keepsake of oneself to a revered friend or family member. The will of W. E. Gladstone's daughter, Mary Drew, for instance, sets her bequests within a larger web of intimate relationships and shared experiences. Spencer Lyttelton, the brother-in-law of Mary's friend Laura Lyttelton, who had herself recently died, was to have "*The Imitation* [*of Christ*] which Laura gave me the night before her wedding."[21] Patricia Jalland recounts how Ada Lovelace bequeathed, in 1852, her leather writing-box to her former lover John Crosse, stipulating it must be given to him with its contents exactly as they were when she died, in order to remind him of their "many delightful and improving hours."²² And fragments of the lives of lost people shine out of so many Victorian novels and poems, attesting to the popularity of the practice of secular, secondary relic collecting, such as Hardy's mayor of Casterbridge, who holds onto a few of his daughter's cast-off belongings – gloves, shoes, and a scrap of her handwriting – knowing he will never see her again. Some of the magical healing properties of Esther Summerson, in *Bleak House*, imbue her monogrammed handkerchief so treasured by the brickmakers' wives and, later, by her mother, Lady Dedlock. In Gaskell's *North and South*, Margaret Hale wants some object that belonged to her dead friend Bessy, and she is happy to carry off her drinking cup. Freighted with significance, these stray stuffs are emblematic of the meaning the things of death could hold during the Victorian era.²³

Not only did Victorians have an especially elaborate and ritualistic mourning culture, but they also had a particular relationship to certain types of material objects.²⁴ Death mementos held a special status in the proliferation of consumer goods in Victorian culture. Indeed, they hark back to an earlier relationship to things. They are the kind of objects that Elaine Freedgood describes as peculiarly early Victorian; they are tied steadily to a concrete place and time; they are nonreproducible, have no monetary value, and are in no way alienated from their human origins. They make up a part of "a more extravagant form of object relations than ours, one in which systems of value were not quarantined from one another and ideas of interest and meaning were perhaps far less restricted than they are for us."²⁵ As I explored in the introduction, relics have a unique place in the emergent field of "thing culture."²⁶ They are certainly fetishes of the type that Peter Logan explores in that they are inanimate matter given a particular kind of aliveness, an "overvaluation" not attributed to most material goods.²⁷ Herbert Spencer, in his investigation into mummy worship among Peruvians, Egyptians, and other cultures, defines what he calls "fetichism" as, first, the idea that "the soul, present in the body of the dead man preserved entire, is also present in preserved parts of his body."²⁸ He then goes on to remark on "the primitive belief that each person's nature inheres not only in all parts of his body, but in his dress and the things he has used."²⁹ Although Spencer does not relate this cultural belief of the "savages" to his own culture, the connectedness is abundantly clear. We can conclude, then, that the Victorians were even more inclined to be fetishistic than Logan surmises, when the vast realm of death culture is taken into account.³⁰ Indeed, death mementos work as ideal material for "thing theory," inhabiting as they do the "troubling intersections between clear categories," as John Plotz describes the materials ripe for such theory.[31] More than any other possessions, relics enact such troubling. Bill Brown finds "things" worthy of interest when they have been infused with a metaphysical dimension. While he does not explore relics as such, they are the *most* metaphysical of objects, the ones with ideas *in* them, the ones that carry something like a "soul."[32] Yet relics do not have the duality of what Plotz calls "portable property": "at once products of a cash market and, potentially, the rare fruits of a highly sentimentalized realm of value both domestic and spiritual, a realm defined by being anything but marketable."[33] They can be classed with what the anthropologist Annette Weiner has called "inalienable possessions," things transcendent and kept out of circulation that are "imbued with the intrinsic and ineffable identities of their owners." She sees such possessions as knitting communities together since they "recreate the past for the present," providing a stabilizing force in the midst of change.[34] Death souvenirs can thus have a conservative, nostalgic place in the culture, although, as I argue in Chapters 4 and 5, in certain cases they can be deeply radical and disruptive.

Secular relics also held a dash of magic. In ancient folk customs, death had a strange and secret influence on the lives of objects. Many of these superstitions still maintained power over the British in the nineteenth century, either actively – consciously – or as a residual and forgotten origin for certain practices still in effect. Ruth Richardson recounts what she calls a popular "folk theology" about death in the early- to mid-nineteenth century, a mixture of "orthodox, obsolete, and ersatz Christianity and what can only be called quasi-pagan beliefs."[35] For instance, when death approached, inanimate objects might act strangely. Clocks would stop, many believed, when their owners died, "as if the machine was somehow identified with the allotted span of a particular human life."[36] Covering mirrors or any reflective surfaces upon a family member's death is a holdover from the fear of omens or haunting, as evil spirits could come to reside in the reflected image.[37] Windows and doors would be left open to let the spirit or soul easily waft out, and conversely, mourning hangings and clothing provided protection from malignant forces that hovered around death.[38] The material world could thus be influenced by the afterlife; somehow the place of death could reach back and inspirit inanimate things residing among the still living. Emily Brontë, deeply involved in her writing with questions of death, love, and how these two forces influenced material objects, brings just such an enchantment to *Wuthering Heights*. Her work was influenced by aspects of both the Romantic and

Victorian periods, carrying, as she does, notions of the Gothic and of the sublimity of nature into her writing. In *Wuthering Heights* can be seen the special status of secondary relics as shrines for the ordinary dead and as the substance that holds a love that transcends death.

"Like a child reviving"

Emily Brontë's *Wuthering Heights* is perhaps the single most celebrated representation of undying desire in nineteenth-century English literature. Famously praised by David Cecil in 1934 as a love "revealed against the huge landscape of the cosmic sphere," the novel's status as *the* text of two souls melding into one has only increased in subsequent years.[39] In J. Hillis Miller's assessment, for example, Brontë's masterwork stands as "the climax and endpoint of the long tradition making love a private religion."[40] Yet at the heart of this love lauded for its immortality is found, at all turns, the mortal. Indeed, the recounting of this legendary romance narrative occurs entirely postmortem. When the novel opens and our narrator Lockwood arrives at the hostile Wuthering Heights, Heathcliff is already a bereaved man, with Catherine a ghost knocking at a dream window. The story Nelly Dean then unfolds for Lockwood and the reader has a certain staleness to it because the end has already been given away – Catherine dies young, and Heathcliff is left to long. Given the retrospective character of its central love narrative, *Wuthering Heights* is a book that seems reluctant to share this rich, wild relationship with the readers and even the characters themselves. Strangely, the only unmediated glimpse the reader has of this love in full flower, each lover alive and communing with the other, comes in the form of a few lines from Catherine's diary. She writes that the two of them, still "groaning and shivering" children, flout Joseph and the "tyrant" Hindley and race off – "half savage and hardy, and free" – for a "scamper" on the moors.[41] But already the decline of their love has set in. Not long after this foray they peek into the window of Thrushcross Grange, the bulldog Skulker bites Catherine's ankle, and she is carried into the genteel world of the Lintons, Heathcliff decidedly shut out as a "villain," "Lascar," "American or Spanish castaway," or merely a "wicked boy" (76). Thus the process of their inexorable separation begins, and the few scenes left to them consist of struggle: Heathcliff must watch or listen as Catherine moves toward, then into, marriage with Linton. When Heathcliff returns from his mysterious absence – a wealthy, soldierly gentleman – the two are given a few passages of strife and pain, climaxing in Catherine's final illness when she springs at him and their bruising embrace ends with Catherine fainting and Heathcliff gnashing and foaming over her "like a mad dog" (170). "I wish I could hold you," Catherine cries, "till we were both dead!" (168).

Catherine and Heathcliff's premortem love story never really gets told, whether it is because both the citified outsider Lockwood and the too-conventional Nelly Dean "lock" the reader out of the radical narrative of Cathy and Heathcliff's love, as many critics believe, or because the "Prelapsarian" history is static, outside time, or just uninteresting as accounts of happiness are wont to be.[42] In this way, their love shares qualities with the natural world in the novel, which is never much described for the reader. Margaret Homans points out that the absence of nature proves its very centrality, "Both Brontë and her Cathy avoid description of nature or of events in nature because there is no way to name nature without making it secondary. Primary nature neither needs to be nor can be referred to."[43] Forced to imagine what is so liberating and magical about those moors, the reader must also construct a fantasy about what a Heathcliff and Catherine happy together would be like. It is the very invisibility of this love, perhaps, that has made it so exemplary – that gives it its spacious, mythic quality; that lends it an emptiness that readers find worth filling.

Love unfolds as a play of absence, with death its steady background. *Wuthering Heights* is more a tale about longing for the dead than it is one of earthly love; as Steven Vine sums it up, it is "a love that is inseparable from mourning."[44] In a representative formulation of the liebestod of the novel, Elisabeth Bronfen finds that when "their love aims to attain the static union before and beyond social divisions and compromises, it transforms into a love for death."[45] Pulling one of its deepest meanings out of its figuration of death, *Wuthering Heights* troubles, again and again, the life–death divide – caught up in the activity surrounding death, in imagining what happens after animation has left the body, in being in love with the perished. Heathcliff's amorousness comes to be about peering into, touching, and eventually trying to get into a postlife place. Dwelling with death means, in this novel, dabbling in its tangible, touchable presence: in grave clothes, in coffin wood and nails, in dead hair and flesh. Understanding mortality – and, in fact, the love between Catherine and Heathcliff – in the novel, I will argue, means "reading" material, texture, and the weight and heft of objects. Things find animation through being touched, irradiated even, by death. It is in the elemental – and the elements – that Catherine and Heathcliff's relationship has its liveliness. My aim in what follows is to show that their love, interwoven inextricably with the afterlife, has its fullest realization – perhaps its only realization – in stuff and substance. Brontë's situating of mythical passion in the materials of death makes her, at least in this instance, not an anomalous, morbid pagan, as many critics have constructed her, but rather fully steeped in the evangelical death culture of her contemporaries.[46] A reading of the material culture of the novel foregrounds the ways in which the love between Catherine and Heathcliff is typical of the period (if exaggerated), rather than sui generis, as it is more traditionally understood. Yet because the novel is primarily about love for someone who has died, its presentation of this love includes intimations of an afterlife, thus giving the love a kind of mystical invisibility (and bringing about a need to give it material "containers").[47] The eternal question of what happens to the "self" when its fleshly vehicle rots is a central theme of the novel, although one addressed only indirectly. Material things hold a fragment of that selfhood, Victorians believed, and seem to "prove" that this self still exists in some sort of afterworld. This would be the most startling aspect of Victorian death culture to the twentieth century: its treasuring of the physical manifestations of dying and the body, its reverence for relics.

To die in *Wuthering Heights* – and so many do – usually means to be bundled speedily offstage, ungrieved and soon forgotten.[48] As an everyday matter, death is not to be met with much fuss.[49] Characters expire in most of the rooms and beds of Wuthering Heights and Thrushcross Grange, and the still vigorous sweep in and continue the daily activities of sleeping and eating in them.[50] The patriarch, Mr. Earnshaw, for instance, passes away while seated in front of the hearth with his children and servants around him. As his sleep changes to the eternal sleep, Catherine, without realizing what has occurred, jumps up and puts "her arms around his neck" (71). It is the feel of his dead weight that brings her to understand he is gone. Death has a physical presence in the common round of daily tasks in the novel; not only are many characters found dying or dead (Hindley's corpse is discovered "changed into carrion ... both dead and cold, and stark" [190] on a settle in front of the same hearth, as it happens, where his father died), but others often bump into deanimated matter. A heap of perished rabbits drapes a cushion at the Heights. One of the most vivid images of a family in the novel is a lapwing nest, full of starved little skeletons. The local chapel lies in a hollow near a swamp, and its "peaty moisture is said to answer all the purposes of embalming on the few corpses deposited there" (54). Domesticated and even made a bit comic in its profligacy, death in the novel loses some of its sting.

Even Catherine's mortal passage, from which the central plot unfurls (not to mention Heathcliff's titanic passion and need for revenge), comes to hold some consolations. Catherine's absence brings with it a curious kind of presence. The clearest explanation for her undead state comes from the novel's steady belief in an afterlife of some sort or other. Even as children, Heathcliff and Catherine busied themselves picturing what happens at the life–death boundary. When Earnshaw shuffles off this mortal coil, they comfort each other with visions that Nelly describes: "no parson in the world ever pictured heaven so beautifully as they did, in their innocent talk" (71). Nelly follows this remark with her evangelical fervency about death's goodness: "I could not help wishing we were all there safe together" (71). As they reach adulthood and face their own demise, death for Catherine and Heathcliff seems to bring liberation, a release into unmappable narrative, a return to childhood. While definitive proof "that the dead are not annihilated" (309), as Heathcliff himself describes it, does not exist in the novel, the evidence piles up. The ghost sightings must be considered: Lockwood's dream of Catherine's girl ghost; the little shepherd whose sheep will not be guided because the dead lovers block the road; the "country folks" in general who, referring to Heathcliff, "would swear on the Bible that he *walks*" (311); and Joseph, who affirms "he has seen two on 'em" (311) on every rainy night. Both plan to stay animated in this world after they die. Catherine will, she insists, merge with the moors and become a revenant to remain a torment to Heathcliff. She angrily cries, of her future grave, "they may bury me twelve feet deep, and throw the church down over me; but I won't rest till you are with me – I never will!" (141). And Heathcliff comes to see death as a simple stepping over into a space close by, one inhabited by the still-vivified Catherine.

Catherine certainly believes that death leads to vitality, in fact, perhaps a more joyous revivification, rather than cessation. Her life becomes ever more insupportable as she ages. She feels ripped apart by her dual selves – one being the proper lady who marries the gentleman Edgar Linton and the other the wild child of storm and strife, wedded to the heath and cliff. Living comes to feel like a "prison": "I'm tired," Catherine exclaims, "tired of being enclosed here. I'm wearying to escape into that glorious world, and to be always there; not seeing it dimly through tears, and yearning for it through the walls of an aching heart; but really with it, and in it" (169). Nelly's description of Catherine's death opens up the possibility that she really does pass into a state of being intensely with and in the world. She went "quietly as a lamb! . . . She drew a sigh, and stretched herself, like a child reviving, and sinking again to sleep; and five minutes after I felt one little pulse at her heart, and nothing more!" (174). Catherine's dying body suggests that she moves into the regenerative world of childhood, into the liberation of immensity.[51]

Even inanimate matter might serve as a window onto the vigor that occurs after death, such as Catherine's oak-paneled bed at Wuthering Heights. When the novel opens, Catherine's sleeping chamber is alive with absence. Lockwood describes it as "a large oak case, with squares cut out near the top, resembling coach windows," and also "a singular sort of old-fashioned couch ... [that] formed a little closet, and the ledge of a window, which it enclosed, served as a table" (50). Its uses multiply: a writing and reading space, a coach for traveling and a couch for relaxing; it is also a girl's private chamber, full of fantasies and passionate thoughts, with an escape hatch opening out on the wind-licked firs and the stormy moors. Entering it by sliding back its panels, Lockwood feels immediately that it is permeated by the presence of the deceased Catherine. She has carved her name – Catherine Earnshaw, Catherine Heathcliff, Catherine Linton – repeatedly on the window ledge. She has inscribed the mildewed books to be found there with "Catherine Earnshaw, her book."[52] Not only has she scribbled in them her extensive commentary on the works, but in the margins of a devotional text she has recorded her diary. If Lockwood's imaginings are not merely nightmares but actual events, Catherine literally haunts the bed. Lockwood dreams that she, long dead, appears as a girl-ghost, tapping her "little, ice-cold hand" (56) on the window, begging to be let in. All of the broad themes of Catherine and Heathcliff's lives cluster here. As children, they used the closet as a secret hideout of free play, away from the restrictive, hostile adult world. It is here that Catherine first experiences the great grief of separation from Heathcliff. Intricately linked with her life, her very identity, the bed is where Catherine wishes she could be in her final illness and madness. "'Oh, if I were but in my own bed in the old house,' she went on bitterly, wringing her hands. 'And that wind sounding in the firs by the lattice'" (139). When she wants to escape her "home of clay" into death, it is into this bed, which represents, among other things, her child's body, that she wants to move.

The bed also works as a coffin of sorts. For Heathcliff's escape from his deathly living, into a postmortem animation for which he pines, he chooses this oak box, window open with a storm coming in off the moors. The bed, a memento of death, "speaks" to those who can see the shadow play of memory over it; the lost past inheres in its solidity. Yet it functions as more than just a container for the past. It becomes a location where the line separating life and death seems to become porous. Here matter and space do more than hold traces of the dead, they act as evidence. They "prove" not only that Catherine did once exist, but also that she still does, somewhere. Heathcliff, although he reacts to Catherine's death with anger and torment, has never believed that Catherine is gone for good, but rather that she is just temporarily unlocatable. "Where is she?" he cries when he first hears of her death. "Not *there* – not in heaven – not perished – where?" (175). He calls on her to haunt him, and he comes to believe that she does. After Lockwood reports his nightmare, Heathcliff, in a "passion of tears," wrenches open the lattice enclosed by the bed and sobs, "'Come in! come in! . . . Cathy, do come! Oh, do – *once* more! Oh! my heart's darling, hear me this time – Catherine, at last!'" (59). Thus Heathcliff lurks in the wooden berth, not merely because it reminds him of his lost Cathy, but because he finds here a statement that Catherine's vital spark still roams. The material thing links him to some animated place. To be in Catherine's bed is to touch absence and to actively, dynamically, feel the permanent end of that absence. Heathcliff describes this: "And when I slept in her chamber – I was beaten out of that – I couldn't lie there; for the moment I closed my eyes, she was either outside the window, or sliding back the panels, or entering the room, or even resting her darling head on the same pillow as she did when a child, and I must open my lids to see. And so I opened and closed them a hundred times a night – to be always disappointed!" (273). The ability of their love to exist over the life–death continuum shimmers through this wooden bed. The object holds the suspension of the two: stark loss and eternal union.

A more flexible understanding of sentience and its ability to roam from bodies to objects existed during the late eighteenth century and the first half of the nineteenth in the sciences and religion. Catherine Gallagher and Stephen Greenblatt describe a widespread willingness to understand vitality as lurking practically everywhere: "in electricity, in magnetic 'force,' in a subtly all-pervading liquid; indeed it can be latent in the whole of inorganic, or inanimate, matter."[53] Following other scientific disciplines, physicians debated the nature of "suspended animation" – the capability of a person to seem to be dead but to be still alive – and many held to a belief in a general "vitalism." While the bodily functions shut down, a "vital principle" might persist, and it could then "leak out of its usual vessels" and move to other forms of living and inanimate material.[54] In *Wuthering Heights*, Catherine's vital presence comes to enliven all types of objects, making her death an opening into truly being with and in a wide-ranging vivification. Vitalism also permeated evangelical death culture – as will be explored further later – giving the corpse and its traces an odd ability to be revivified.

The Evangelical Good Death

The corpse itself is another kind of object – the body is "a thing among things," as Bill Brown, quoting Merleau-Ponty, reminds us – that might provide a glimmer of the "glorious world" that Catherine perhaps dissolves into with her demise.[55] As Nelly keeps company with the just-dead body, she peers at Catherine's countenance and finds there a "perfect peace": "My mind," she explains, "was never in a holier frame, than while I gazed on that untroubled image of divine rest" (173). She goes on to remark of all the remains she has looked on, "I see a repose that neither earth nor hell can break; and I feel an assurance of the endless and shadowless hereafter – the Eternity they have entered where life is boundless in its duration, and love in its sympathy, and joy in its fullness" (173). Nelly's words mirror Catherine's hopes for death – plenitude, a filled-up joy – but also prove her to be an evangelical of a moderate stripe. While being of rather indeterminate religious belief herself, Brontë could not avoid the evangelical revivals of the 1830s and 1840s, precisely the time period when she was conceiving and penning this novel. Emily's father Patrick was an evangelical clergyman, who held the perpetual curacy of Haworth, a district with a long tradition of Methodism.[56] Her Aunt Branwell, who became a mother figure to the children after their mother died when Emily was three years old, was a Methodist who attended both Anglican services and Methodist cottage meetings.[57] Brontë carries the most tyrannical characteristics of this Methodism into the novel with the servant Joseph, who tries to force young Catherine and Heathcliff to read typical evangelical tracts entitled *The Helmet of Salvation* and *The Broad Way to Destruction*. The Reverend Jabes Branderham, featured in Lockwood's nightmare, works as a parody of a strident Dissenting preacher.

Yet it is in the lingering that happens around Catherine's remains that the evangelical influences on the novel have their broadest outlines. Nelly's conviction that Catherine's body provides a window into the "shadowless hereafter" comes from the evangelical belief in the "good death," based on Catholic tradition.[58] As Patricia Jalland explains, death could work as a kind of triumph because it was the moment at which the dying passed into a rapturous state, into a heaven peopled by the loved ones that had died before them.[59] Not only could the moment of death express a holy joy, but in the dead flesh itself might be seen gleams of that state of spiritual salvation. This view of death as a "window" influenced the wider population, Jalland points out, including those with little religious leanings whatsoever. It might seem natural to point to the Oxford or Tractarian movement, a Catholic-inflected revival of the 1830s and 1840s led by John Henry Newman, John Keble, and

Edward Pusey, as a force in the rise of relic culture. Although it did have some impact, the movement as a whole did not spread across all classes and influence the daily lives of ordinary people as did evangelicalism. Jalland argues that, despite the differences between the Catholic-leaning Tract-arians and the "low church" evangelicals, the understanding of death (and the emphasis on the "good death" model) remained similar across both movements. As one of these average believers, Nelly describes Catherine's corpse in a way that echoes popular evangelical tracts recounting beautiful deaths – often called "Happy Deaths" – where the visage of the lifeless appears like that of an angel or a saint, a vessel for an ethereal light.[60] A hymn by Charles Wesley, originally published in 1746 but repeatedly printed throughout the nineteenth century, includes this passage:

> Ah! lovely appearance of Death!
>   No sight upon Earth is so fair;
> Not all the gay Pageants that breathe
>   Can with a dead body compare.
> With a solemn Delight I survey
>   The Corpse, when the Spirit is fled,
> In love with the beautiful Clay,
>   And longing to lie in its stead.[61]

Marked on the face of the one who has exchanged this form of life for another are "surprise and rapture," expressions of moving into a redemp-tive realm.[62] Nelly finds in the cadaver itself a kind of link to that place where Catherine seems to still exist. When she wonders where Catherine goes upon her death, she had no doubt when "in the presence of her corpse" because "it asserted its own tranquility" (173). Evangelicalism thus participated in the vitalism found in the sciences: in the body and its material adornments, which have become inanimate matter through death, moves a flicker of vital energy, lent to them from some form of afterlife. The Victorian evangelical revivals also drew on Romantic emotionalism and esteem for the heart's promptings. Indeed, despite the disparate belief systems that underpinned them, the evangelical "good death" and the Romantic "beautiful death" both grew out of similar needs to find signifi-cance and passion in the act of dying and its physical remnants.[63] Brontë's art fed on all three movements.

The evangelical belief that the materials of death might work as evidence of the soul's passing into a better place helped fuel the secular relic culture already established by the cultural forces discussed in Chapter 1. Intimate objects, such as the oak-paneled bed, could be suffused with the presence and absence of the lost one. In *Wuthering Heights* any thing could be cherished, preserved, because it belonged to, or was part of, the dead. Nelly says of a letter from Isabella, "any relic of the dead is precious, if they were valued living" (148). After Catherine dies, all the matter of life becomes, for Heathcliff, replete with that tragedy. "And what does not recall her? I cannot look down to this floor, but her features are shaped on the flags! In every cloud, in every tree – filling the air at night, and caught by glimpses in every object by day – I am surrounded with her image! . . . The entire world is a dreadful collection of memoranda that she did exist, and that I have lost her!" (301). Her absence has left traces of intensity in the objects touched by her, or associated with her, not so different from the saints who were believed to sanctify the clothing, crosses, and other objects that their bodies pressed, sweat or bled on, and the places they had frequented when alive. Early Christian saints infused certain sites with their blessed spirits, the faithful held, which linked them to eternity. Catherine thus takes on the status of a kind of secular saint (as did many of the "dearly departed" during the period, whose remains and associated places were revered). She herself has a vision of just such a radical sense of subjectivity before she dies – that her self resides not merely in her living body, but could be in some way with and in other people and things: "What were the use of my creation if I were entirely contained here?" (103). Her image, stamped everywhere for Heathcliff, sanctifies objects but also causes them to glow with her departure to another sphere. In the novel, love and loss of the beloved have the potential to pervade all things, all materials of earthly life.

Objects in *Wuthering Heights* contain little narratives of lives, just as people are themselves "containers" for stories and even for things (a bag of bones). And relics are the most "speaking" of objects; to one who treasures them, they tell the story of a lived love and open a narrative of postdeath vitality. Through these objects, Heathcliff doesn't just accumulate "representations" of Catherine, he believes he gets to *have* her again.[64] Ingrid Geerken makes a similar argument, contending that Heathcliff attempts to reassemble Catherine through her remains: "a perfect assemblage of parts will resurrect the dead."[65] Keepsakes of death in the novel work figuratively – Catherine's body represents an animated postdeath state – but they also stop figuration in that they hold the status as being *the thing itself.* Catherine's corpse (and any dead body) moves us because it has become mysteriously stilled with death; subject has become bald, blank object. Death stops meaning. But then, as Brontë claims for the characters in this novel, it might start up again, if the vital spark still lives; the object might open out into more meaning, a more perfect meaning.

That objects and bodies might contain or represent both the hard facts of this life – in that they are what decays, rots, become useless – and the possibility that life does not ever end takes us right to the heart of *Wuthering Heights*. The novel's frame of death expresses precisely this paradox. Although Catherine is gone and Heathcliff pines, there yet might be consolation for the immense pain of bare mortality, in fact, the ultimate consolation, that there exists another state of being where all injustices might be swept away and where all desire is satiated. The novel holds both, side by side: the bereavement and the hope. From this mystery of exist-ence – its tenuousness discovered through the body that decomposes and its permanence found in the same place – arises the mythic passion of the novel, its ultimate tragedy, and its final hope, postmortem.

Before he dies, Heathcliff's need to feel Cathy in the physicality of everyday living is such that he must have not just her spirit. Not only for Nelly does meaning pool in Catherine's remains; much tarrying happens around her body. Heathcliff steals into her death chamber and, finding a locket around her neck that contains Linton's curl of light hair, tied with a silver thread, he tosses it on the floor and replaces it with his own black lock.[66] Including another's hair in the coffin was not uncommon in the nineteenth century; Keats had a lock of Fanny Brawne's hair buried with him.[67] John Callcott Horsley, a popular painter, recalled in his diary how, upon his wife Elvira's death in 1852, he hung around her neck a little red velvet bag that contained the locks of hair of her husband and her children. She had planned this herself before her death, cutting off each of the locks and labeling them with names and the date they were snipped.[68] Both Edgar and Heathcliff desire that their bodies, or a synecdochic fragment of their bodies, persist in the place where Catherine is going. This is the grave, of course, but it is also a region or state of being where bodies matter. And it is the body part – the hair in this case – that constitutes the tenuous filament connecting this life with the next. More than this, the afterlife, as it is formulated in this novel, has a materiality to it. A place that will have bodies and things in it, "eternity" will be reached through the materials – *the things* – of this life.

Nelly cannot get enough of gazing on the corpse, but Heathcliff takes this one step further. He must press his flesh against it, as if he uses his own body to make a cast or a death mask. He disinters Catherine, not once but twice. He explains to Nelly his actions and future plan:

> I'll tell you what I did yesterday! I got the sexton, who was digging Linton's grave, to remove the earth off her coffin lid, and I opened it. I thought, once, I would have stayed there, when I saw her face again – it is hers yet – he had

hard work to stir me; but he said it would change if the air blew on it, and so
I struck one side of the coffin loose – and covered it up. . . . and I bribed the
sexton to pull it away, when I am laid there, and slide mine out too . . . by the
time Linton gets to us, he'll not know which is which! (271)[69]

Catherine's body, preserved in peaty soil, still means *Catherine* to
Heathcliff. An element of sympathetic magic can be found in Heathcliff's
belief in the power of her mortal cast-offs: if the flesh is still preserved, so
too is the animation that was once contained in it. What he digs up are,
in effect, not merely "remains," but, in some essential way, Catherine
herself. Heathcliff imagines the yearned-for death not as spirits meeting,
but bodies dissolving into each other. In the very decay he finds future
vigor. His need for Catherine remains enfleshed: he wants to find,
postmortem, Catherine "resting her darling head on the same pillow
as she did when a child" (273). It does not matter if his heart is "stopped
and my cheek frozen against hers" (271). Heathcliff believes, and needs
to believe, that materiality is carried over into death, a way of imagining
that the beloved will be the same in the afterlife. In death, nothing
is lost.[70]

Heathcliff imagines a bodily consummation with Catherine when he
dies. Somehow what should be an erotically infused coming together
becomes a death-infused one, as if sex and death change places in
Wuthering Heights. The essence of this celebrated love can be located
not in sexual consummation but in the mortal body, in its state of
becoming more and more a part of matter. Indeed, to be together means
to become objects together.[71] The notion that the body continues to exist
after death was a familiar element of Victorian death culture.[72] In
evangelical family hymns, mourning letters, diaries, tracts, and sermons
of the 1830s and 1840s, the afterlife is depicted as a recognizable place,
similar in characteristics to the earthly home. In this home waits the dead
beloved, for the living mourner to die. The reunion in the afterlife is
envisioned as perfect and eternal, leading to the kind of love and unity
impossible in the chaos and vicissitudes of life itself.[73] Michael Wheeler
observes that in heaven "love, both sacred and profane" found "its
perfection, or completion, or consummation."[74] In his survey of sermons
preached on the deaths of the famous in nineteenth-century England,
John Wolffe finds a heavy emphasis on the dead as active in heaven – still
growing and moving about – and watching over the living, waiting in
anticipation to be reunited.[75] And bodies were carried to this home-like
place, to make such a consummation complete. Typical consolation

letters of the time mirrored these sentiments, such as the following written by a young woman to her friend:

> It takes away all the mystery and horror of the grave, to think that when we die we shall only pass from the loving hearts and arms here, to the arms of those who have gone before us. I am sure I often feel, even while talking and laughing, as if I could turn round and clasp my arms around my darling sister at my side, who has stepped across those awful shores, to take my hand and kiss me.[76]

This girl imagines the tender touch of her sister, her very arms embracing her once again, there in another world where bodies still move and breathe.[77] When the daughter of the feminist Josephine Butler died in 1864, her words about heaven were recalled by Butler, a fervent evangelical, with some comfort: "'Mammy, if I go to heaven before you, when the door of heaven opens to let you in, I will run so fast to meet you; and when you put your arms round me, and we kiss each other, *all the angels will stand still to see us.*'"[78] The lips and hands still hold their warmth in this imagined heaven.

Christian ideas about death mingled with pagan superstitions. The practice of carefully preserving one's teeth throughout one's life to be buried with the corpse so that the body would be complete upon the resurrection on the "Last Day," for instance, survived in certain parts of England well into the middle of the nineteenth century.[79] Grave goods still went down with the coffin, just in case belongings might be needed in that "other place."[80] Ruth Richardson explores a popular confusion during the period about the metaphysical nature of the corpse – whether the soul slept in the grave with the body until judgment day, for instance, or, perhaps, the soul was judged right at death and then was reunited in heaven with the body.[81] The dead must be carefully tended and watched until burial, so that whatever might happen to it after death would not be meddled with. This was the primary reason, Richardson explains, for the violent protest against human dissection. If the body would be raised to heaven, then it must maintain its completeness as much as possible.[82]

It is not only Catherine who seems to exist embodied – somewhere – postlife. Eventually Heathcliff comes to believe that he, too, will pass into that place of intensity. First he sees Catherine – locates her – in things, but then he begins to see through things to her. He finds Catherine drawing him toward death, over to that place where she is. Living becomes hard work. So obsessed does he become with attempting to caress and feel Catherine, that he takes little interest in his daily life. "I hardly remember to eat and drink" (300). "I have to remind myself to breathe – almost to remind my heart to beat! And it is like bending back a stiff spring – it is by compulsion that I do the slightest act" (302). The "stiff spring" must be bent back to remain alive, and death would be a relaxing of the visceral tension that runs through his body. It is in his very flesh that he comes to feel the contiguity of mortality and immortality. His body craves the release of death, as if it desires to assert its status as material. Heathcliff never properly separates himself from objecthood. As Leo Bersani states it simply, "Heathcliff is a reminder of our ties to matter."[83] When he first arrives at the Earnshaw household, emerging fairytale-like from Mr. Earn-shaw's cloak, he is described as an "it": "when it was set on its feet it only stared round . . . and Mrs. Earnshaw was ready to fling it out of doors . . . not a soul knew to whom it belonged" (65). Catherine later calls him "an arid wilderness of furze and whinstone" (121). He gains humanity by being named, but his name is taken from a child who died. Thus does Heathcliff just barely emerge out of death, out of being vitalized matter, and in his final passages he seems to meld back into objecthood, a state seemingly natural to him.

Oddly, this death seems for Heathcliff to be a quivering into life, or, to state it differently, a quickening to death. "[H]is teeth," Nelly describes him, "visible, now and then, in a kind of smile; his frame shivering, not as one shivers with chill or weakness, but as a tight-stretched cord vibrates – a strong thrilling, rather than trembling" (304). His flesh thrills to the tune of death, a state and a place he comes to be able to see and feel, as if it were a location just out of reach of the living. In his frame he feels the anticipation of transformation. He tells Nelly that "I am within sight of my heaven – I have my eyes on it – hardly three feet to sever me!" (305). Georges Bataille calls Heathcliff's dying "a curious state of beatitude."[84] Dying once again comes from plenitude, from a moment of such intensity, one simply passes through a thin scrim, to a spot *just there*. It is a movement of the body toward its object-state, but one that appears to involve a Lazarus-like resurrection. Nelly "reads" the afterlife in Heathcliff's face, as she did in Catherine's. His eyes are "so keen and fierce" and a smile lingers. His entire aspect shines with a "life-like gaze of exultation" (310). A triumphant future is marked on the flesh.

The postmortem of *Wuthering Heights* is not located, it is true, in some ethereal place, far away, as the Christian heaven is often pictured. It represents a kind of here and now, a type of presentness. Catherine's being "really with and in it" involves staying with and in this earthly life, in a place that appears to be congruent or contiguous with this one. In the oft-quoted passage in which Catherine dreams of going to heaven, she finds it not her home, but rather she breaks her heart "with weeping to come back to earth; and the angels were so angry that they flung me out, into the middle of the heath on the top of Wuthering Heights; where I woke sobbing for joy" (101–2). The immanent status of the afterlife gives it the same sort of shimmer of absence and presence that both love and nature hold in the novel. Too essential to be laid bare, to be written about, the afterlife runs hidden underneath the plot and all the material objects that swarm around it. To die in *Wuthering Heights* means not to be with God, but to be with the material, natural world. Stevie Davies finds in the moorlands and the world of nature in the novel (and in Emily Brontë's life and work in general) "at once a site of loss and decomposition and an area of reconstitution and composition." She notes that "it is the wildness and wilderness of the moorlands that speak of life and death matters."[85]

The wind speaks Cathy when she dies, as do the "moths fluttering among the heath and hare-bells" (312). Being absorbed into nature means infusing the daily objects of life with the presence of death. J. Hillis Miller describes the "divine" of the novel as "universal intimacy, the copresence of all things and persons in perfect possession of one another."[86] Objects in the novel have a special vitality because they feed on an afterlife hidden just out of sight, as if their liveliness emerges from death. This can be seen most clearly in the fir branch knocking on the window that becomes, in Lockwood's dreamscape, the hand of the dead. But here is an explanation for the magic of the ashes in the grate that stir to life as a brindled cat and the mirror at the Grange that seems, to a sick Cathy, to be the black press from her room at the Heights, haunted by her face, unrecognizable to her. Even more prosaic things shimmer with a mysterious life, such as the windows that "reflected a score of glittering moons" (113) and the "weather-worn block" with a hole, Nelly explains, "still full of snail-shells and pebbles which we were fond of storing there with more perishable things" (126). Something just on the edge of vision animates the objects of the novel, and this something is a postmortem world, lying just beneath. Thus must the reader, like Nelly, give "due inward applause to every object" (80).

But as objects find vigor from death, so do still-living people. When Heathcliff dies in order to join Catherine, he clears a space for another love, one formed for success premortem. Catherine's daughter and Hareton repeat many aspects of the love between Catherine and Heathcliff. Heathcliff sees Hareton as another version of himself: "'Well, Hareton's aspect was the ghost of my immortal love, of my wild endeavors to hold my right, my degradation, my pride, my happiness, and my anguish'" (301). Again, the young man, treated like a servant and left uneducated, unkempt, and ignorant of society, finds his desire spurned by the genteel woman. The cruelty that results between the two replicates the need for torment between Catherine and Heathcliff. But through their more forgiving natures, they are able to work out their love, in this life. Brontë implies here that Catherine and Heathcliff's impossible relationship must fail and lead to death for a successful repetition to reach fulfillment. From within the anguish of Catherine and Heathcliff springs forth the possibility of a love that can be openly experienced between two life-filled bodies. J. Hillis Miller creates an eloquent argument that the second generation of this love can succeed because the deaths of Catherine and Heathcliff liberate "energies" from the region of death, which is one of "boundless sympathy."[87] Energy seeps into the lives of people and objects. But not only do the animate and inanimate things of the novel draw their magic and truth from death, so too do they draw from love. The passion of Catherine and Heathcliff that has become so legendary serves Brontë as a means to reimagine and reinvigorate the flat gloom of death and what might happen after. This hope can then be injected into living and make lively the weightiness of the materials of everyday life.

Being attentive to materiality in *Wuthering Heights* means understanding how death can come to inspire life, giving it a vigor and richness lost when the presence of death is denied, forgotten, or shut out of the everyday. Philippe Ariès affirms that in the nineteenth century, unlike the centuries before it (and after it), "daily life was never free of death, for death was everywhere present and cultivated. The fashion was not to fear it, but to live gladly in its presence."[88] Furthermore, the notion that the dead body and the objects it touched held essential meaning served to give materiality itself a special value. Through their linkage with death, stuff and substance could tell stories, could take on the vibrancy of concrete singularity. Starting forth, shining out, material maintains its connection to the work and productivity of breathing bodies primarily through the death that infuses all things with the life of narrative.

CHAPTER 3

The many faces of death masks: Dickens and Great Expectations

Nothing like dissection to give one an appetite.
—Bob Sawyer, *Pickwick Papers*

Death masks

As Dickens died on June 9, 1870, his daughter, Katey, watched his face smooth out and begin to radiate a "beauty and pathos."[1] After the sudden "fit" that struck him down over dinner and the terrible hours of unconsciousness that followed, his demise came, to his watching family, as something of a pained relief. Gazing on "the beautiful, calm face, they could but thank God that he was so peacefully at rest," Katey reports.[2] To fix for good this last expression of the famous man, John Everett Millais and Thomas Woolner travelled out to Gad's Hill together on the morning of June 10th. Millais made a pencil sketch of the stilled features; Woolner covered the face with an oily mixture, then spread over it a thin layer of soft plaster, which quickly conformed to all the grooves, wrinkles, and crevices that a too-busy, worried life had written on his flesh. Once the cast had mostly dried, he lifted it carefully off and then used it to fashion a bust of Dickens.[3] In addition to these souvenirs of the moments just after death, a lock of his hair was cut by his sister-in-law, Georgina Hogarth. Dickens would hardly have been surprised at these attentions. When his beloved sister-in-law Mary Hogarth died at the age of 17, not only did he snip a curl from her head and place it in a special case, but he also slipped a ring off her finger and transferred it onto his own. He also held onto her clothing, taking garments out and caressing them long after her death. Dickens expressed a fervent wish to be buried with her.[4] Like many of his contemporaries, he believed that the dearly departed might be able to take ghostly form and come back to speak to those they felt passionate about. He felt – and wanted to feel – that Mary Hogarth looked down on him from some eternal spaciousness.[5] His only consolation, he remarked on numerous occasions, was "the thought of one day joining her again where sorrow and separation are unknown."[6]

In Dickens's life and especially in his novels, secular relics and post-mortem art have a bustling existence. Such art, which includes drawings, paintings (and, later, photographs), as well as casts of faces, hands, feet, or entire bodies of the corpse, had a steady and broad popularity during the nineteenth century. Indeed, despite the long history of such recordings of death (which predate even the ancient Greeks and Romans), the practice became more common in England in the nineteenth century than in previous centuries.[7] From the sixteenth to the nineteenth centuries, death masks recorded the sacred features of saints, such as St. Francis Borgia's, taken in 1572, and St. Veronica Giuliani's from 1727, thus keeping a transferred image of their countenances incorrupt. The very lines and marks of the body were impressed on them. The healing properties of sacred materiality could be transferred, it was believed, from the blessed face of the saint to its aesthetic representation (the cast), then to the believer who touched or stood near the mask, as if it radiated a benevolent light.[8] The royal death expression became memorialized during these centuries, as well as various "celebrities," such as Oliver Cromwell and (allegedly) Shakespeare.[9] Private citizens who could afford it would take a record of the postdeath body, such as Lady Digby's husband, who on her death in 1633 had a painting of her corpse made, as well as plaster casts taken of her face, hands, and feet.[10] The dead features of the gardener, traveler, and collector John Tradescant were represented in an oil painting around 1638.[11] (Paintings, drawings, and photographs of the dead – the latter are discussed in the afterword – do not function as true relics, however, because they have not "touched" the dead and thus are not able to attest to the material existence of the singular body.) Of the many literary celebrities whose death we still hold recorded in effigies, some of the most famous include Keats,[12] Coleridge, Sir Walter Scott,[13] Thackeray, D. G. Rossetti (see Fig. 7), and Robert Louis Stevenson.[14] The postdeath art that proliferated in the nineteenth century represented the motionless features of the unknown, too, along with the famous. Ordinary lovers of others had such memorials created, such as Josephine Butler, who had a death mask made by the sculptor Alex Munro of her little girl Eva, who died in a fall from the staircase in their home. Butler found this plaster cast initially distressing because "every little mark was reproduced," but she later found consolation in the "peaceful expression."[15] Patricia Jalland recounts how one John Horsley had a cast of the head and shoulders of his 3-year-old son taken after the boy's death from scarlet fever in 1854.

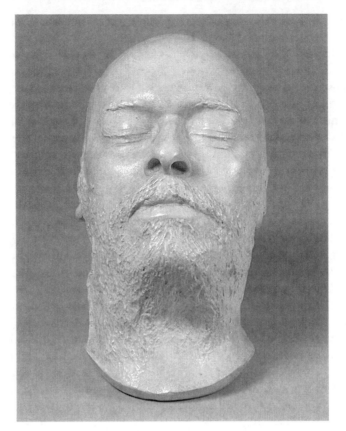

Figure 7.   Plaster cast of Dante Gabriel Rossetti's head incorporating
his death mask. National Portrait Gallery, 1699, 1882.

He displayed the result on a table in his dressing room.[16] When Woronzow
Greig died in 1865, his widow Agnes commissioned a death mask. This
became not only a cherished souvenir but also a kind of window into the
place she believed he was; she found in it "the calm of heaven."[17] In *Aurora
Leigh*, Elizabeth Barrett Browning uses the device of a picture of Aurora's
mother done "after she was dead" as a means to mull over the contradict-
ory influence of the deceased mother on the budding poet. The painting,
hung on the wall of the home and both feared and adored by Aurora, is
described in mystical terms: "That swan-like supernatural white life,/Just
sailing upward from the red stiff silk/Which seemed to have no part in it,
nor power/To keep it from quite breaking out of bounds" (I, lines 139–42).

The mother's spirit expands out of her restraining ("stiff") dress; uncontainable, it seems to float heavenward.[18]

As we have seen, one explanation for the popularity of an aesthetics of death during the period comes from the peace that believers found in these likenesses. The "calm" patina of features likely to have been chaotic in dying (or in unhappy living) was taken to be evidence of the soul passing into a better place, marked on the face, hands, and feet of the body.[19] As discussed in Chapter 2, the evangelical focus on the "good death," revitalized during the Victorian period and pervasive even among nonevangelicals, surrounded the moments of death and the time just after with a glow of the sacred. Rapture, peacefulness, a holy light: these were all signs, read on the body of the dying and deceased, that they were being transported to an afterlife. Josephine Butler described the death of her daughter this way: "She opened her eyes and seemed to see some glory approaching, and her face bore the reflection of that which she saw. Her look was one which rebuked all wild sorrow, and made earthly things sink into insignificance. It was as if she said, *'Now I see God.'*"[20] Frederick Tennyson, the brother of the poet, found the dead face of their father "strikingly lofty and peaceful, I trust it was an image of the condition of his soul, which on earth was daily racked by bitter fancies, and tossed about by strong troubles."[21] Dickens describes little Paul Dombey's last embrace with his sister as illuminated by the "golden light" that came streaming in through the window. As he dies, he exclaims, "the light about the head is shining on me as I go!"[22] Dickens may have been thinking here of the light that was reported to shine from the faces of saints – before, during, and after death – as proof of divine irradiation. It was said of St. Rita of Cascia, for instance, that she was "divinely accorded" a thorn wound in her forehead while alive. Dying, "her cell was filled with an extraordinary perfume, light emanated from the wound in her forehead and the bells of the city are said to have been joyously pealed by angels."[23] Although Dickens was known to be a virulent antipapist – even condemning the ritual of worshiping the relics of saints in some of his writings – he also admired many Catholic practices. This is especially apparent in his descriptions of his trips to Italy. Many Dickens scholars have speculated on his dream while in Italy of the dead Mary Hogarth trying to convert him to Catholicism. Like a good Marian cultist – and, paradoxically, a Victorian Protestant who secularized relics – Dickens subtly equated his Mary with the biblical one.[24] Whatever his complex feelings about Catholic practices, Dickens had a fervent belief in an afterlife – like so many of his contemporaries – where those who had gone before were waiting, arms open to welcome those yet to arrive at this domesticated heaven.[25] The corpse of Little Nell, his most "saintly" heroine, is "so beautiful and calm . . . She seemed a creature fresh from the hand of God."[26] Imbued with the consolation that the vital flame still flickered somewhere, the inanimate flesh called for fixing, for copying.[27] For this reason, viewing the spectacle of dying was seen as an important moral lesson; it was like watching one be saved, through the "book" of the body.[28] Philippe Ariès points out that in the nineteenth century, belief in the afterlife "contributed to the exaltation" of death. "The primary memory to be fixed and perpetuated," he explains, "was that of the individual in death, not in life . . . one senses a determination to preserve at all costs the memory of the *moment of death*."[29] Dickens certainly privileges dying in just such a way in his novels – as a kind of revivification, a fall into the grace of childhood. One version of perishing that he returns to repeatedly is "in the guise it wears when life has just departed: when a young and gentle spirit has but an instant fled to heaven, and the gross air of the world has not had time to breathe upon the changing dust it hallowed."[30] In death the cares and sorrows of a cruel, grasping world pass off the face "and leave heaven's surface clear . . . It is a common thing for the countenances of the dead, even in that fixed and rigid state, to subside into the very look of early life; so calm, so peaceful do they grow again, that those who knew them in their happy childhood kneel by the coffin's side in awe, and see the angel even upon earth" (*Oliver Twist* 192). When Little Nell dies, the question is asked: "Where were the traces of her early cares, her sufferings, and fatigues?" And answered: "All gone. Sorrow was dead indeed in her, but peace and perfect happiness were born; imaged in her tranquil beauty and profound repose."[31] Thus to record the now-inanimate flesh was to create a souvenir of that movement into a place of regeneration.

Although Dickens became a central force in promoting the didactic "good death," he also found in the stilled body and its aesthetics a means to speak in other ways about endings and their materiality. Dickens's attitude toward the dead body had its exaggerated aspects, as will be examined later, but he also picked a thread out of the larger culture and wove it into his more personal preoccupations. Dickens celebrates the dead body and its parts; this is something he finds in his contemporaries, and, by bringing it into his fiction, he works to popularize the idea. Mary Elizabeth Hotz makes a related point, in writing about *Our Mutual Friend*, that Dickens had "an insistent need to accept death, and, simultaneously, a need to be open to death's power to shape life in new ways."[32] For those who lived in close intimacy with corpses – in the nineteenth century, most had watched over or "waked" a body, inhabited rooms where someone had died, or prized death keepsakes of various sorts – death was another stage in the narrative of a body's existence. Ariès's history of postdeath art of the period traces this fluidity between animacy and inanimacy: "Such scenes were apparently born of a desire to represent not just a person but a dead person. The portrait was used not only to preserve the features of a living person, but to fix them in death. It is as if death gave him an extra measure of personality."[33] The movement into matter gave the self a new character, a fresh expressiveness. More than any other novelist of the era, Dickens imbued dying with a personality, and he carried postmortem themes and figures into the common round of the daily living of his characters.[34] Death in his writings was not only a lovely escape into a place "where sorrow and separation are unknown," but it also cohabited with life. Like his contemporaries, Dickens didn't see hanging a postmortem photograph or a death mask on the wall of one's home as gruesome morbidity, but rather as a frank admittance of death as giving life one of its central meanings. Thinking of the body as a "thing" (or a collection of "things") served as a means to accept the demise and decay of the body as part of the natural chronology of existence.

Much writing has been done on the theme of death in Dickens as linked always to the tropes of resurrection and rebirth – those extraordinary occurrences that happen to some mortals, such as John Harmon, who need to "die" first to redeem their lives and those of the individuals around them.[35] But I aim to argue that he also pulls the cadaver and its accoutrements into his fiction to point to those more mundane, little deaths that happen to us all – the faces we put on then discard, the liveliness (or deadliness) we pass on to others, the selves we shed or take on as we move through our being. The focus in this chapter shifts from the use of the relics of another to find a death-in-life to discovering it in the relichood of oneself. The latter is a Keatsian move; he self-relicized in and with his poems. Dickens studies the relics of selfhood (along with those of the other) with the characters in his novels. The finding of the materiality of death in the self, however, moves seamlessly into finding the other in postmortem matter. To think of this in a different way: both are means of imagining that objects can hold subjectivity, through intimacy with the body. Dickens spreads his interest across self, other, and object; he says to us that death shapes all steps in life, all gestures of the vital and deanimated body, a philosophy that situates him firmly in the death culture of his contemporaries. Rather than the stopped narrative, the corpse had an intimate relationship, for Dickens and the Victorians, with reading and the book as an object, as I will explore. Dickens's novels probe the porousness of the life/death boundary and the way that animation could move smoothly, both ways, along a continuum: from vitality into matter, and from dead matter into a kind of liveliness. The thing-ness of the body emerges as an important trope for *Great Expectations* especially and the dangers and, perhaps, joys, of self-ossification, fixedness, as well as leaving in one's wake permanent impressions, epitaphs, and memorials.

The corpse as collage, frieze, or waxwork

The plot of *Great Expectations* moves within a thick air of the elegiac. Given that it is not a book obviously about death, this fact needs some excavation. Although actual deaths and deep disappointments occur to be mourned (Pip's sister and Magwitch die, for instance, but also rend Pip with their actions while living), the narrative has a spreading mist of grieving that rises mysteriously from small, unconsidered moments, from the objects of daily being. Much of this background of loss comes from Pip's feelings of existential belatedness. He rarely wants what he has until it has become inaccessible to him – Joe's simple goodness and Biddy's wise warmth, the care he can take for Magwitch after he is mortally wounded. And he wants desperately that which he will never be able to possess, Estella being the most obvious example, or a past cleaned of class shame. Pip has trouble coinciding with himself, which in turn leads to a measure of self-haunting. Even more perilous for him is his deep regret over his lack of mastery of his own story. Suffused often with shame over his powerlessness, he mourns his victimhood and longs to be someone else. *Great Expectations* is a novel full of disappointed characters, or ones struggling to stop the seep of the paralyzing poison of bitterness, regret, and defeat. Many mourn their failures, as if they have already died and must transfer life to others: Miss Havisham to Estella, Magwitch to Pip, Pip to the second Pip. These elegies at the back of events often burst out with a startling concreteness. Little memorials come seeded throughout the novel, whether it is the opening scene with Pip reading his familial gravestones, the death masks cluttering Jaggers's London chambers, or the mourning jewelry dangling from Wemmicks's coat front. By some mysterious process the elegiac tends, in the novel, toward the effigic. Not only do the departed leave small testaments of their existence behind, but even the still animated have the tendency to fossilize into hardened versions of themselves or become moving memorials to what they might have been or once were. In other words, the materiality of death enters the narrative of being inextricably.

Death presses in from all sides, making its appearance in the daily round in all registers – as farce, tragedy, as dull everydayness (dragging the weighty body through the hours). Magwitch appears to be "eluding the hands of the dead people, stretching up cautiously out of their graves, to get a twist upon his ankle and pull him in."[36] The deceased seem to surround the walking and breathing, massing themselves on the other side and ready to pluck one into their swelling ranks. The gibbet, with its display of hanging, rotting flesh, awaits Magwitch as if he were "the pirate come to life, and come down, and going back to hook himself up again" (7). Magwitch could be always a decaying carcass, then, about to, Pip surmises, "drop down before my face and die" (18), or, always looking for that light to go out as it finally does toward the end of the book. Pip also seems balanced along that permeable boundary. Mrs. Joe stipulates, before Joe and Pip head out to join the chase for the convicts in the marshes, "if you bring the boy back with his head blown to bits by a musket, don't look to me to put it together again" (33).[37] Miss Havisham, who will be discussed at greater length later, teeters on the edge of her grave, always with a "deadly lull" upon her, making Pip alarmed she will cause him and Estella to "presently begin to decay" (89).[38] Most characters come associated with some death emblem – Jaggers's carved garlands on the paneled walls of his home that look like nooses, Mr. Pocket who takes the attitude of the "Dying Gladiator" – as if they are friezes on ancient Roman tombs, surrounded by pictures of the objects most akin to them (images of shoes next to a portrait on a cobbler's tablet, for example). It is as if they carry their death around with them, in bundles of awareness of last things. Or, if we keep in our sights postmortem art, their deaths are already etched into materiality, in the form of effigies, epigraphy, and more humble and commonplace relics.

The aesthetics of death in Dickens lead always back to the body and its availability for becoming a thing, a relic predeath. The plaster casting of the faces and hands of cadavers reminds us that these are the most expressive parts of the body, the most vulnerable; they hold the secret of personality. Through their gestures, tensions, puckered or relaxed parts, they act as windows into emotional states such as shame (blushing), sorrow (drawn-down lines), and interiority in general. Because they are so intricately meshed with being, they are prime candidates for shining with undeath, or thingness that maintains the vitalism of the postperished. Faces and hands find a good deal of play in *Great Expectations*, reminding us of life and death masks and casts of hands and bodies. Characters are introduced by pushing their faces and heads to the foreground of the narrative, such as Camilla, of whom Pip finds it "a Mercy she had any features at all, so very blank and high was the dead wall of her face" (81) signifying, of course, her false and greedy nature – the mask is all she is, through and through. The same remark could be made of Sarah Pocket, who has "a small face that might have been made of walnut shells" (87). Jaggers is first introduced as a burly man "with an exceedingly large head and a correspondingly large hand" (83), giving the reader immediately a flavor of his bullying nature. Wemmick floats out of the sooty backdrop of London as "a square wooden face" (171), which Pip finds out later, to his delight, *really is a mask*, hiding an interior that has give. Estella haunts Pip's vision often as just a face "in the glowing fire . . . extracted . . . from the darkness of night to look in at the window of the forge and flit away" (236).[39] Pip feels most painfully his class shame through his hands after Estella calls them "coarse."[40] He comes to see them as "vulgar append-ages," wishing he could be detached from them because they represent a part of his selfhood he would like to annihilate. John Carey points to the separable quality of many of the bodies of Dickens's characters, seeing it as "a deeply ingrained imaginative habit to see bits of people's bodies as if they have come adrift from the rest, or to make them handle parts of themselves as if they belonged to someone else."[41] David Copperfield's caul works as a startling example. Believed to protect the owner from drowning, the birth membrane was often sold. First advertised in a newspaper, David's caul is eventually won in a raffle by an old lady.

Pip's body-as-thing points to the soft material of faces and hands, which express traces of the interior, but can also easily take the impression of things, gain layers of meaning from other objects rubbing off on them. Jaggers tries to wash his clients off his hands and face, as if they create a film of corruption that overlays his very flesh. The countenance of Molly, Estella's mother and Jaggers's servant, carries with it a sense of being "disturbed by fiery air" (212), as if her murderous actions in the past agitate the atmosphere in front of her features. After leaving Newgate on a visit with Wemmick, Pip muses on the way that the "taint of prison and crime" starts "out like a stain that was faded but not gone" (264) and seems to linger on his body.[42] London impresses Pip the most as a place where people and things pick up dust and grit that lay thickly everywhere, just as Smithfield seems to stick to him, with its filth, fat, blood, and foam.[43] Sometimes the smudging substance causes what is underneath to shine forth more clearly, such as when Magwitch tries to disguise himself with powder, which was like "rouge upon the dead; so awful was the manner in which everything in him that it was most desirable to repress, started through that thin layer of pretence, and seemed to come blazing out at the crown of his head" (338). The body, a kind of artwork, like a collage, picks up narrative as it moves about, becoming both a "speaking" thing and, inversely, a multilayered secret, harder and harder to "read" as it gains a carapace of living. Just as they can be impressed upon, so can the face and hands – and any furniture of the body – leave their trace on their environs, being the oily, flakey, grimy implements they so often can be. It is no surprise to find that since the walls of Jaggers's office are "greasy with shoulders," so, too, do the staircases have a dark wash of sweaty limbs from their "shuffling up and down the staircase for years" (199).[44] Such leavings and the ability to be marked provide an ever-present reminder of how bodies are not just the container for "selves," but they are also substances that leak and rot, that can be creased and smeared. *Great Expectations* is a story aware of the objecthood of all people (not just Pip), how one might be "fished up by the hair" (12), might "deliver himself at the door . . . like coals" (173), or might be "an animated rag bag whom she called her niece" (327). Such examples proliferate exponentially if Dickens's other novels are taken into consideration. Oliver Twist is called a "bag o' bones" (32); when Oliver's mother dies, the doctor calls her "Mrs. Thingummy"; and all, in *The Mystery of Edwin Drood*, are merely "dust with the breath of life in it," to give just a few examples out of hundreds.

Dickens had a lifelong fascination with the thing-ness of the body. A frequent visitor to the Paris morgue (where the unclaimed dead were put on public display), he felt "dragged" there, as he says in the guise of the Uncommercial Traveller, "by invisible force," though he admits to being often horrified by what he saw.[45] Something about the grotesque mesmerized him, but he also wanted to see the corpse becoming corpse: there is hardly any other way to explain his attending two public hangings in England and a beheading when in Rome. John Carey remarks of Dickens that he "never missed a human carcass if he could help it."[46] The intellectual – and emotional, even – acceptance that the body was finally just an inanimate object brought a curious kind of joy for him. He adored Holbein's *Dance of Death*, and when a young journalist, he sent a business card to an editor that read "CHARLES DICKENS, Resurrectionist, In Search of a Subject." (A "resurrectionist" was a grave robber of the Burke and Hare stripe. Jerry Cruncher, in *The Tale of Two Cities*, is one.)[47] Death, cadavers cavorting about full of fun, corpses stolen, all these struck Dickens as a bit humorous, but also essential, in ways that will be explored further later, as a means to tell stories.

Some of this humor came from viewing death as a safe place, placid enough for poking fun. Like so many of his fellow novelists of the era, Dickens presents the imagined space of death as a site of comfort, a realm to be yearned for by characters still vigorous. In *Our Mutual Friend*, Jenny Wren creates a rooftop eyrie with Lizzie Hexam, which, with its light, air, and peace, she calls "being dead." "'Oh, so tranquil!' . . . 'Oh, so peaceful and thankful! And you hear the people who are alive, crying and working and calling to one another down in the close, dark streets, and you seem to pity them so! And such a chain has fallen from you, and such a strange good sorrowful happiness comes upon you!' "[48] In the famous scene that opens *Great Expectations*, where we find Pip sitting terrified in the graveyard, a secret desire comingled with a deep dread floats within him, unmoored and subtle: a desire to be dead, like his little brothers who "gave up trying to get a living, exceedingly early in that universal struggle" (3). Magwitch expresses a similar sentiment in the same graveyard: "I was a hiding among the graves there, envying them as was in 'em and all over" (352).[49] To want to end before you begin describes a temporality common to *Great Expectations*. The grave, then, might be a welcoming home, just the right fit for a weary body. Dickens picks up on a common understanding of death in nineteenth-century Britain, when the tomb was made so that it coincided exactly with the body; sometimes a little footstone would be set at the feet of the corpse, like the footboard of a bed frame (with the grave marker acting as headboard).[50] As a means to complicate the chronology of a life span, as if dying might come first, or at any time during being and then animation could come after, Dickens brings the grave and funerary art into his characters' narratives. Dickens, whose characters' names take up such an important place in his fictions, found many of his best names from frequenting graveyards. ("Fanny Dorrit" can be found on a marker near Rochester Cathedral, and from three tombstones at a Chalk church he read off these names of the dead: Guppy, Twist, and Flight.)[51] Joe and Pip cross their fingers when Pip's sister is in a "cross temper," so that their fingers are "like monumental Crusaders as to their legs" (22). This is a reference to the belief (erroneous, incidentally) that if an effigy of a knight on a medieval tomb had crossed legs, this meant the man had taken a vow to proceed to the Holy Land as a crusader.[52] Pip himself is "put upon a tombstone" (286) as a child, a placing and imaginative space that is recalled with profound significance in his adulthood.[53] In a literal sense, this refers to Magwitch forcing Pip to sit atop a grave marker, of course, but implicit here is also the idea of Pip's effigy or epitaph "put upon" a tomb. His parents and brothers are "put upon" tombstones in that their epitaphs are all that is left for Pip to know them by.[54] He attempts to "read" their identities from these material carvings: "my first fancies regarding what they were like, were unreasonably derived from their tombstones" (3). The font of these engraved letters seems to him to mirror the character of their bodies: "The shape of the letters on my father's, gave me an odd idea that he was a square, stout, dark man, with curly black hair" (3). The art that death leads to – in this case epigraphy – works as a commentary on their life story. All relics have a profoundly narrative quality, as was discussed in Chapter 2, but postdeath art lends itself especially to "reading." In the death mask, we read the tale of the body moving through being – marked as it has been by being bumped, scraped, and ravaged by experience. If bodies or their aesthetic remnants can be texts, then texts have an intimate relationship to bodies, here, specifically, dead ones. J. Hillis Miller considers written texts as akin to death masks. The living hand writes a text, which becomes a kind of "replica" that survives the death of the author: "The hand that writes and its double, the face, are in their replicas both survivors of and survived by the text that the living hand has written." The text, like a death cast, gives a "face" to the absent, the dead; "The text survives as the cast or simulacrum of the events it records." Reading, he continues, might then be a fitting of the death mask to our own faces, "the cast to our own hands, [we] shape our hands and faces to their shape."[55] Texts write us as we give them life, just as we pick up death from them, and out of death comes narrative, just as Pip attempts to give himself a face (and tries to revive the faces of his family) by reading a text of death.

Because the opening passage – an essential scene of origin for Pip – is not only his first "impression of the identity of things" (3), but also his first awareness of his own identity, somehow who he is becomes linked to a marking of his death, actual or figural, just as his family is understood through their grave markers. Before teasing out the implications of Pip's beginning coinciding with his ending, a brief exploration of funerary art is helpful. Dickens, who wrote about tombs and the "bodies of deceased saints" on his trips to Italy and around Britain, would have been aware of the fact that, starting around the fifteenth century, tomb sculptures were often whole-body effigies, either fashioned from studying the features of the subject just after death (sometimes, right at the moment of death) or, more concretely, by taking actual casts of the hands and face of the corpse.[56] As a child, Dickens used to gaze on a tomb at Rochester Cathedral that had a "staring" effigy "bursting out" of it. The corpse would often be arranged on the bed exactly as the tomb effigy would then be fashioned, with hands crossed, legs orderly and straightened, and the feet carefully aligned.[57] It is as if the body becomes effigy, hardening directly from flesh into stone. Dickens imagines this with Mrs. Gamp, who muses about her patient, not yet dead, in this way: "a horrible remembrance of one branch of her calling took possession of the woman; and stooping down, she pinned his wandering arms against his sides, to see how he would look if laid out like a dead man. Hideous as it may appear, her fingers itched to compose his limbs in that last marble attitude."[58] But Dickens was particularly attuned to and, as I will argue, makes a theme in *Great Expectations*, the way that art – here, the funerary sculpture – also influenced the fleshly body. The "recumbent figure" – a representation of the dead, as if they are sleeping on their own tombs (see Fig. 8) – became so popular that the influence began to flow the other way: the corpse would be made to imitate the eventual sculpture, the artistic style thus coming to shape the view of the body itself. A variation on the tomb statue came from the popular practice in England and Europe from the fifteenth to the eighteenth centuries of creating effigies of kings and queens that would, in effect, *replace* the corpse. Placed on the coffin for the procession and sometimes displayed to the people as a stand-in for the body, the sculptures, called, interestingly, "representations" (also "personas," or "pictures"), could be formed from wax, plaster, or wood.[59] Sometimes the craftsman would set up an armature, pack it with straw, and build the exterior "walls" of plaster or wax (the effigy of Queen Elizabeth of York was made this way, for instance).[60] Boiled leather worked, in some cases, as an approximation to skin with hay as the "entrails," such as in the case of the effigy of Henry V.[61] Death masks or

Figure 8.   Bronze recumbent effigy of Prince Albert, modeled by Carlo, Baron Marochetti, RCIN 45185. The face is based on a death mask.

copies from such masks generally were used for the faces (like the representations of Edward III and Henry VII, where a death mask was set into the wooden head and then painted), and human hair would often be used to make wigs to cover the heads.[62] These likenesses provided a material presentation of the theory of the king's (or queen's) two bodies: the natural body of the now-dead man or woman (the cadaver) and the "body politic" (the effigy), now transferred to the living king.[63] Another type of "dummy" is the "auto-icon" – figures that included parts of the body, such as the one Jeremy Bentham arranged to have made of himself in 1832 that incorporates his bones.[64] Many displays of the saints in churches contain a kind of mixture of old flesh and "representations"; St. Catherine Laboure's "incorrupt" body, one example of many, is composed of human remains except for the wax hands.[65] Dickens was enthralled by such representations, especially the waxworks of dead children at the Museum of National History in Florence. He called them "admonitions of our frail mortality." The thing itself and its material replacement become meshed, reminding us of the body as always a member of the world of things.

Dickens presents a conflation of the practice in *Oliver Twist*, when he imagines the cadavers as themselves wax copies: "A many, many beautiful corpse she laid out as nice and neat as wax-work" (194). The corpse itself works as artwork, a frieze of the purity of the deaths of the poor and their graceful stepping off the edge, after a disorderly life of suffering. Art comes, at long last, with death. With postmortem art generally, the body transforming into an object at death has an additional stage, with the corpse becoming another object, whether it is an effigy, sculpture (auto-icon), painting, or photograph. The art comes to then inform those still animated, as if they are always ready to become their effigy. Carrying the corpse back into the narrative of being, postmortem art carves the ontological out of the eschatological.

In Dickens, as in the history of funerary art recounted earlier, "representations" can sometimes hold more truth than originals, or to put this another way, there is often more than one version of the self, and these multitudes can be effigic (and elegiac). Characters have complicated relationships to their effigies, to their selves that memorialize, solidify, become frozen. The best example is poor Bradley Headstone, from *Our Mutual Friend*, who walks around, already his own tomb. Miss Havisham effigizes quite readily. When Pip first lays eyes on her, he recalls a "ghastly waxworks" he saw at the fair, "representing I know not what impossible personage lying in state" (58). Like royalty, she has "two bodies," or more obviously, she turns herself into an auto-icon because the thing itself is still contained therein. Not only is she her own effigy, but Pip also compares her to various versions of disinterred corpses: "Once, I had been taken to one of our old marsh churches to see a skeleton in the ashes of a rich dress, that had been dug out of a vault under the church pavement" (58). He also thinks of "the discoveries that are occasionally made of bodies buried in ancient times, which fall to powder in the moment of being distinctly seen" (60). Miss Havisham's undeadness has the three stages mentioned in funerary art: the body mobile, the corpse (in various stages of decay), and the "representation."[66] Despite seeming to hover between three options, Miss Havisham finds herself stuck in place, in one state. Her tragedy comes from effigizing at a single bitter moment – when she receives the jilting letter, at twenty minutes to nine. Her death mask is, in some sense, taken just then, like a snapshot (as all casts or masks are); those are the seams and ravages her face will always carry. Transferred onto her body and the objects around her is the gall of her rejection, just as faces and hands can be smudged by soot and dust. And she impresses her embittered ridginess onto others, most notably Estella. Like taking a lump of clay and shaping it, Miss Havisham takes "an impressionable child to mould into the form ... [of] her wild resentment" (399). Despite her own fossilization, she gains a demonic power, as Elisabeth Bronfen describes it, to fashion the stories of others "by speaking from the position of an empty grave."[67] In other words, her relationship to death makes her a powerful generator of narrative. Bronfen understands *Great Expectations* to be about how "the act of storytelling involves listeners and speakers that are absent from the world."[68] Gallagher makes a similar argument, writing of *Our Mutual Friend*, that "apparent death is the condition of storytelling and regenerative change."[69] In the end, Miss Havisham reaches a final effigic state. She wants her family to imagine her laid out on her bridal table when she dies, where the rotten cake now sits, and which makes Pip worry she might climb up and become "the complete realization of the ghastly waxworks" (85). In some sense, this is exactly what she does. Mortally wounded in the fire, she is laid there, wrapped in cotton-wool like a mummy, with "the phantom-air of something that had been and was changed" (403). Slowly becoming what she has always meant to be, she turns from mobile body to postmortem art.

What is to be feared here is not perishing, then, nor even becoming inanimate, but losing the capability to be many selves. A fearful example of this is Pip's mother, reduced in death to merely "Also Georgiana Wife of the Above" (3). One of the most successful characters at fluidly moving between versions of the self is Wemmick. These different selves are marked, of course, on his face. When in the City his countenance holds its wooden, mechanical appearance, but when inhabiting his pleasant home in Wal-worth, kept with his "aged parent," a softness loosens his features. Pip notes the movement from self to self when they walk together into the City from the suburbs: he "got dryer and harder ... and his mouth tightened into a post-office again" (210). Wemmick's relation to postdeath art appears clearly with the mourning jewelry he wears, such as the four rings and "a brooch representing a lady and a weeping willow at a tomb with an urn on it" (171).[70] Keepsakes given to him by condemned criminals, these amulets don't represent grieving at all. As "portable property," they work rather as embellishments for his jacket, markers of not only the dead (unmourned) but also of his past movements through the City, his work, and his visits to Newgate to press the hands of the soon-to-die (who are compared to plants that he tends).[71] A flexibility and even humor characterize Wemmick's relation to memorialization and the effigic. Other selves will always come to supplant earlier ones, just as new shoots will spring up at the prison to replace those that have been cut down. Wemmick balances successfully the requirements of becoming, at times, a fossilized self with, at other times, being a pliable self, open to transformation.

Pip has the tendency not so much to get stuck in one sorrowful moment, like Miss Havisham, but rather to feel that the current self, whatever it is, is not the real self. Somehow those other selves he might have been (a born gentleman; happy being a blacksmith and never having met Miss Havisham and Estella; a fellow promised to Estella with Miss Havisham as his benefactress), or once were (a simple boy at the forge, loving Joe) are the true ones. Pip always bears this shadow with him; he mourns these other versions that flit about him like revenants. But at times they become more substantial. From this backdrop of elegy, reminders of these lost beings emerge in various material ways. For instance, when Pip finds out that Magwitch is his real benefactor, he sees himself as Victor Frankenstein's creation: "The imaginary student pursued by the misshapen creature he had impiously made, was not more wretched than I, pursued by the creature who had made me" (339). Pip imagines himself here as both the student who made the creature and the creature itself (and pursued, in any case). In the sense that Pip has always seen himself as guiltily, secretly – and mysteriously – linked to the outcast and felonious, he "made" this alternate self, Magwitch, who now runs him down and must be accepted. But Pip is also the poor deformed creature, made out of parts of the corpses of a variety of people, all of them criminals or outcasts. His many selves, then, become connected to dismembered body parts, the castoff meat of the unmourned dead.

Pip's identification with the tombs in the graveyard, discussed earlier, represents a potential self, one that died as an infant (another Pip he sometimes longs to be). The water of the Thames makes him think of what he might have been, "all drifting by, as on the swift stream of my life fast running out to sea!" (428). The Pip that is the successful lover of Estella floats about him, represented by a ghostly mask of Estella's features, seen sometimes in the fire of the forge, other times through the windows at night, when he would fancy that he "saw her just drawing her face away" (108).[72] Onto the face of the other are transferred one's own desires, a kind of cast of yearning, an ephemeral souvenir of a land never to be found. Other potential identities for Pip that push themselves forward, like faces crowding in a window, are ones he has feared becoming and that spark their own type of grief. He is saddened by the ways he might be like the Miss Havisham auto-icon, an effigy of a broken heart.[73] The sooty death masks in Jaggers's office that reappear repeatedly in the narrative represent some layer in Pip's identity connected to criminality. As a boy, his general feeling of guilt, augmented by robbing his sister's kitchen to feed Magwitch on the marshes and then having to spin lies about those events, bring him to believe he's speedily on his way to prison himself. When the soldiers come to the house on their way to chase after the escaped Magwitch and Compeyson, Pip is sure that the handcuffs are for him. Upon his first arrival in London, Pip waits in Jaggers's office alone, wondering about the relics of the criminals strewn about. Pip finds unbearable the stare of "two dreadful casts on a shelf, of faces peculiarly swollen, and twitchy about the nose" (164) that sit on a "dusty perch" gathering blacks and flies. They remind him of the time when Magwitch put him on a tombstone, as a child and thus take him back to that formative moment of victimhood and association with a "depraved" class. The suspended animation of the faces, complete with the grooves, lines, and wrinkles transferred from the bodies, call up Pip's worries about becoming ossified in a hateful state and then being permanently remembered as such. When he is convinced he'll die by Orlick's hands, what he fears most is being misremembered: "And so quick were my thoughts, that I saw myself despised by unborn generations" (425). Pip wants to beget a loving memorial or epitaph, but his guilt and sense of self-belatedness make him feel this is impossible. Another reason Pip sees these relics as versions of self-fossilization is because he feels a victim of his fate. These are casts of his debasement (as he sees it at this point in his life), his forced identification with the lowest strata of society. In *Great Expectations*, the criminal we come to know best – Magwitch – is painted as a victim of a cruel social order that abandons him as a young child, leaving him no choice but to find food and shelter through dishonest means. Pip sees himself saddled with similar injustice and thus doomed to be always with the outsiders and, finally, effigized as such. What Pip will come to realize, however, is that such little entombments are scattered throughout living and can, ideally, be points of continued narrative rather than full stops. The body represents this deanimation, but it might be merely caught in a kind of suspended animation and be able to jump up again, participate in the *danse macabre* that is being.

The jovial, dancing cadaver to be skinned, eaten, or read

The postmortem art that resonates with the most meaning in *Great Expectations*, and that seem to hold some special key to death's placement in existence, are the death masks in Jaggers's office. Casts of a murderer and a forger hanged for their deeds, they were made in Newgate directly after the men were taken down from the scaffold. Dickens possibly modeled them on ones he viewed of executed criminals, shown to him by his friend and family doctor, Dr. John Elliotson.[74] Dickens had a deep interest in criminality in general, and he especially found murderers fascinating.[75] The features of two "resurrectionists" who were executed for their murder of an Italian boy, John Bishop and Thomas Williams, were fixed in death masks, and Dickens saw them at an exhibition at Newgate Prison.[76] He would visit the scenes of murders and buy "last confessions" that were sold on the street around the time of execution.[77] Mrs. Jarley, in *The Old Curiosity Shop*, has numerous murderers in her collection of wax-works, who are posed in ways reminiscent of their crimes, such as Jasper Packlemerton, whose fingers are curled as if in the act of tickling because he destroyed his fourteen wives "by tickling the soles of their feet when they were sleeping."[78] Dickens is referencing an important subset of relic-love, common in eighteenth- and nineteenth-century England and America: collecting souvenirs of criminals, including post-death art.[79] In addition to casts, postmortem photography became a means, popular especially in America, as a way to document the successes of lawmen and to feed public fascination with these celebrities. A stereoview photo of Jesse James in his coffin, from 1882, was sold widely in America. Another of Rube Barrow, a celebrated train robber and murderer nicknamed "Lone Wolf," killed in 1890, shows a coffin standing up with the "Wolf" stuffed in it, along with his guns and holsters.[80] Wemmick also keeps souvenirs of celebrity malefactors in his home, such as "the pen with which a celebrated forgery had been committed, a distinguished razor or two, some locks of hair, and several manuscript confessions written under condemnation" (209). The popular relish for such mementos of crime moves against the grain of my central argument about the practice of treasuring the remains of ordinary loved ones. Here we have a desire for sensationalism – the drama of lives in which extreme events occur – connected closely to the "celebrity" relic collecting described in Chapter 1. Collectors feel they become part of a larger history with such objects, imaginatively stepping into a more passionate, deviant, and perhaps clever set of experiences than their own. Keepsakes of crime and of the dead loved one, however, share the quality of being coveted because meaning inheres in these remains of lives.

Another reason Dickens and so many others felt a need to fix the features of criminals was because of the popular belief in physiognomy. If one's character traits could be read in the furniture of the face or in the bumps (or shape) of the skull (phrenology), then to save important examples of the criminal "type," after death, casts and/or photos were needed (see Fig. 9).[81] Wemmick certainly "reads" the depraved actions of these two men in their casts, seeing in both of them "the genuine look" (200). Magwitch recalls that when he was deemed a "hardened one," "they" measured his head, as if this might be a way to discover the source of his felonious behavior. When Dickens saw the death mask of John Bishop, he joked that it "exhibit[ed] a style of head and set of feature, which might have afforded sufficient moral grounds for his instant execution at any time, even had there been no other evidence against him."[82] In *Great Expectations*, the fact that one might be fated from birth to live a hard life full of injustice is what Pip – and the novel – grieves. "Fixedness" (hardness) in general works as a figure for injustice in Dickens, whereas the supple, the soft, has redemptive qualities. And when one becomes "fixed," as is inevitable, then the best one can do is to be open to transformation. A means that Dickens uses to signal this transformative possibility is through humor, especially the tragicomedy of criminality.

An additional reason for the Victorian interest in criminal relics, and this was particularly true for Dickens, was a sort of macabre humor – another side to the Victorian materialization of death. Jaggers's death masks manage, despite the tragedy they come to represent for Pip, to have a comic liveliness more expressive than the countenances of many characters, like Sarah Pocket's nutlike features. When Wemmick takes them off their shelf to show them to Pip, he suspects one has "come down in the night and been peeping into the inkstand" (200). During Pip's

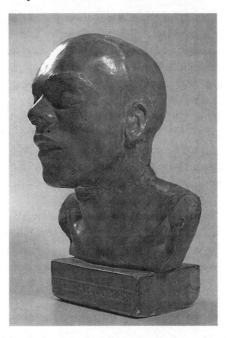

Figure 9.   Cast of the death mask of William Corder, hanged in 1828 for murdering
his lover Maria Marten. The marks of the rope can still be seen on his neck.
Artifacts from the "Red Barn Murder" of 1827, as it was called, are in the same
collection, including part of Corder's scalp, a piece of the barn turned into a
shoe-shaped snuff box, and more. Moyse's Hall Museum, Bury St. Edmunds.

confrontation with Jaggers about his benefactor, the effigies seem to
"attend to the conversation" (286), looking "as if they had come to a crisis
in their suspended attention, and were going to sneeze" (289). These
effigies bring us again to the jaunty humor surrounding death that inter-
mingles with the elegiac in the novel. When beginning to write *Great
Expectations* in 1860, Dickens felt that the "pivot on which the story will
turn" was the "grotesque tragic-comic" conception, as he explained it in a
letter to John Forster.[83] Dickens's interest in Holbein's *Dance of Death* is
instructive here. The image of the skeleton jovially prancing about,
plucking the reluctant living to join in the dance, calls to mind the
absurdity of fate and the body – how strange and arbitrary it is that one's
body stops functioning at a certain point and becomes a pile of flesh and
bones.[84] Writing in *The Uncommercial Traveller* about his visits to the
Paris morgue, Dickens found a certain sad humor in imagining the corpses

there springing to life: "This time, I was forced into the same dread place, to see a large dark man whose disfigurement by water was in a frightful manner comic, and whose expression was that of a prize-fighter who had closed his eyelids under a heavy brow, but was going immediately to open them, shake his head, and 'come up smiling.'"[85] Philippe Ariès finds the art of the "danse macabre" "in the contrast between the rhythm of the dead and the rigidity of the living." ("The dead lead the dance," he adds, "indeed, they are the only ones dancing.")[86] In the world of Dickens, stiffening can happen to those stuck in their lives, while becoming a corpse or its representation can bring a measure of suppleness.[87] Imagined cadavers, in Dickens more generally, seem able to assert their presence in ways that the still-vital body can't, just as when Monks fantasizes about Oliver dead and buried: "'If you buried him fifty feet deep . . . I should know, if there wasn't a mark above it, that he lay buried there" (283). The elegy that runs underneath the story – like an underground spring – glimmers forth in a melodramatic sorrow or a dark jollity, the two not being enemies but holding hands.

The fluidity across the life–death boundary in so much of Dickens's fiction appears through these two moods; a macabre hilarity is seeded throughout *Great Expectations* and so many of Dickens's late novels, especially *Bleak House* and *Our Mutual Friend*. Such tone shifts are used by Dickens to carry us with him in his delight in the body as a thing (and also – and somehow at the same time – the deepest tragedy of existence), as just another part of a crowded landscape of objects to love and hate. Disembowelment and the idea of being eaten or feasted upon provide opportunities for this kind of humor and are also ways to imagine the body as transformative and ready to be aestheticized. Magwitch, upon first meeting Pip in the graveyard, threatens to have Pip's "heart and liver out" if he's not brought a file and "wittles." Orlick, when still at the forge, seems often about to run a red-hot bar through Pip's body or either to be "jiggered" or to "jigger" someone, which to Pip sounds like something "savagely damaging" done to one's body "with a sharp and twisted hook" (131). Being skinned or eaten seems like rather a droll way to go. Wopsle appears to be flayed when he has his Shakespearean stockings taken off. Magwitch exclaims, when he first meets Pip in the graveyard, "'Darn Me if I couldn't eat 'em . . . and if I hadn't half a mind to't!" (4). This is the first of many references to the delights of cannibalizing Pip, sometimes raw and other times cooked.[88] The fictitious fellow escapee that Magwitch makes up to scare Pip wants, he claims, to tear Pip open and roast and eat his organs. During Christmas dinner, the adult diners like to imagine, for the sake of an argument about how privileged he is, Pip as "a four-footed Squeaker," whom the butcher disposes with his "penknife" (27), landing him on the table as the main course of the meal.[89] Miss Havisham finds a grim amusement in imagining herself as corpse, laid out where her rotting bridal cake sits, with her greedy relatives around her, ready to partake of this new decomposing dessert. "'Now you all know where to take your stations when you come to feast upon me,'" she exclaims. "'It's very hard to be told one wants to feast on one's relations – as if one was a Giant'" (88) Camilla grumbles in response.[90] There is something funny about imagining being eaten – the many children's tales about consumption by giants and the giggling response of children attest to this. Picturing the body as transformative in general brings pleasure: turning into an animal or a whimsical machine, for instance, or growing gigantic or tiny, as Alice does. Thus does the body seem to have many lives or selves. Being eaten is being incorporated into another's breathing and moving self, transforming into another, being plugged back into vital being.

Transformation works as a key term for so much of Dickens's fiction, which serves to emphasize the permeability of the life/death boundary – the possibility that a body might reanimate after becoming life-drained. Or that the vital body might fall into dormant states. To be in the midst of change, not quite one thing or another (a rotten carcass ambling about or a nutrient being chewed up), describes the state of many characters peopling *Great Expectations*, whether it is Miss Havisham becoming carrion, Pip "a model with a mechanical heart to practise on" (323), or Wemmick's mouth a post-office. Indeed, the prefix *trans-* becomes essential to Dickens's presentation of death and deathlike states in his fiction, floating about and attaching itself to various gestures and movements. Postmortem art transfixes the self at the moment of death (or soon after); the seams of the face and hands are transferred onto the death cast; death brings to the body a transfiguration, a shining radiance (to die without dying is to be translated – like Enoch and Elijah – a term also used when the relics of saints' bodies were moved to a new site). The "transi," as mentioned in Chapter 1, was the figure of a decaying corpse (worm-infested, rotting flesh peeling off, the skeleton showing through), which became popular from the thirteenth through the fifteenth centuries in funerary art, frescoes, and other visual arts and in poetry about death. But the *trans-* in *transfer* has a privileged place in Dickens's use of posthumous aesthetics in his fiction, as well as in the history of mourning and death culture in general. As a critic of Victorian funeral practices (he satirizes them in *Great Expectations* when Pip's sister dies and Trabb and Co. "put in a funeral execution"

[279] – and in numerous other writings, such as *Oliver Twist* and *Martin Chuzzlewit*), Dickens was clearly steeped in various folk customs and beliefs about the corpse and mourning still common in the first half of the nineteenth century.[91] Some of these ancient practices involved trans-actions or transfers of meaning between the loved one's body and visitors to the deathbed. Touching the corpse was one such gesture: with a motion of the hands or lips, the mourner pressed or kissed the brow or cheek. A mysterious transfer would take place, according to believers, either from cadaver to griever or the other way around. To caress the corpse might be a way to gain the deceased's strength, for example, or to gather to one the good luck the dead might otherwise take with her.[92] This certainly happens with the kissing and hugging of Little Nell's body by her grand-father, who hopes to thereby hold onto her angelic nature and, past all hope, transfer his life and warmth to her rapidly cooling body. The corpse, in these cases, worked as a useful site, a space for transference and transformation, for stories to be passed on.

The mourner might also bless the corpse through such transfers. Can-nibalizing the dead body, not literally but metonymically, was another way to glean meaning from the dead. Funeral feasts have their origin in a number of traditional beliefs, among them that the food consumed stands in for the body of the moribund. In this sense the mourners are "eating" parts of the corpse, reincorporating the materials of death back into the motions of vigorous bodies. One could "consume" positive attributes from the deceased, or even take on the "sins" of the soon-to-be-judged. A destitute or marginalized person was sometimes hired for this purpose, called a "sin eater."[93] Dickens imagines a deceased child as something to be eaten in *The Uncommercial Traveller* when he visits a crypt for the poor. Stretched out in its coffin and having been dissected – "it had been opened, and neatly sewn up" – a baby appears somehow palatable. "It looked as if the cloth were 'laid,' and the Giant were coming to dinner. There was nothing repellent about the poor piece of innocence, and it demanded a mere form of looking at. So, we looked at an old pauper who was going about among the coffins with a foot rule, as if he were a case of Self-Measurement; and we looked at one another."[94] The transfer of gazes makes the adults feel that they will, too, soon enough, be "food." Such a repast here is delectable rather than "repellent," as if eating the baby might be a means of eating (and thus, impossibly, redeeming) the sins of society. This has something of the quality of Christians eating the host, claimed to be Christ's body (and the wine his blood). In addition, imagining becom-ing oneself such a delicious bundle has a consoling quality. All food, all with a capability to be eaten, we might all enter back into that alimentary circle. Becoming-object (meat) has a purifying aspect, in Dickens.[95]

These practices of "using" the cadaver (to put it bluntly), whether it be "swallowed," kissed, patted, embalmed, sculpted, painted, snipped of hair, lead logically to discussions about "recycling" the corpse that circulated in the nineteenth century. Catherine Gallagher points to Gaffer Hexam's use of corpses pulled out of the Thames for his livelihood, in *Our Mutual Friend*, as a form of trafficking in human flesh.[96] Dissecting bodies for medical and scientific purposes is another obvious way this was done, but what is of interest here is how the body was utilized to produce some other material object, thus transforming and aestheticizing it. Venus, in *Our Mutual Friend*, is not only a taxidermist, but he also "articulates" human skeletons, making his trade from "turning bodies into inorganic representations of themselves," as Gallagher explains.[97] Ruth Richardson tells of a radical whose 1829 anonymous text criticizes the practice of burial as a "romanticization of human remains." Instead, he felt everyone should follow his lead and create a will that directs his executors to not only dissect his body, but tan his skin and use it to upholster chairs. His bones are to be given to a turner to be made into "knife-handles, pin-cases, small boxes, buttons, etc."[98] Using tanned human skin to bind books – called anthropodermic bibliopegy – is one case of such reuse, a rather grisly form of recycling. The "leather" that covers these books makes them surprisingly beautiful (if terribly poignant) objects, the skin generally of a pale-cream color and soft and buttery to the touch (similar to pigskin) – often with the pores still visible. Although not a frequent practice in nineteenth-century Britain, binding in this fashion went through various fads, especially in the first half of the century, and legends sprang up about a wider practice.[99] The master binder Joseph Zaehnsdorf, who was originally from Budapest and established his business in London in 1842, was rumored to have taken orders from doctors, lawyers, and other well-off patrons to sheath books using the integument of unclaimed corpses of the poor.[100] Although there is no evidence to support this, he certainly finished a handful of books in this manner most notably a copy of Holbein's *Dance of Death*.[101] As with the Holbein, many of these books' trimmings reflected their contents, such as anatomy and other medical books (the English pornographer living in Paris, Frederick Hankey, boasted that he wanted his copy of the Marquis de Sade's *Justine* bound anthropodomerically).[102] But the most common instances of the practice involved the skin of criminals, thus drawing on the same fad as the death masks made of celebrated felons. Most of these volumes were either autobiographies of the executed person whose skin bound the text or accounts of their crimes, trials, and deaths. They became all-inclusive "packets" about criminality, containing a specimen of the thing itself, a kind of secular reliquary or auto-icon (like Jeremy Bentham's). A volume kept at the Bristol Royal Infirmary, bound in "the true skin of John Horwood," tells the story of Horwood's murder of a little girl, his trial, execution, and dissection in 1821.[103] At the Moyse's Hall Museum, in Bury St. Edmunds, Suffolk, a number of relics of the famed "Murder in the Red Barn" of Maria Marten in 1827 by William Corder are on display (see Fig. 9), including an account of the trial proceedings bound in the executed murderer's skin (and, oddly, a part of his scalp).[104] Although these "relics" are in many ways the opposite of saintly and secular ones, made because the donors were abhorred rather than revered, there is still a common theme to be traced. This skin, like those of the saints as explored in Chapter 1, is akin to paper; the body is engraved, becoming itself a piece of writing, a continued narrative to be read like postmortem art more generally.

Most of these felons had no choice in how their bodies were treated after their ignoble deaths. Before the Anatomy Act of 1832, the bodies of condemned criminals were the only corpses that could be legally used for dissection, seen by many as further punishment for their crimes, pursued even after death. Dickens wrote of this practice with sympathy for the executed: "Imagine what have been the feelings of the men … of whom between the gallows and the knife no mortal remnant may now remain."[105] Yet some criminals requested that their flesh be tanned and integrated into a book about themselves. At the Boston Athenaeum, for example, there are two volumes of the autobiography of the American George Walton, a professional thief who requested that the copies be bound with his own skin after his execution in 1837 (see Fig. 10).[106] Not only would his story survive, but even some of his body itself would live on, as a container for his narrative, just as the body contains the self (or soul). Such books are like little crypts; the word made flesh, the life story materialized. They also give us a strangely tactile sense of the idea of a *corpus*. The book becomes an epitaph, a grave marker, a proof of death but also a way to keep it "speaking." (There is an interesting reversal here from the royal effigy, where leather was used as a stand-in for skin.) These books remind us that all books eventually become crypts of a sort when the author dies, or death masks, as Miller claims, and when the world (and a particular language culture) that produced the book is long gone. Books are a form of postmortem art; manuscripts are secondary relics (touched by the hand of the now deceased), the printed book at a further representational remove, like tomb art based on the

Figure 10.   Autobiography of George Walton (also called James Allen),
bound with his own skin, 1837.

corpse. Gallagher imagines texts in a different but related way: "a text, in short, was another form of suspended animation, holding not only ideas but also their animating motive power."[107] She pictures Dickens, with *Our Mutual Friend*, dying "into that commodity [the book], where he remains immortally suspended."[108] In writing about Romantic and Victorian poets, Samantha Matthews makes a similar point about the book and the dead body of the author: "The metaphor of the book as a body has resonances beyond the conventional and figurative; the book functioned as a substitute for and transformed incarnation of the poet's body, and in some cases through biography ties the works to the decayed authorial body itself, sending readers back to the site of the mortal remains."[109] In his will, Dickens stipulated that he wanted his friends "on no account to make me the subject of any monument, memorial, or testimonial whatever." Rather, he wanted his "published works" to do the work of a commemorative marker.[110] As readers, we en-skin (enflesh) these dead words again, enlivening the corpse of their narrative. Our warm hands holding the book touch these "casts" of the hands of the author (also the book), or the very skin, in the case of anthropodermic bibliopegy. Tactile narrative transforms into more tactile narrative, moving from moribund author to animated reader.

Books bound in human skin remind us of the way that bodies themselves are texts, with skin that holds secret "writing" inside that others want to read. These multiple selves, hidden from others and some of them unknown, perhaps, even to ourselves, prefigure death in their inaccessibility. This is one way to read the well-known, and somewhat mysterious, passage in *A Tale of Two Cities*, where people are compared to books that can never be read in time and the still-animated to the buried corpse: both hold their secrets. The passage deserves quotation at length:

> A wonderful fact to reflect upon, that every human creature is constituted to be that profound secret and mystery to every other. A solemn consideration, when I enter a great city by night, that everyone of those darkly clustered houses encloses its own secret; that every room in everyone of them encloses its own secret; that every beating heart in the hundreds of thousands of breasts there, is, in some of its imaginings, a secret to the heart nearest it! Something of the awfulness, even of Death itself, is referable to this. No more can I turn the leaves of this dear book that I loved, and vainly hope in time to read it all . . . It was appointed that the book should shut with a spring, for ever and for ever, when I had read but a page. . . My friend is dead, my neighbour is dead, my love, the darling of my soul, is dead; it is the inexorable consolidation and perpetuation of the secret that was always in that individuality, and which I shall carry in mine to my life's end. In any of the burial-places of this city through which I pass, is there a sleeper more inscrutable than its busy inhabitants are, in their innermost personality, to me, or than I am to them?[111]

Death might close that book that we hastily try to read but never can. But then, the book is closed even before death. In fact, death might make the loved one more readable (if only slightly), especially if he or she takes on the character of a representation. Here we again have a formulation of the representational removes involved in materiality and language. Truth is located in the secret heart, which is then "represented" by the body, the house, the city. The body is a text we try to read, in our desire to get at the thing itself. Such mediation might take us away from meaning or might bring us closer, as it does sometimes in *Great Expectations*. But then again, as Dickens suggests in *Great Expectations*, we carry our death representations, like our secrets, around with us, our death mask already made. There is something biblical about this idea: "I die daily."[112] Thus does the ending always touch the beginning and does meaning flow out from death, backward along every point of a life. As with Magwitch and Miss Havisham, all bodies already contain their rotting corpses inside them, their status as objects, as carrion.

Great Expectations, then, is a book of the dead. Pip's journey is, at all destinations, touched by last things. Accepting death, for Pip, comes to signify accepting his lack of mastery (a common piece of Dickensian didacticism). Plots happen to one; the true self (or selves) might ultimately be unrecognizable to the self (Magwitch as Pip's benefactor and emblematic of his essential self, rather than Miss Havisham). To put this another way, identity is comprised of various friezes of experiences, or tableau vivants of past encounters (the graveyard passage, for example, is a stilled image that reappears later as a seminal scene, when Magwitch reenacts it in Pip's London flat), which are little endings, small death markers that move one toward more permanent ones. Pip reaches a measure of Dickensian knowledge when he recognizes the need to move through many selves, to incorporate endings into his being. Pip's redemption comes through a willingness to be worked on by fate, to let the body go the way it must. He comes to take into account his objecthood. Yet another didactic message in *Great Expectations* is that stilled material can be stirring, and can stir, even when dead. Death's fixedness reminds one, Dickens seems to be teaching the reader, not to be fixed, but to be supple among many selves always (even ones long gone or never had, like so many of Pip's), comically fluid even in the midst of sorrow. Dickens believed, along with many of his contemporaries, that the living were incomplete and lonely without the vast realms of the dead, among whose membership the living could already count themselves. Seeing these dead is realizing one's powerlessness over the life of the body. One must learn, in Dickens, to be dead without bitterness, ossification.

CHAPTER 4

The elegy as shrine: Tennyson and In Memoriam

> . . . when the steam
> Floats up from those dim fields about the homes
> Of happy men that have the power to die,
> And grassy barrows of the happier dead.
> —Tennyson, "Tithonus"

Spaces of intimacy

A shrine encloses a space hallowed by a beloved or revered dweller. Often encircling objects as well as air, a shrine can encompass both secondary relics – things touched by that venerated body – and a more nebulous sense of metonymy. A little area has come to be, through association, imbued with the presence of the now-lost other.[1] A space can be filled with memories, can trigger a narrative of the past. Somehow it is as if the space "witnessed" the living of the loved one. If a space had eyes, then the shrine "saw" the life events of the departed. As such, shrine spaces can work as "proof" as other relics do: proof that the person really had been a breathing, moving being. Shrines can also be used as evidence of passion and love. This is the place (*hic locus est*), they seem to say, where those emotions came to life. A room, a house, a natural locale (field, path, stream, grove, grotto), a cathedral; desire comes to define a space, mark it out from the rest of the earth as having singular meaning. Even if such spaces were not made specifically to house a relic, they have come eventually to hold one or more than one – the "relic" possibly being something as insubstantial as just a location. For instance, if a shrine is a spot in nature – say, a little opening in the trees – then the presence of the beloved deceased might seem to hang in the very air, become a *genius loci*. It is not that any one object carries the presence of absence, but the sense of something here that is now gone seems to be layered onto the general site. Shrines have been closely related to reliquaries from their early history. The smaller the shrine or reliquary, the more "concentrated" that essence might become. Yet, the stronger the passion, the larger the space the shrine might cover. One can imagine a longing so profound that it might encompass an entire country.

An elegy, like a shrine, also functions as a kind of "witness," a figurative marking out in words of the space the dead used to occupy. They both express a need to continue to "dwell" with, or near, those lost. Elegies and shrines not only share a similar history, which will be traced later, but they both emerged from the same impetus and desire: to mark the bones of a longed-for body and to celebrate its story. The production of both grew from a deep need to "prove" that the loved one had been here – a proof provided by relics more generally – to verify that her presence and loss could still be shaped in earthly forms, whether it be printed words on the page or the walls and furniture that make up a room. The Victorians' attentiveness to death made the elegiac mood pervasive in their literature. As Carol Christ observes about the era: "Literature, particularly poetry, was often used to perform a kind of mourning work."[2] In some of its most famous iterations, this literature of sorrow foregrounded not only the materials of death but also the way that the lost one might define expanses. If a literary form could be a shrine, then the elegy would be the best candidate (or, another way to think of this: if relics were a literature instead of objects, they would probably be elegies, little fragments of stories, replete with "thingness"). This braiding of the elegy and the shrine leads to the twofold argument of this chapter. First, the Victorian love of the elegiac and of shrines were both part of the same movement toward a need to locate the dead in *place*. As discussed in Chapter 1, this sense of the local emerged with Romanticism, particularly Wordsworth's need to link character to natural scenery. Tennyson's *In Memoriam* will be the focus of this exploration of the elegy's relation to death's materiality because of its immense influence on Victorian elegies and death culture more generally during the latter half of the nineteenth century. Tennyson was himself shaped by the understanding of death of his contemporaries, especially topical forms of doubt in religious faith and a traditional afterlife. Around the same time that Tennyson's great elegy was published, Spiritualism spread around Britain as a popular belief and pastime. Another piece of the larger history of relic culture traced throughout these chapters, Spiritualism contributed to relic love and to the spatial understanding of pre- and postdeath that informed shrines and elegies. Although Tennyson was never himself a Spiritualist, his understanding of the presence of the dead emerged from the same nexus of belief systems and desires during this historical moment. The second strand of this chapter's argument explores the use of these two types of memorials to affirm a singular personality in time and place, one that might have been annihilated for good. Elegies could provide a countermovement to the evangelical use of memorials and relics of various sorts to confirm the eternal. The more radical savoring of such memorials came from their confirmation of doubt and transience, a notion that, I will argue, can be found in pockets of Tennyson's elegy.

Saintly and secular shrines

As with other relics discussed in this book, shrines can be traced back to the beginnings of religious faith.[3] As sites associated with Christian saints, shrines already had a thriving existence by 400 AD. From the Latin *scrinium*, "shrine" originally meant a chest, case, cabinet, coffer, or coffin that held something dear or sacred.[4] The Ark of the Covenant stands as probably the most famous *scrinia*. Like the Ark, fabled to have held the tablets on which the Ten Commandments were inscribed (among other miraculous objects, such as Aaron's rod and manna), scrinium often contained venerated writing, books, or papers. Thus shrines had, from the very start, a close relationship to inscription, epigraphs, and language, a lineage to be explored further later. By the Middle Ages, a shrine came to mean a space that held the relics of a saint or of Christ, and thus it became bound intimately with the reliquary. The original Christian shrines in late antiquity and the early Middle Ages, also called *martyria* or *memoriae*, consisted simply of tombs built on the graves of the martyrs, outside the city walls. Many of these spaces were large enough for funeral meals to be held within them, an early Christian practice.[5] Roman towns banished their burial places to the outskirts, but the spread of Christianity brought a radical shift in attitudes toward the corpse and its geography: the cult of the saints carried the dead into the heart of the towns, to be buried near or in the church. With this changing cartography of the dead, an altar came to be defined, in Roman canon law, as "a tomb containing the relics of a saint": *sepilchrum continens reliquas santorum.*[6] To be near a saint's tomb was a means to call on the intercession of the interred, and the magical presence of remains came to enliven an ever-wider circle. The artifacts of the saints drew the faithful, who desired to be interred *ad sanctos*, as mentioned earlier, or to be among those who "deserved to rest among the saints" (*qui meruit sanctorum sociari sepulcris*).[7] Gradually corpses came to inhabit areas adjacent to living spaces, as if dying might mean simply slipping into the next room. Philippe Ariès observes that the ancient opposition between the dead and sacred – remains were thought to be unclean and needed to be kept far from altars to the gods – became inverted because of the worship of saints. "The dead body of a Christian created by its very nature a space if not altogether sacred, at least ... religious."[8] Cemeteries sprang up around the place where the saints' relics were kept, but the word *cimeterium* eventually came to signify not just a place to bury bodies, but also "an area of asylum around the church," a refuge or sanctuary enshrined by death's materials.[9] Great cathedrals and their environs function, at their most basic level, as huge and elaborate altars, tombs, or reliquaries, spaces built to "hold" the enchanted presence and those – still breathing or inanimate flesh – who want to be near it. (Ariès explores the practice, fairly frequent during the early Middle Ages, of destitute or troubled people being welcomed to make their habitations in the cemetery.) Thus did remains help to redefine space and beliefs about where different types of bodies, whether still breathing and vigorous or deanimated flesh, could dwell. Cadavers influenced how areas might be bounded or enlarged or how a certain sanctity might be able to move or travel. As mentioned in Chapter 1, a shrine not only housed the corporeal parts of the saint, but also he or she was thought to be present, even to lodge in a ghostly sort of way, at the site. This is why many reliquary chests, boxes, or coffers were fashioned to look like miniature cathedrals, houses, or other types of habitations (see Fig. 11).[10] An example of a reliquary shaped like a small Gothic church, called the "Reliquary Shrine of Saint Barbara," is displayed at the Metropolitan Museum of Art, New York.[11] A casket containing portions of St. Blasius, at the Kunstgewerbe-museum, Berlin, takes the form of a lighthouse. Thus it was sometimes the case that the bones and flesh would be domiciled in a tiny "room" that was itself housed in a much larger one: the treasury, the cathedral, the walled-in cemetery, the town.

Corpses not only transformed towns and the spaces of those still animate, but they could also cause populations to move about, sometimes in drastic ways. The traveler to Rome, Canterbury, Jerusalem, or Santiago de Compostela – to name the most popular medieval shrines – went to see, perhaps even touch, the bodies of the saints and their surroundings. Pilgrimages resulted in contact with this magnetic presence, tethered as it was to the stuff of the saintly body; the pilgrim could stand in the space consecrated by the little body parts contained therein. To be a pilgrim was to bring one's own body into the "joy of proximity," as Peter Brown eloquently calls it, a joy that resulted initially from a kind of "therapy" of travel to a shrine. Those who were willing to close the distance might be

Figure 11.   Bronze reliquary in the shape of the Church of the Holy
Sepulcher, German, late 12th century, RF.2006/104.

granted a miracle in the here and now – be healed of a sickness, for
instance – or might obtain remissions for sins, a kind of promissory note
for the postdeath future. A pilgrim might activate the technology of the
relic or shrine in other ways, bringing forth various types of holy occurrences. Climbing the Holy Stairs – the Scala Santa in St. John Lateran in
Rome – on one's knees would, it was claimed, release a soul from
purgatory. A pilgrim could take a bit of this enchantment home with
him or her in a "souvenir." As proof that he or she had made the journey to
Jerusalem, for example, the pilgrim would be given a token of a palm; for
the shrine to Saint James in Compostela, a scallop-shell medal would be
awarded.[12] Other types of souvenirs might be carried back, such as little
stones at the Holy Sepulcher, or for the intrepid and felonious, a more
sanctified relic might be stolen, such as "part of the pillar at which Christ
was scourged," bits of the holy manger, or an actual body part, like the
piece of finger bone that, the story goes, an English bishop bit off while
pretending to kiss the hand of the skeleton of Mary Magdalen, under the
watchful eyes of the monks who kept it in their monastery in France.[13]

Thus not only did human remains work as a spur to move people toward their environs, but also individuals might carry fragments away, thus creating new magnetic spaces. Shrines begot shrines, and divine materiality became dispersed over ever-wider areas.

To simplify the history of Christian shrines for the purposes of this chapter, we could say that the movement was from the grave itself as that which determined the site of the shrine, to larger and more diffuse spaces, such as churches and their surroundings, where the "essence" of holiness hung in the atmosphere.

The history of secular shrines follows a similar trajectory. Although they can be traced back at least to Virgil's grave, which became a site to visit after his death in 19 BC, they didn't become widespread in Britain until after the sixteenth century, when shrines to the saints disappeared. Veneration for the spaces infused by sainthood moved gradually to the worship of spaces associated with the illustrious dead. Yet it wasn't until the late eighteenth century that literary pilgrimages began to be fashionable, as Nicola Watson explains, and the practice didn't become widespread until the nineteenth century.[14] In Britain, Chaucer's tomb in Westminster Abbey brought about, from the 1550s, the first stirrings of post-Reformation "necro-tourism." Such pilgrimages really started to capture the general imagination with the first public celebration of Shakespeare's birthday in 1769.[15] Thus began a steady stream of visitors to Shakespeare's grave.[16] Yet like their sacred version, secular shrines followed a pattern of a loosening of the need for a direct connection with the tomb. The growing force of secularism led, as we have seen throughout this book, to the idea of death becoming, for many, unmoored from its association with church and the sacred space of the cemetery. Thus could the "presence" of Shakespeare expand out to include the room where he was born, in the house on Henley Street. Other examples of early sites for literary pilgrimages that set the stage for their proliferation in the Victorian period are the places associated with Robert Burns's birth, life, and literature and Walter Scott's house, called Abbotsford. (When Keats visited Burns's house, he wrote a sonnet that imagined his own body moving toward death, there: "This mortal body of a thousand days / Now fills, O Burns, a space in thine own room" [lines 1–2].) As visiting the spaces where revered literary figures had dwelled or wrote about became more widespread in the nineteenth century, such travels took on an increasingly sacralized quality. Such is the paradoxical nature of Victorian death culture: as the figures worshiped became more secular (from saints to ordinary individuals) and as the cherished spaces also became increasingly secularized (from church and cemetery to house and natural setting), the possibility for sacralization spread. Anyone or anything could become sacred when enough personal desire and emotion was felt for her or it. These pilgrimages thus became more "Victorian." Just as with saint's shrines, not only did the divine presence expand to the rooms where the literary genius had dwelled – including the furniture and clothing contained therein – but visitors could also take away "souvenirs" to carry with them some of that sacred presence (such as pieces of the thorn tree that Burns reputedly stood under as he parted from his Highland Mary).[17] Some literature lovers wanted to be buried close to or in sites associated with the authors or texts they adored, not so different from being buried "ad sanctos." (Nicola Watson tells of the fashion starting in the 1840s for burial near Alloway Kirk, immortalized in Burns's *Tam O'Shanter*.) Such spaces spoke of the person who had touched, inhabited, or wrote about them, the Victorians felt, so much so that it became common to use these shrines and the objects they contained as a means to interpret the writings or art of the absent dweller. Numerous studies of this sort came out in the nineteenth century, one of the most popular being William Howitt's *Homes and Haunts of the Most Eminent British Poets* (first published in 1847 and running into many editions). Other well-known titles of a similar nature include the 1859 anthology of essays, *Homes and Haunts of the Wise and Good or Visits to Remarkable Places in English History and Literature*; *The Last Homes of Departed Genius* of 1867, by T. P. Grinstead; the many-volume series by Elbert Hubbard published in the late nineteenth century, called *Little Journeys to the Homes of English Authors*; and the 1895 *A Literary Pilgrimage among the Haunts of Famous British Authors*, by Theodore Wolfe.[18] Tennyson, the Brontës, and Dickens were especially favorite shrine subjects, perhaps because of their own interest in areas and objects sanctified by the dead. Not so different from pilgrimages to the great shrines of the Middle Ages, the Victorian literary pilgrimage often involved some sort of intangible, personal gain. With the saints one might be healed or earn credit for the afterlife, but from the secular shrine the visitor might further understand or commune with the dead genius. An admirer who was a writer or artist herself might draw the magic of inspiration for her own work. Because personality could seem to sink into objects, just as it could seem to be held in the atmosphere of the place, it could be transmitted to the minds and perhaps bodies of pilgrims. The belief in the capability of personal possessions and dwelling spaces to "hold" personhood was so strong that some pilgrims didn't wait until the death of revered literary figures, visiting and taking away souvenirs from the homes of still living authors, such as Tennyson at Freshwater and Dickens at Gad's Hill.

The influx of pilgrims to the shrines of the famous was paralleled by the emotion and desire infused into the sites that held the ordinary and obscure. Following in the footsteps of saintly shrines, memorials to loved ones began with places linked to religious ritual. Tombs of unexceptional individuals in Britain became increasingly revered by those who loved them by the end of the sixteenth century, in part because the saints' shrines had been demolished.[19] Beginning in the seventeenth century, family chapels and mausolea were "rooms" built apart from the church, not only to house remains but so people could visit them. (An epitaph on the seventeenth-century tomb where the Tradescant family is buried, in St. Mary's Churchyard, London, expresses this idea; the space is identified as "A World of Wonders in one Closet shut.")[20] Starting around the middle of the eighteenth century, mausolea were occasionally constructed on private land, a sign of the beginning of the detachment of corpses from religious spaces. Many post-Enlightenment shrines had a completely secular character, containing not a single Christian symbol.[21] The historical shift toward sanctifying and celebrating rooms entombing the obscure dead included a new attitude, in the late eighteenth and nineteenth centuries, about visiting the cemetery. Ariès explains that the tomb and its environs became places where the physical presence of the ordinary, dead loved one was thought to linger, as if the individual dwelled there, similar to the saints inhabiting the area around their remains (see Fig. 12). Thus not only did the grave become a destination for remembering, praying, and mourning, but also the cemetery itself was a place for meandering, to feel the shades of the dead and to meditate on melancholy ideas.[22] Such cemetery strolling contributed to – and, indeed, helped to create – the eighteenth-century "cult of tombs" and the Graveyard School of poetry, mentioned in Chapter 1 – a certain gothic sensibility that retained much of its strength in the Victorian period, especially among the "late Romantic" writers. Not only did the mausoleum become free standing and secularized during this era, but, for the first time in the history of the Western world, funerary art became a fashionable accessory for one's garden or park. "Follies" that had no corpse were built because of their voguish, gothic character, such as the "picturesque arch masquerading as a 'Mausoleum'" in Charles Hamilton's garden at Pains Hill in Surrey.[23] Sir John Soane had something of an obsession with the funerary, and the mausolea he designed were often meant to be "theatrical spectacle[s]," as Howard Colvin observes, to be visited even by strangers (one had a visitor's book).[24]

As graveyard ornaments began to leave the cemetery and be "domesticated," so too did the "presence" of the lost loved one. One might feel the companionship of the dead in the fields, the trees, in one's very home.

Figure 12.   An example of a Victorian-era tomb shrine that was made to be actually
inhabited. Isabel Burton had this stone "tent" built for her husband Richard Burton,
to mimic the types of dwellings he slept in on his travels. Isabel would sometimes
take up temporary abode here. Mortlake Cemetery, London, 1891.

As relics became more secularized, they could be brought into the actual home (rather than being domiciled in an artificial abode, such as a house-shaped reliquary or a church). With inscribed hair jewelry, not only would a fragment of the corpse be domesticated, but the epitaph would also. (The majority of hairwork had tomblike inscriptions, which will be explored further in the next chapter.) Finding the presence of the dead lingering in specific areas had its roots in certain strands of early Christian belief. Ordinary individuals might remain at the scene of their sins or death, to request masses and prayers to release them, or perhaps to give valuable information (such as the father in *Hamlet*, who asks his son for revenge for his murder).[25] A variation on this type of "spirit" of grove or field were the "pseudopurgatories" of the Middle Ages, fixed places on earth where sinning individuals were held and punished for a time and which any person might stumble on and witness. Such ideas continued in the more secular world. The presence of the beloved dead might have some chance of revivification in spaces that had been dear to her. The outline of her life, of her very form, might then be traced once again. But that lingering "essence," those memories that were housed just there, could also call up the pain of that vanished form, limned so clearly in the rooms and furniture of being.

The elegy as shrine

The basic function of both the shrine and the elegy is to keep memories astir. Revisiting the past could mean touching memory objects (relics), visiting memory places (shrines), writing some form of memorial (an elegy, for instance), or simply contemplating inwardly. Such latter brooding has, historically, been imagined as palpable, tangible. From classical antiquity through the Middle Ages a recurrent way to picture the holding of memories in the mind has been as words or representations inscribed on objects, such as, for example, waxed tablets. "Memory was thus figured as a written surface and as part of a process involving the inscription or marking of the body," the anthropologists Hallam and Hockey explain.[26] Memories were also envisioned as spatial, as if they were something to be gathered in parts of the brain and perhaps sorted or organized. The mind might be a strong room containing treasures, a library or a set of compart-ments for books, or a hive (with honey). It could be a cave with inner chambers, or even a shrine containing relics – an idea especially popular during the Middle Ages. This sense of the mind as a mansion with many rooms continued through the nineteenth century and can still be encountered today. Gaston Bachelard, in his *Poetics of Space*, takes this idea further by arguing that we come to form our selfhood not so much temporally as spatially. Our history can be summed up by considering the rooms we've passed through, which have contained and formed us. He calls this "topoanalysis": "at times we think we know ourselves in time, when all we know is a sequence of fixations in the spaces of being's stability."[27] If we seem to put memories into the spaces of our minds or inscribe them onto its tablet, and if the creation of our being happens, at least partially, in and with the stretches and tracts we inhabit, then it is easy to see how the absent could be understood to themselves continue to occupy spaces, whether in the chambers of our heads, in tombs or cemeteries, or houses and in nature itself. The mind can be understood as a sort of shrine where the memory of the lost one might still dwell, or be englobed. Or, to revisit an earlier idea, perhaps the mind works as a slate or tombstone with the epitaph or elegy for the dead loved one inscribed on it, giving memories and memorials a kind of inward, written permanence. To externalize these imagined spaces or "tablets" is to set up a material shrine in one's house or to write an elegy or have it printed in a book. Memories were made material, legible, "things" or words that celebrated the lost self who had always been embedded in the object world and the sphere of language.

Like shrines, words point to absence and, at the same time, attempt to fill it up. Language can try to crowd out the void opened by death, but it can also come to be about little else. Jacques Derrida plays with the idea that language is a kind of crypt because its inexact quality means it always refers to a sort of emptiness. What we as singular individuals experience can never be precisely expressed using a means of communication so general that everyone can use it. What can't be said or written falls into a place of loss, or of death (a crypt), as Derrida imagines it. The elegy often sings of the disappearance that results from language's inability to express singularity – of the speaker or of the subject. In a similar vein, words themselves can be seen as coming from the dead. Giorgio Agamben remarks that all words are dead letters, part of "a dead language handed down to us by the dead."[28] Words are a type of found object, Gerald Bruns asserts, something we pick up, dust off, and reuse.[29] In this sense, they always refer to a past, to what has been dead and is now being revivified. Words are a bit like relics, then, which are also found objects (things that had another use and are taken up and "reused") that gesture to previous users. Diana Fuss asks: "Is not every literary utterance a speaking corpse, a disembodied voice detached from a living, breathing body?" But we could reverse this detachment and bring this corpse back, retracing its relationship to language – specifically, the elegy – and recognizing again its importance as a material thing.

Actual corpses did generate writing that was tethered closely to the body. Writing on the tomb, grave, or vault has been, during much of Western history, a tangible means to hold onto the memory of the deceased, a *monumentum* or *memoria*. The epitaph and the effigy were arts that developed to perpetuate memories of the dead; they are versions of biographical writing. As the nature of tombs shifted from the saintly to the secular, inscription about the dead on the markers of remains came to be increasingly personal. Ariès makes a clear historical connection between the art of the epitaph and that of the elegy; indeed he sees them as, at least early in their history, the same thing. The elegy was often what was carved into the tomb or gravestone. Ariès points out that the French called these little memorial poems *tombeau*.[30] Inscribing the poem on the tomb makes it not just a text about and *on* the mortal remains but also a marking of the bones and flesh, something like a textual shrine or language that actually "contains" a corpse. The history of the epitaph is a familiar one: at first such texts told the story of a saintly or heroic life, but they became increasingly written for the ordinary dead. They also grew to be centered on the regret and grieving of the survivors rather than merely celebrating the deceased. In eighteenth- and nineteenth-century Britain, not only might the elegy be engraved in stone, but it was also sometimes pinned to the catafalque during the funeral ceremony. Occasionally elegies were thrown into the open grave, sometimes along with the pen with which they were written. In his 1868 history of Westminster Abbey, the Dean of Westminster, Arthur Penrhyn Stanley, describes Spenser's hearse being attended by mourning poets who tossed their verses and writing instruments into his tomb.[31] The elegy flows into the epitaph and the eulogy, all corresponding to the French *tombeau littéraire*.[32] As writing out of and on the tomb, the elegy also became unmoored from the corpse, a poem written on paper. An elegy recorded in a book worked as a type of cenotaph – a memorial without an actual body buried in or underneath it.[33] Elegies can be understood as portable and dispersible shrines, similar to "souvenirs" or relics of pilgrimages that could be carried on the body to any new space.[34] Samantha Matthews makes a related point about the book that "carries" the elegy: "the physical volume that enshrines a meditation on the lost body may be read as a form of personalized and mobile memorial, a metaphor for the body which, like the body, is also material."[35] Elegies were a means to move the longing for the absent around; to relocate a shrine. One has to travel to be in the presence of an epitaph carved in stone or marble and marking the actual location of body parts, but an elegy can be brought to and kept in the home, on one's person, or even "engraved" on one's own mind. Conversely, rather than turning an epitaph into a peripatetic elegy, a visitor to a shrine might inscribe her name or a bit of verse on the walls or furniture of the dwelling places of those they revered, or on other objects associated with them, such as trees, tombs, or churches. During the eighteenth and nineteenth centuries pilgrims left traces behind as a means to communicate with the dead. Tennyson became part of this tradition when he visited the room where Shakespeare was born and penciled his name on the wall, along with the thousands of others already scribbled there. "I was a little ashamed of it afterwards," he admitted.[36] Just as an elegy is a way to bring two names and experiences together – that of the author (or speaker) and of the one mourned – pilgrim graffiti works to mark the bringing together of two existences in the same space.

The most important elegy of its time, Tennyson's *In Memoriam* became consolation literature for a nation and helped shape other acts of memorialization.[37] Queen Victoria in particular found great solace in the poem when her husband died and turned to it as much as to the Bible. Excerpts from the poem became popular epitaphs and remain so today in Britain and America. Strolling through most large cemeteries, one can read on gravestones carved after 1850 lines from *In Memoriam*, used to mark the placement of the corpses of the ordinary dead. In fact, it was common in the nineteenth century for those who didn't have the leisure, literary accomplishments, or money to acquire and read long printed poems to walk through cemeteries and peruse, and sometimes copy down, epitaphs, for their moral edification (or merely for pleasure). Many thus encountered Tennyson's lines for the first time *not* as part of an elegy with his name attached to it, but rather as an epitaph inscribed on a grave. In addition to these uses, *In Memoriam* also became a voice, I will argue toward the end of this chapter, for those questioning their religious faith.[38] The Victorian historian James Anthony Froude remarked that Tennyson spoke to those who wanted to investigate religion without "a preconceived resolution that the orthodox conclusions must come out true."[39] More important for my argument, however, Tennyson's poem is interested not only in the beloved corpse, but also in attempting to "locate" or find a space for this body or its palpable absence. We might think of the longer poem of *In Memoriam* as a reliquary – a *wunderkammer*, house museum, collection, or shrine of the type discussed in Chapter 1 – a container for the many relic-like smaller poems or poem "objects." Peter Sacks connects *In Memoriam* to the Victorian love of collecting, with each poem an accretion adding to the larger collection of moments. Creating a powerful poetics of loss, Tennyson's elegy affirms the importance of keeping loss an open question or "room" as a means to honor the absent.

In Memoriam's shrine space

When Tennyson's closest companion, the 22-year-old Arthur Hallam, was dying in Vienna on September 15, 1833, Tennyson happened to be writing him a letter. The distance between them meant that it would be October before Tennyson heard about the death and weeks later before the body, borne back by ship, arrived on British shores. Time and space – and the writing that might bridge them – were knocked out of joint. Writing a direct address to what Tennyson thought was the still-breathing body in that distant country speedily became writing about and to a shadowy outline, one whose material status became an open question to be pondered. Where was that addressee to which Tennyson had, with such natural complacence, directed a letter now never to be delivered? Could writing serve to find out? Just as penning a missive can function to help one imagine the site of the desired one, writing an elegy might be a gesture of incantation, of magical recreation or transubstantiation, whether the still-echoing space summoned be heavenly or earthbound. Tennyson attempts, with *In Memoriam* but also many of his other poems, to embellish the emptiness wrought by the vanished corporeality, to carve out an edifice of sorts for it.

Death's dark space had drawn Tennyson well before Hallam's demise; it was part of his attraction to the belated and too late. As his friend James Spedding said of Tennyson in 1835, he was a "man always discontented with the Present till it has become the Past, and then he yearns toward it, and worships it, and not only worships it, but is discontented because it is past."[40] This "passion of the past," which has been discussed copiously by Tennyson scholars, had been a well of inspiration for him for a number of years.[41] Dipping into it often meant finding its embodiment through touch, sight, and sound. As a child, Tennyson thrilled to stormy days because he liked to think that, when he spread his arms to the gusts, he could "hear a voice that's speaking in the wind."[42] Just after his father died, Tennyson slept in his bed to increase the chances he might see his ghost. Contact with the deathbed was important to Tennyson, as if revivifying the father could come by fleshly touch with the place (thing) that might still hold the impress of the body. In a similar gesture during the funeral of his friend Sir John Simeon, Tennyson, instead of attending, went off in Sir John's hat and cloak, smoking his pipe, to walk the gardens his friend had loved. This act seemed, to him, to bring him closer than the more formal rituals. The things around him might provide a point of connection with the sphere of the departed, which Tennyson described soon after his son Lionel died in 1886, as "a great ocean pressing round us on every side, and leaking in by a few chinks."[43] Wedging open a chink became an obsession when Hallam merged with the enchanted realm of "far, far away." Although Tennyson, on Hallam's demise, "suffered what seemed to me to shatter all my life so that I desired to die rather than to live," he also let this magnetic pull toward death bring with it a flowering of his best verse.[44] Forming poetry might search out those "chinks." Writing about Hallam, whom he thought of as his "half-self," led not only to attempts to reconstitute Hallam's selfhood, but also his own. Losing himself – and perhaps finding himself again – emerged as a deep desire and an impetus for writing on and about the dead.

In Memoriam marks death, at certain junctures, as productive of the richest meaning, while at the same time it is the most lacerating, blackly terrible, and unspeakable event imaginable. Without death and unending grief, love does not shine in its deepest luster: "Let Love clasp Grief lest both be drown'd, / Let darkness keep her raven gloss. / Ah, sweeter to be drunk with loss, / To dance with Death, to beat the ground."[45] Yet, in a turn of emotion characteristic of the different colorings of each of the poems that make up the larger one, it is death that makes the long street unlovely, the call for the "tender day" unending, the darkness vacant. Similarly, rendering death legible might let Tennyson slip, at least temporarily, into the refuge of verse, somewhat like the Christian cemetery – a sanctuary because strewn with bodies. Such a place of provisional calm can be found in the regular beat of verse and rhyme: "But, for the unquiet heart and brain, / A use in measured language lies; / The sad mechanic exercise, / Like dull narcotics, numbing pain" (5, lines 5–8). The measured mechanism of the poetic form creates an aural blanket to soothe somewhat the lacerated self. It is also a kind of mourning clothing that will cover the body frozen with grief: "In words, like weeds, I'll wrap me o'er, / Like coarsest clothes against the cold; / But the large grief which these enfold / Is given in outline and no more" (5, lines 9–12). Yet the writing's help, like the scratching of the alliterative "c" in "coarsest," "clothes," and "cold," is only roughly effective. It can only partially envelop the great void that has opened up. Conversely, words can only give the body of grief "in outline."

As the first stanza of lyric V has it, "I sometimes hold it half a sin / To put in words the grief I feel: / For words, like Nature, half reveal / And half conceal the Soul within" (lines 1–4). Words hide that which one might want the relief of revealing (a theme to be found also in "Break, Break, Break," where the speaker laments: "I would that my tongue could utter / The thoughts that arise in me" [lines 2–4]), like Derrida's crypt opening onto emptiness and dead space. But one might also hide out in verse, and use it as a transformative or secretive space.

Thinking of a poem as a kind of chamber has a long history, stretching back to Christopher Marlowe's famous characterization of the sonnet as "infinite riches in a little room." Among the many Victorians who liked to think of poems in this way is D. G. Rossetti, whose sonnet sequence *House of Life* treats each poem as a little room of the soul. As explored in Chapter 1, poems of any sort – but sonnets especially, of course – have a structural tightness lacking in prose, so that they can seem like closed systems, with the possibility of much (even infinite) inward action and depth. They enclose a space, if you will, that both reader and author might step into and inhabit for a time. If we can imagine Tennyson's *In Memoriam* as a space, then it opens onto other rooms and bounded areas. The most obvious would be a tomb or grave, with the title of the poem working as a traditional (classical) inscription carved in stone: *In Memoriam A.H.H. Obiit MDCCCXXXIII.*[46] As Darrel Mansell contends, *In Memoriam* works as a type of architecture, specifically a memorial tomb.[47] But given that one of the poem's key themes is the way dying can sanctify many types of places (perhaps even any), the elegy also leads the wayfarer to other enclosures or captivating pathways. Tennyson found this poetic gesture pleasing in past writings, one that he picked up from Keats and Wordsworth, among others. In an early poem heavily influenced by Keats's cherishing of the melancholy mood – about a stream in a valley in Cauteretz visited with Hallam – he draws an enchanted circle around the synthesis of the local, temporal, and emotional:

> Check every outflash, every ruder sally
>   Of thought and speech; speak low, and give up wholly
>   Thy spirit to mild-minded Melancholy;
> This is the place. Through yonder poplar alley . . .
>   And all the haunted place is dark and holy. (lines 1–4, 8)

The valley (Tennyson would later write that "love is of the valley") is a little church or cathedral because joyful experiences happened there – love and intimacy with Hallam. Be silent there, he exclaims, as one hushes the voice in sacred places. Tennyson returned to this valley after Hallam's death, becoming a pilgrim to a shrine, in search of miracles. From Wordsworth, Tennyson borrowed the rooting of the sublime in landscape: he took "Tintern Abbey" to heart. Gazing on the ruins of the Abbey and thinking of Wordsworth's poem, Tennyson found himself caught up in his grief for Hallam – the sorrowful pile became a vessel for his passion about his friend's disappearance into death. The poem "Tears, Idle Tears" emerged from this confluence of memory, locality, and poetic influence. "This song came to me," Tennyson explains, "on the yellowing autumntide at Tintern Abbey, full for me of its bygone memories. It is the sense of the abiding in the transient."[48] In it he imagines a room where someone lies dying.

> Ah, sad and strange as in dark summer dawns
> The earliest pipe of half-awakened birds
> To dying ears, when unto dying eyes
> The casement slowly grows a glimmering square;
> So sad, so strange, the days that are no more. (lines 11–15)

The room, the window, and the sounds and light that pass through it take on a meaningful and poignant patina of mystery because seen for the last time by someone just about to "cross the bar." Leaving – to die – estranges and enchants what was touched, seen, heard, or last inhabited, pulling it out of the ordinary, making it, perhaps, a point of access to another realm. The room in "Tears, Idle Tears" reflects the poem as a "space" that mirrors the "shrine" that is the ruins of Tintern Abbey, a place itself tethered to the Wordsworth poem.

Given his personal attentiveness to the materiality of death – good Victorian that he was – Tennyson saw his pining for Hallam seem to infuse landscape, rooms, walks, artifacts, and most essentially, the body lost.[49] Part of his impetus for this sentimental materialism came from his belief – not untroubled or unwavering – in the "good death," shared with so many of his contemporaries. Such sentiments are scattered throughout *In Memoriam*: referring to the dead, he remarks, "'They rest . . . their sleep is sweet'" (30, line 19).[50] Yet Tennyson didn't witness Hallam's dying, good or otherwise, nor did he ever view his inanimate body (nor did he, incidentally, attend his funeral or visit his tomb until many years afterward). This lack of embodiment for his yearning set his imagination even more adrift; he felt the need to picture the place of death, the corpse in different contexts, the funeral, and the gravesite again and again and, of course, trace them in verse. He wanted to picture the "dead face."

He addressed Hallam thus: "So, dearest, now thy brows are cold, / I see thee ... and know / Thy likeness" (74, lines 5–7). A tradition of criticism has developed that attempts to make the corpse disappear in Tennyson's elegy. Darrel Mansell, for instance, continues an argument by Peter Sacks in his contention that the "elegy ingests the body as words."[51] I want to put the body back into *In Memoriam*. The truth of the other most often resides in his felt presence, Tennyson affirms repeatedly in numerous writings, in the "touch of a vanished hand, / and the sound of a voice that is still" ("Break, Break, Break," lines 11–12). In other words, it is found in the visceral experience of the warmth and sound of being with the corporeal other. Peter Sacks also explores the many "images of physical touch or possession" in *In Memoriam*, which he connects to the "Victorian passion for collectables."[52] "Be near me" Tennyson calls to Hallam repeatedly, in a litany of need. The loss of the body's presence is keenly missed in *In Memoriam*, particularly the hands, their gestures and work. He mentions Arthur's hands ten times in the poem. Most famously, in lyric VII:

> Dark house, by which once more I stand
>   Here in the long unlovely street,
>   Doors, where my heart was used to beat
> So quickly, waiting for a hand,
>
> A hand that can be clasp'd no more (lines 1–5).[53]

The hands were often cast postmortem, as was discussed in Chapter 3 because they, like the face, expressed the unique personality, carrying their years of living in their seams and texture. What was lost, in all its singularity, is modeled in three dimensions. The material with which Tennyson would like to "cast" Hallam's now-stilled hands is his own flesh. He envisages grasping those other hands, as if his own hands could still hold the shape of absence, like a garment or plaster. He also feels with his arms – and his whole drowsy body – like "the widower, when he sees / A late-lost form that sleep reveals, / And moves his doubtful arms, and feels / Her place is empty" (13, lines 1–4). Another "casting" is the elegy itself. A "thing poem" steeped in death, *In Memoriam* tries repeatedly to form a space that will surround, embrace, or contain Hallam's embodied self.[54] We might compare it to that copy of Shelley's *Adonais* that contained his heart.

Tennyson uses the sweep of numerous stanzas to conjure up – as much as he can – not only that animated Hallam, but also his silent, quiescent corpse. John Rosenberg, in his reading of *In Memoriam*, finds a "transgressive quality" in Tennyson's "corpses in motion or embraced underground," but we can see this as another example of the Victorian embodiment of death culture, therefore not transgressive at all but rather commonplace.[55] In lyrics IX to XX, he fervently imagines Hallam's deanimated form – "my lost Arthur's loved remains" – being carried home to England on that fateful boat. Placing himself, imaginatively, on that "fair ship" he can "hear the noise about thy keel" and "hear the bell struck in the night." Tennyson struggles with the unfathomable mystery of the subject made object – can, will that "thing" move again? The unimaginable stillness of the beloved body, no longer able to move on its own, is so disturbing that Tennyson pleads for *any* movement, even if it is only with the sway of the deep ocean. Envisaging the smooth lapping and rocking of the waves, he hopes the body will find a similar rhythmic rest: "and dead calm in that noble breast / Which heaves but with the heaving deep" (11, lines 19–20). Some pleasure is to be found in visualizing a possible shipwreck, which would mean Hallam ("thy dark freight," he names the body, addressing the ship) would be buried at sea. Then those hands might find a new, bewitching life: "Than if with thee the roaring wells / Should gulf him fathom-deep in brine, / And hands so often clasp'd in mine, / Should toss with tangle and with shells" (10, lines 17–20). Hallam's relics might serve to sanctify the entire sea, not to mention the now "sacred bark," a floating reliquary and shrine. *In Memoriam* sacralizes Hallam's body and self repeatedly; he is "the man I held as half-divine" (14, line 10), not so different from Christ or the saints. Hallam's remains are "sacred dust" (21, line 22); his words were "sacred wine" (37, line 19). Indeed, as mentioned earlier, if we focus more on the little poems that make up the larger one – the parts rather than the whole – we are reminded of the collections of relics so important to the power of certain Catholic institutions. According to Caroline Walker Bynum, fragments of saints and the things they touched were brought together in large reliquaries to gesture toward divine wholeness. Somehow, she argues, the fragments, by their very fragmentation, come to point to the endless, the infinite. Tennyson brings together a collection of little "relics," each one pulsing with its own meaning, set in the "reliquary" of *In Memoriam*.

Tennyson echoes, in his lines about Hallam at the bottom of the sea, an equally famous elegy, deeply important to the history of the form. In Milton's "Lycidas" the subject of the elegy – Milton's schoolfellow Edward King – died when his ship capsized near Ireland.[56] His body, unlike Hallam's, was in actuality lost at sea and unlocateable (but certainly not impossible to imagine, indeed, perhaps easier to imagine because not in reality seen). In the ship/sea poems of *In Memoriam*, Tennyson is referencing the lines of "Lycidas" in which Milton desires King's bones, wherever they may be, to be brought home or to heaven as a final home.

> Ay me! whilst thee the shores and sounding seas
> Wash far away, where'er thy bones are hurled,
> Whether beyond the stormy Hebrides,
> Where thou perhaps under the whelming tide
> Visit'st the bottom of the monstrous world ...
> Look homeward angel now, and melt with ruth:
> And, O ye dolphins, waft the hapless youth.[57]

The ocean becomes a vast, echoing container ("The moanings of the homeless sea," as Tennyson calls it [35, line 10]) for these precious relics – a crypt because of those remains – and a place of redemption where kindly sea creatures might carry the youth back to familiar shores. Tennyson, thinking of "Lycidas," calls to the ship to bring "such precious relics ... the dust of him" home, to be buried in "English earth" (17, lines 18–19). Both poems try to open in the elegy a stretch of spaciousness to hold the bones, to domicile them in friendly surroundings.

Tennyson also discovers some consolation in imagining Hallam's body buried in the domestic earth, despite the fact that, being of a wealthy and well-known family (his father was an MP), he was buried in a vault beneath the church. But a church needs no shrine-creating bones, being already a sacred space; thus to write Hallam's remains into the earth is to find a reason to let the bones sacralize the homely landscape.[58] (The grave is "a little house" [35, line 2].) "'T is well; 't is something; we may stand / Where he in English earth is laid, / And from his ashes may be made / The violet of his native land" (18, lines 1–4). To find in his decomposing flesh "food" for plants is to desire a regeneration, a fresh living thing coming out of his moldering corpse. The "native" violet is local; its roots clinging to Hallam's bones keep him local. Regional plants emerging from his "ashes" affirm that Britain is the home of his tomb, but they also turn the environs of his relics into a domestic shrine. Even the plants partake of his divinity. The corpse infuses meaning and animation into landscape and language. Yet the landscape doesn't necessarily need the bones to become sacralized. Memories can suffuse place so that anywhere can become a shrine, as long as the associations are strong enough. Patrick Scott explores the "topographical narrative" in *In Memoriam*, and he encourages a rereading of the poem "as elegizing not a person ... but a place."[59] Throughout *In Memoriam* Tennyson attempts to shape these spaces, such as Hallam's

London house and street; the rooms at Cambridge he had occupied; and the shadow under the trees at Somersby where he had cooled himself. Also: "The path by which we twain did go, / Which led by tracts that pleased us well, / Thro' four sweet years arose and fell, / From flower to flower, from snow to snow" (22, lines 1–4). The paths where their love happened are now imbued not only with past scenes but also with the very fact of death. Hallam's disappearance leaves behind traces glowing with significance, with the vibrant tenor of death's dark drama.

If Tennyson could feel again Hallam's selfhood, the feeling would come by situating Hallam's presence in a domestic space. This is indeed what happens: at Somersby, Tennyson has his miracle at the shrine of his saint. Peter Sacks calls these "near-religious rites" in this most-famous lyric.[60] A nighttime scene is bounded with still, unflickering tapers and bats going "round in fragrant skies": "The trees / Laid their dark arms about the field" (95, lines 9, 15–6). A charmed circle is thus traced. As Tennyson reads Hallam's words, in letters from long ago, he has his epiphany: a discovery that Hallam can be found infusing this place with eternity, as the saints were thought to do. Suddenly, "the living soul was flash'd on mine" (95, lines 35–6). Tennyson feels at one with his friend's soul, and then he can catch "The deep pulsations of the world" (line 40). An existential wonder overtakes him and, taking the death of his beloved as an integral part of being, he finds all interfused and endless: "And East and West, without a breath, / Mixt their dim lights, like life and death, / To broaden into boundless day" (lines 62–4). Not only does he make of this place a shrine, but the poem, too, becomes a sanctified abode, walled by words. It is a "frame / In matter-moulded forms of speech" (lines 45–6).[61] He slips into the chamber of verse to find his Hallam, to discover a transformative space. Tennyson also encounters himself here, after losing himself in the death of the other. John Rosenberg sees the mourning that Tennyson does with *In Memoriam* as holding "his life together, expressing and ordering his inmost being."[62] Within the disappearing act of the elegy, he comes to know that losing himself is part of knowing being.

Spiritualism and loss as loss

The exploration of the sacred spaces of *In Memoriam* brings to mind the notion of haunting. One way to imagine the presence of Hallam in the climax poem discussed earlier (lyric XCV) is as a sort of ghost, called up through the medium of writing, or the letters written by Hallam. Part of the era's fascination with the life/death boundary, Spiritualism was another system of belief that found power in the materiality of death. Tennyson's invocation of Hallam shares ideas with this movement, which was just coming into fashion in 1850 when his poem was published. Spiritualism celebrated the idea that not only did the dead still have a being in a postlife place, but they also remained tangibly among us.[63] Spiritualists believed that the worlds of the living and the dead, the absent and the present, were permeable and that this could be proven most solidly through materiality.[64] If those "gone before us" were loved strongly enough, if their memory was kept fully alive, then perhaps they might crowd in on the still living. Believers most wanted proof of the presence of the unique dead – that loved one the "sitter" in a séance most desired to locate once again. In its most basic form, the dealings with the perished that Spiritualists conducted involved the ghost "speaking" through everyday things: knocking or "rapping" on walls, tables, or other furniture, or moving heavy objects (such as levitating the séance circle's table). Spirits might, it was reported, play on musical instruments with invisible hands, guide the medium to write down their chatter (called passive or automatic writing) or even be "materialized," the most difficult task a medium could accomplish. Materialization might occur when the medium was affixed to a chair in a closet, as Alex Owen explains in her history of the movement, and as the audience watched, the form of a deceased person would seem to emerge from the closet – a ghost, supposedly, but one that had enough substantiality that the audience might "prove" its existence by touching, grasping, or kissing it. What most convinced the séance goers was this solidity of the spirit, its seeming embeddedness in things. These wispy forms were made up of a kind of "ectoplasm," it was believed, a type of mesmeric fluid or force that could be caught in photographs.[65] "Katie King," the spirit that the celebrated medium Florence Cook claimed to materialize, would sometimes, as part of her performance, cut locks of her hair and hand them to audience members.[66] The "spirits" could have the vigor and humor of breathing beings, but they often also had a connection to corpses. The revenant that the medium Mary Rosina Showers would occasionally materialize, called "Lenore," would at times be only partially formed and would exude, audience members reported, "a charnel-house smell . . . as if she had been buried a few weeks and dug up again."[67] This desire to call back the material form of the deceased, even in the form of a semiputrid corpse, kept alive a need to believe that the dead were companions that might occupy, sound on, or infuse objects.

It was in rooms that revenants could most be felt, usually in domestic spaces. Spiritualism deepened the already strong love the Victorians had for shrines and pilgrimages. Believing that spirits might float around or return to the spaces associated with their living and dying selves meant that in such places – and in the thingness of them – might be found their presence. Such beliefs fed a cherishing of relics and souvenirs, and relic lovers were the most likely ones to take up Spiritualism. Queen Victoria, to give a famous example, felt haunted by the presence of the dead Prince Albert and had a difficult time, as explored earlier, consoling herself for his loss. "I feel now to be so acquainted with death," she wrote to the Princess Royal, "and to be much nearer that unseen world."[68] She conducted séances and "table-turnings," feeling convinced he still lingered. "The thought, the *certain* feeling and belief that her adored Angel is *near* her," the Queen wrote, referring to herself, "*loving* her, watching over her, praying for her and guiding her – is – next the blessed Hope of that Eternal reunion – her only comfort in her overwhelming affliction."[69] Queen Victoria was evangelical leaning, as were many Spiritualists, but a more radical set dallied with Spiritualism as well. Secularists of many sorts, included full-blown atheists, found solace in Spiritualism as evidence that the loved one was not annihilated, but might still be called up, felt in rooms, worshipped in shrines, and photographed.

Dante Gabriel Rossetti, discussed in Chapter 1 in relation to the beautiful death, was another séance attendee. He believed the spirit of his wife floated about him; for a period, he "*saw* her ghost every night!" according to his friend John Marshall.[70] Like the Queen with her husband, Rossetti tried to speak with his wife, attending his first séance in 1864, arranged by the traveling spiritualists the Davenport brothers.[71] At his rambling mansion, Tudor House, Rossetti began to hold his own spiritualist gatherings. "It seems Gabriel's wife is constantly appearing (that is, rapping out things) at the séances at Cheyne Walk – William affirms that the things communicated are such as only she could know," commented one friend.[72] Although the core philosophy behind Spiritualism is belief in an afterlife, it also had strong ties to other nonreligious systems, such as animal magnetism, sympathetic magic, and scientific rationalism. Historians of Spiritualism argue that its rise in the middle of the nineteenth century signaled the looming doubts of modernity.[73] Janet Oppenheim develops the theory that the immense popularity of Spiritualism was a symptom of the growing insecurity of religious faith of the time.[74] Like the beautiful death and relic love, a belief in ghosts was an anxious grasping after permanence of the authentic, unique individual. Spiritualism can be seen as an effort to hold onto the belief that the beloved individual is a perpetual being, an idea increasingly threatened by the rising forces of secularization: scientific discovery, rationalist philosophy, new forms of history making, and rampant consumerism. While these forces will be explored in Chapter 5 and in the afterword, I want to return here to *In Memoriam*.

Although Carol Christ is certainly correct when, in her exploration of Browning's poetry and death, she points to "Tennyson's attempt in *In Memoriam* to connect body to text in a way that restores Hallam's presence," I want to suggest that this is not the whole truth.[75] This presence that he wants is very much embodied, of course. But what Tennyson often desires is to keep loss palpable, to be not consoled, but to feel true death – annihilation – as an inspiration for poetry and being. I agree, then, with James Kincaid's argument that Tennyson celebrates loss rather than vanquishing it, but my emphasis falls differently. Kincaid finds that Tennyson "actively erases substance" in order to not foreclose loss.[76] I contend that it is in *substance* that this loss in located. *In Memoriam* is a poem caught up in the struggle with faith and with deep doubt, and it therefore shares the struggles of many Spiritualists, like Rossetti. The question of what the dead body might mean and if and how it lingers with the still living sits at the center of this troubling. At certain turns, believing that "dust and ashes" retain meaning becomes a bulwark against the flood of the existential abyss:

> My own dim life should teach me this,
>   That life shall live for evermore,
>   Else earth is darkness at the core,
> *And dust and ashes all that is.* (my emphasis, 34, lines 1–4)

Thus recovering a sense of the infinite in the finite, in the trace of the once alive – the dust and ashes – becomes a key movement in the shoring up of faith, in the fight against the idea that "Man dies: nor is there hope in dust" (35, line 4). While in the long view of *In Memoriam* consolation and belief in the afterlife are affirmed, the individual poems can be read as, in Timothy Peltason's words, "pockets of rebellious and unassimilated intensity," or statements of pure grief, of doubt unconvinced.[77] Doubt arises again and again in the poem, of course, such as here: "Yet oft when sundown skirts the moor / An inner trouble I behold, / A spectral doubt which makes me cold, / That I shall be thy mate no more" (41, lines 16–20). In Tennyson can be found a more complex emotional approach to remains than the evangelical popular discourse, one that was more common than the simple feeling of consolation in the relic, the sense that the corporeal fragment's referent was the still existing. Even many

Christians found that it was in the insupportable loss of the loved one that their belief intermingled with doubts. The very rhyme scheme enacts just such sentiments. Susan Gates notes that the abba stanza form expresses the mourner's desire "to continue missing Hallam rather than to cease loving him."[78] Christopher Ricks finds "the exquisite aptness of Tennyson's choice of stanza ... which can 'circle moaning in the air,' returning to its setting out, and with fertile circularity staving off its deepest terror of arrival."[79] Tennyson keeps open a little space for Hallam to be embraced.

As with Victorian relic culture more generally, the incantatory elegy is a means to respect the irreducible self lost. In his history of the elegy, Peter Sacks finds that *In Memoriam*'s central conundrum is the need to represent the unique and "irreplaceably personal" self and its attachments.[80] Tennyson locates in the elegy, the shrine space, and other relics what Roland Barthes calls, in his twentieth-century exploration of photography, the "punctum." Relics can be fruitfully compared to photography, especially the nonreproducible, hard-plate type most common in its beginnings. The elegy and relic objects had a "punctum," a quality in a photograph that can bruise, prick, or be poignant. The punctum, Barthes explains, is "undevelopable ... [it is] what cannot be transformed but only repeated under the instances of insistence (of the insistent gaze)."[81] The elegy – and the relic – can bring a kind of pure grief that doesn't change or develop, but bruises freshly again and again: loss crystallized and inescapable. Tennyson weeps "a loss forever new" (13, line 5). His grief was deeply personalized, was felt for *one man*, without ritual, generalization, or stylization. In writing about the death of his mother, Barthes expresses a similar idea. The photograph and the relic both prove that the absent loved one has been there, that she "has been absolutely, irrefutably present."[82] This *that-has-been* can open a "wound" (Barthes) of longing because what has been lost – and both the photograph and the relic attest to this – was an utterly unique, singular being, a whole that can never be replaced, duplicated, encompassed (even in memory). As Barthes comes to discover through the process of writing *Camera Lucida*, the photograph of his dead mother "achieved ... *the impossible science of the unique being*."[83] When his mother died, he lost a living, changing entity, the "grace" of "an individual soul," and the photograph brings this wholesale loss back to him, all at once. Relics hold this same quality; they are the material sample of a being that will never be given to grow, to be seen, or felt again. Emblematic of the "radiant, irreducible core," relics speak of the truth of the loved body, which is a particularity that cannot be universalized, just as the relic can never be reproduced, copied, multiplied.[84] A kind of "dead commodity," it attests to the never before and the never again.

Found everywhere in *In Memoriam* is this passionate belief in the unique soul. If one truly loves, this philosophy goes, then the lost beloved and the loss itself can't be absorbed into a general religious belief or sphere of commonality. To give up this loss is to be like everyone else, is to liken the beloved body to every*thing* else. Even after death, Tennyson affirms that Hallam cannot be subsumed in the "general Soul," but must remain what he has always been: a "separate whole," eternally. Tennyson must still "know him when we meet" (46, lines 1–8). As with a saint, death and the elegy that sings it link the subject to the singular moment in place and time – *hic locus est*. Although Tennyson and Hallam's time together lasted only five years ("those five years in richest field"), it encompassed "the eternal landscape of the past." In other words, "O Love, thy province were not large / A bounded field, nor stretching far" (46, lines 13–14). The sharp grief, Tennyson appears to say, comes from precisely this bounded quality – the specificity of the thing and person – but it is this singularity from which his love emerges. Integral to the project of *In Memoriam* is the "undeniability of immediate experience," as Peltason eloquently puts it, "the refusal to place the moment in history."[85] Tennyson, in the more radical of these poems, repudiates the work of mourning. Mastering the "complex art of saving loss itself," Tennyson uses the elegy as a kind of relic, a means to continue to see and know absence.[86] Peter Sacks sees *In Memoriam* as an "accretion of moments" that he collects and accumulates, which "gives each stanza a self-encysted quality, an effect of being withheld from time."[87] And *In Memoriam* is the edifice – the cathedral even – built as an act of reverence to house (and celebrate) the relics of Hallam.

Saving loss is a Keatsian move, of course, and Tennyson takes from Keats the importance of keeping darkness dark.[88] The death chamber opens into life; it serves "to enrich the threshold of the night" (29, line 6). Another means of stating this is to point to the way that "knowing Death has made / His darkness beautiful with thee" (74, lines 11–12). There is no better way to keep this darkness of loss animated – to keep Hallam's death singular, irremediable – than in language, fallible as it can be. Tennyson finds that the poem is a shrine that keeps love memorialized. With the poem, he shares the death of his friend with all, taking from that life completed, as Walter Benjamin would see it, a story to limn. Tennyson partook of the Victorian willingness to dwell with the loss of the irreplaceable, to hold onto it. The Victorians expressed a desire to touch the death that surrounds life, to feel its presence as material, vital. Such a culture sees death, and the body itself, as a starting place for stories rather than their annihilation.

CHAPTER 5

Hair jewelry as congealed time: Hardy and Far From the Madding Crowd

Bracelet of bright haire about the bone.

—John Donne

Making of the moment something permanent

When Hardy's cousin Tryphena died, he wrote a poem about wishing that he had known her better, spent more time witnessing her life in the places where it had its day. "Thoughts of Phena at News of Her Death" laments having no material trace of her, "Not a line of her writing have I, / Not a thread of her hair."[1] What he wants is to "picture her there" during her span and its environs, and for this he most needs a "relic" of her. The poem was published in his 1898 *Wessex Poems and Other Verses*, a volume filled out with many of Hardy's own drawings. "Thoughts of Phena" is accompanied by an illustration of a dead woman covered closely by a sheet. Other drawings depict graveyards, churches with the underground tombs pictured so that the skeletons can be seen, and bearers of a coffin. As with the other Victorian writers discussed in this book, Hardy's attentiveness to deanimated bodies and what they left behind (or didn't, a thing to regret) runs extensively through most of his writing. There is the elegy sequence written on the death of his wife Emma, *Poems of 1912–13*, in which he seeks to rediscover her in locations she adored, like the coast of Cornwall, and he imagines her in her grave.[2] In *The Woodlanders*, he has the young Marty South, the girl most attuned to the rhythm of the woodland, sleep next to her dead father, whose coffin has been set next to her bed: "when the moon arrived opposite the window, its beams streamed across the still profile of South, sublimed by the august presence of death, and onward a few feet further upon the face of his daughter, lying in her little bed in the silence of a repose almost as dignified as that of her companion."[3] In many of his novels, Hardy imagines the Wessex landscape as a kind of palimpsest, with not only the ancient ruins creating a layer of human existence

128

under the current one, but also the graves of the long-dead, the corpse position and grave-goods pointing to cultures so distant in time that they can hardly be understood anymore.[4] In her meditation on the role of death in Hardy's novels, Mary Elizabeth Hotz comments on the material nature of these layers, in *Return of the Native*, "Egdon Heath ... suggests that the cosmos is a seamless entity, unbroken in the connection of artifacts and bodies buried deep in the earth to the lives walking upon the heath to the heavens above."[5] Gillian Beer sees these strata as Hardy's "many time-scales, from the geological time of Egdon Heath to the world of the ephemerons."[6] This chapter considers both temporality and its mark made in materiality, but it moves from the grandiose scales explored by Hotz and Beer to the minute one of the lock of hair.

In her Hardy biography, Claire Tomalin calls the illustrations in *Wessex Poems* "distinctly weird."[7] Part of their strangeness comes from their lack of sentimentality and nostalgia. Not cynical, nor comical in a Dickens sort of way, their mood and function appear simply illustrative. In the drawing of the dead under the church, the impetus seems to be a curiosity about how and where they are positioned down there, under the flags of the floor. The sketch of the dead woman stretched out on the bed also appears to evolve from an uncomplicated desire to picture what such a shape would look like: a female corpse with a sheet wrapping the form closely. Similarly, the snippet of hair that Hardy wants from his cousin's head has some sentimental value, but he also wants to use it as a kind of metonymic tool of imagination. He pines to hold it, hoping that it will help him form an image of what her life had been like, particularly its material ordinariness ("No mark of her late time as dame in her dwelling, whereby / I may picture her there" [lines 3–4]). Some of Hardy's elegies to Emma also hold just such a "weirdness." By the time of her death, Hardy and his wife had become largely estranged (though still living in the same house), their love soured and embittered. His mourning for her had more to do with yearning for that long lost love, buried in the past before she died, than with the actual person who had just perished (although he did have her corpse in its coffin put at the end of his bed, so he could sleep in the same room with her for a few days).[8] The argument in the following pages will focus on Hardy's depiction of death as a hard fact of life, with little of the sublimity, melodrama, sentimentalism, or religious trappings we find in the Romantic poets, Brontë, Dickens, and Tennyson. Hardy's desire to represent a certain rural attitude in his writing, a set of beliefs quite ancient, in line with the time when the Dorset countryside really had been called "Wessex" and based partially on what he witnessed in his Victorian neighbors, colors his representation of death. This view aligns well with what Phillip Ariès, in his history discussed in Chapter 1, calls the early medieval "tame death." Yet interleaved with this representation is Hardy's own brand of atheism, which had much to do with late- and post-Victorian developments in the realm of secularism, science, technology, and consumerism. Nevertheless, these views also foregrounded death as a form of thingness, to be considered in light of materiality. Unlike what we find with Romantic visions of the posthumous and Victorian hankering toward the afterlife in the various forms that have been discussed in Chapters 2, 3, and 4, Hardy's stance, which we find becoming more common as the century moved toward its close, involved not some sort of posthumous realm, but rather only the past and remembrance. As the narrator remarks in *Far From the Madding Crowd*: "Immortality consists in being enshrined in others' memories."[9]

To return again to "Thoughts of Phena," the poem centers on this absent snip of hair as the residue most evocative of that vanished existence. In his desire to write novels that would be somewhat shocking and thus sell well enough for him to live off his writing, Hardy utilized a symbol common to popular novels of the period, especially sensation fiction: hairwork.[10] As I will explain in the following pages, hair relics became ubiquitous plot devices in fashionable thrillers and romances, primarily because they were so common in the larger culture and worked as a sort of dramatic shorthand. Of Hardy's novels, *Far From the Madding Crowd* of 1874 is the one above all others that carries the hair fragment and its relation to a corpse into the center of the narrative. In this novel and many of his writings, Hardy was part of a larger Victorian practice of finding in hair keepsakes a figure for a myriad of ideas, including a crystallization of evanescence, or to state this differently, a certain approach to the life–death boundary. The lock of hair became the most cherished of secular relics in nineteenth-century Britain for reasons easy to surmise, and therefore numerous ideas about death and the body accreted in and around these little things. This chapter will trace, through these mementos, this thick gathering of ideas and gestures: not only Hardy's own special use of them as plot devices, but also a broader secularization of mourning customs, which intersected with a particular culture of consumption and its attitudes toward death, the body, and the individual.

Like the other types of relics under discussion in this book, hair mementos have a long history, yet they reached their apotheosis (and then final decline) in the nineteenth century. Some of the earliest hair jewelry was, not surprisingly, linked to the cult of saints and was thought to have miraculous – or magical – abilities.[11] The sapphire amulet Charlemagne gave his wife in the ninth century, which reputedly contained the Virgin Mary's hair and fragments of the True Cross, was thought to have the power to perpetuate love between them.[12] Reliquary crosses and other wearable jewelry containing saints' hair (kept in interior cavities and sometimes able to be viewed through little windows) can still be found scattered throughout Britain in churches, museums, and archives.[13] Wearing morsels of saints' flesh, bones, or hair could protect one, it was believed, from perils of all sorts. Placing royal tresses in jewelry was well established by the late sixteenth century. Mary Stuart, for example, gave James Gordon of Methlick a brooch representing a laurel wreath, set in the center with a curl of her dark hair under crystal.[14] After the beheading of Charles I in 1649, numerous rings containing his hair commemorated the event, some reportedly dipped in pools of his blood on the scaffold.[15] Interwoven with gold and silver, his locks were used to bind a volume of *Les Heures royalles, dediées au Roy*.[16] Judith Pascoe tells the story of Queen Charlotte's freedom with her own curls, during the mid- to late eighteenth century. One of her subjects praised her for this: "she was told I had wished for a lock of her hair; and she sent me one with her own fingers." Some of these were set in "reliquaries," such as a coil kept in a black box, with a silver plate on its lid inscribed "Queen Charlotte's Hair."[17] When the 5th Duke of Gordon died in 1836, a memorial bracelet set with his hair was made, inscribed with his name and the date of his death.[18] Later, as the bracelet was passed down to other family members, the band recorded each transfer with a new inscription and, sometimes, another curl from the new owner or a recently deceased relative, lending the bracelet a familial, temporal specificity.[19] Marking an eminent historical or military event with reliquary jewelry continued to be popular in the eighteenth and nineteenth centuries. Lady Neville, for instance, prized a brooch carrying some strands from Nelson's mane, given to her husband by the hero himself. The brooch's inscription included such details as, "Lost to his country Oct. 21, 1805." The practice became so pervasive that the hair mementoes collected from the famous are too common to enumerate. Many of these still exist today, such as scraps from Charlotte Brontë, Mary Shelley, and Wild Bill Hickok in the Berg Collection of the New York Public Library. In the Yale Beineke can be found a lock of hair, in the Thomas Hardy collection, tipped into *Jones' Series of Engravings*, as well as curls mounted under glass in the Robert Louis Stevenson collection and snippets of hair from the heads of George Eliot, Alfred Lord Tennyson, and Algernon Charles Swinburne. The Keats-Shelley Memorial House in

Rome has a reliquary containing a wisp of Milton's hair alongside one from the head of Elizabeth Barrett Browning. At the British Library can be found at least twenty-two locks of hair tucked into letters, envelopes, and books. These include tresses that once belonged to Letitia Elizabeth Landon, George Eliot, Felicia Hemans, Christina Rossetti, Lord Nelson, Goethe, and Beethoven. Such a lover of relics as Queen Victoria could not forego the chance to aestheticize Albert's hair after his sudden death. She sent curls to Garrard – the royal jewelers – where they were worked into jewelry. At least eight pieces were made that incorporated his hair, such as a gold pin fronted by an onyx cameo of the Prince with a box at the back for a curl and a bracelet set with tresses from the heads of royal family members, mixed in with Albert's – a present for the Queen from one of her children. Her eight-year-old son wore around his neck "a Locket with beloved Papa's hair."[20]

In Britain, placing the tresses of ordinary mortals in jewelry was an established practice by the early seventeenth century.[21] Men and women wore bracelets woven entirely of hair, given to them as tokens of love, friendship, or familial affection. The bracelets that appear in John Donne's early seventeenth-century poems, "The Funerall" and "The Relique," mentioned earlier, work as symbols of erotic passion linked inextricably with the decay of the material self. In both poems the speaker imagines his body after death, with the hair bracelet still testifying to a love now made secret and unknowable.[22] Popular from the mid-eighteenth century, hair jewelry became such a craze from the 1850s to the 1880s that a busy industry flourished.[23] Hair albums also had their day, as did pictures and wreaths. Advertisements for designers in hair, hair artisans, and hairworkers ran in newspapers (such as the London *Times* and the *Illustrated London News*), and periodicals (*New belle assemblee*, *The Cornhill Magazine*, and others) discussed the fad as it waxed and waned. The London jeweler Antoni Forrer, the best-known professional hairworker midcentury, kept 50 workers employed at his Regent Street shop.[24] Among that accumulation of things that was the Great Exhibition, there were at least eleven displays of hair art, and medals were won for miniatures of the royal family worked in hair.[25] There was even a prize for "a large portrait of Her Majesty Queen Victoria" made of hair.[26] This is another instance of "recycling" the corpse; hair was often bought and sold, a practice and its implications that will be discussed later.

Jewelers accepted curls sent through the mail, for those who lived far from shops, with instructions for the piece to be made. Working in hair became a handcraft for women to practice at home, akin to other types of "fancy work" like embroidery, feather pictures, shell-work, and wax modeling. Popular instructional manuals such as Mark Campbell's 1867 *Self-Instructor in the Art of Hair Work* and Alexanna Speight's 1871 *The Lock of Hair* described how to first boil the hair in order to clean it, then how to weave it using special round tables (which could be mail ordered) with a series of weights to be attached to the strands.[27] Women's magazines often included patterns for hair jewelry, such as the *English Woman's Domestic Magazine*, *The Family Friend*, and *Cassell's Household Guide*. The simplest type of hairwork involved merely placing a curl in a locket or in the compartment behind a watch or miniature.[28] For a bracelet or necklace woven of hair, the ends would be attached to gold (or a cheaper material) fasteners, such as one Charlotte Brontë had made of the hair of her sisters Emily and Anne, after their early deaths from tuberculosis.[29] Watch fobs or chains, buttons, brooches, earrings, or pins all could be made of or contain hair. Rings held hair in a variety of ways: hidden behind a gem that could be slid to the side to expose the plait, displayed openly behind glass or crystal, or exposed completely, backed by gold or another metal. Inscription came to be an important part of these gems, and engravings often had epitaphic qualities. A brooch illustrates the "tomb-like" quality of these jewels; these little "graves" often held the "bodies" of two lovers entwined, in Donnean fashion (see Fig. 13).[30] At its heart and visible behind glass, the brooch has two interleaved curls of hair of different colors (and textures). The inscription on the reverse reads: "Sir Marc Isambard Brunel, Died Decr 1849. Aged 80. Sophia Brunel, Died Jany 1855, Aged 79."

Figure 13.   Gold brooch enclosing the hair of Sir Marc Isambard Brunel and his wife Sophia, 1855, M.21-1972, 1855.

Hairwork became so conventional that the omniscient narrator of Wilkie Collins's *Hide and Seek* (1854) could declare that a hair bracelet is "in England one of the commonest ornaments of woman's wear."[31] And by the time Dickens wrote *Our Mutual Friend*, men's watch fobs made of hair had become a mark of middle-class respectability. That poor seeker of class approval and stability, Bradley Headstone, wearing all that is proper, "with his decent silver watch in his pocket and its decent hair-guard round his neck, looked a thoroughly decent young man of six-and-twenty."[32] While hairwork as part of mourning culture will be at the center of this chapter, such keepsakes memorialized various types of emotional and sentimental situations. Jewelry with hair could be amatory, passed between lovers, such as Edward Ferrars's ring in *Sense and Sensibility*, "with a plait of hair in the center," which causes speculation about the identity of his beloved, the donor of the plait, or the hair bracelet in Wilkie Collins's *Hide and Seek*, which contains the tress of a secret lover.[33] The lock given to Caroline Helstone by Robert Moore in Brontë's *Shirley* acts as a reminder of their early affection, when their relationship has gone wrong; the diamond and hair locket in Mary Elizabeth Braddon's *The Lovels of Arden* is passed among family members until it ends up in the hands of the paramour. Major Dobbin treasures "a little brown hair-chain which he wore round his neck," which was made from Amelia's locks.[34] Hair jewelry could be a vehicle for affection, a gift between family members or close friends, like Margaret's hair ring holding a paring from her still-alive sister Hester, in Harriet Martineau's *Deerbrook*. As time moves forward, however, all hair jewelry inevitably holds the hair of the dead, thus potentially becoming mourning jewelry.[35]

The ubiquity of hair as a revered relic, as opposed to other types of primary relics, came about because of its relative permanence and attractiveness: when every recognizable part of the body had decayed (such as the flesh and eyes), the hair could abide to testify to the unique whole. (Not only does it remain, but the myth that hair continues to grow on a corpse for years after death maintained currency in the nineteenth century, as we have seen with rumors about Lizzie Siddal's corpse.) The most ornamental part of the human body, hair is easily altered. Its appearance through new styles, cutting, dying, and even moods ties it closely to the personality of the individual. It holds its color, shape, and texture when divided from its source and continues to attest to the life era from which it came: the soft, pale baby lock; the shiny, rich adult head; and the grizzled gray of old age. Hair is the part of the body most epochal, susceptible to dating discrete periods of one's existence. It is therefore the relic that has the strongest relationship to moments of the past (see Fig. 14).

Figure 14.   Watch fob made of hair.

Set in its often beautiful and elaborate reliquaries and with a certain
aesthetic significance, the hair memento functioned as another type
of postmortem art. Like the other types explored in Chapter 3, hair
artifacts were sometimes used as consolatory devices, another proof of
imperishability tied to the Christian "good death." An evangelical named
Emily Palmer gave her reasons for wearing the hair of her recently deceased
sister Dorothea.

> Dear Laura [her sister-in-law] has given us each a ring of our Do's hair with
> a small pearl in the middle. I am so fond of it. We chose a ring – and I am
> glad for 3 reasons. First because always wearing it – helps me always to think
> of her – 2nd because a ring seems to be bond of love – 3rd it being round –
> a circle reminds one how one's love and communion with her may and will
> last for ever.[36]

Representing presence, the fullness and plenitude of meaning, the body
and its pieces could express the not-death of the "good" death. The hair
jewel says, for some believers, that *we will meet again*, not that absence will
be forever fixed (see Fig. 15). Yet because the culture of hair keepsakes
became so pervasive across class, gender, and religious boundaries, it also

Figure 15.   Two hair bracelets; a ring with an open hoop revealing a strip of woven
hair; two brooches with sections for the hair of numerous family members, each
inscribed with the initials of the donor; a card case with decorative elements and the
name "Ellen" made with cut and laid hair. Probably English, 1835–55.

could represent a discourse of doubt. Or, in fact, memorial tresses often
represented a complicated play of both faith and doubt. It is this double
movement of comfort and grief that can be found most commonly in
nineteenth-century writing about hair jewelry. A writer for *Cassell's Household Guide* points out that it was the "imperishable nature . . . and the great

brilliancy and beauty which it retains long after it has been severed, and even after the person to whom it once belonged has passed away" that made hairwork a "cherished memento."[37] The relic reminds one of the eternal – the imperishable – and calls up the finite in the one now "passed away." *The Family Friend* remarked, "A lock of hair from the head of some beloved one is often prized above gold or gems, for it is not a mere purchasable gift, but actually a portion of themselves, present with us when they are absent, surviving while they are mouldering in the grave."[38] Marcia Pointon calls hair jewelry "a material figure for memory" because it "stages the death of its subject and simultaneously . . . instantiates continuity."[39] The play of presence and absence begins when the relic is touched – the fragment of the body and the memories are *here*, the being itself, its whole corporeality, *gone*. To cite another example, in Rhoda Broughton's *Cometh Up as a Flower*, when Nell's father dies, she cries over a lock of his hair, "and now the sight of the thin grey lock, so sparse, so almost white, recalled to me with such bitter force the head from which it was severed, that he, being dead, yet spake."[40] The hair brings the dead father back to speak, yet foregrounds, at the same time, the eternal silence. As we shall see in Hardy's writings, hair relics represent the "fatedness" of human life, always in movement toward still objecthood, which then, for a nonbeliever like Hardy, draws all the threads of that life not toward a future, postdeath, but back in a retrospective of memory.

Material magic

Not long after Bathsheba Everdene has married the caddish Sergeant Troy, in *Far From the Madding Crowd*, she finds her worries about his character confirmed when she observes him opening the case at the back of his gold watch, thus "revealing, snugly stowed within it, a small coil of hair" (349). The watch has a long history, some of which is inscribed on its surface, like many of the pieces of hairwork described earlier. Its inscription, the Earls of Severn's motto "*Cedit amor rebus*" ("love yields to circumstance") and a coronet with five points, links it to Troy's familial past and to his romantic future in marrying the wealthy Bathsheba Everdene (representing "circumstance") instead of the more beloved Fanny Robin. The only piece of inheritance he has, the watch embodies a personal and national history; it "has regulated imperial interests in its time – the stately ceremonial, the courtly assignation, pompous travels, and lordly sleeps" (238). Not only does it evoke these skeletons and their earlier states of being, but the hair coil belongs to Fanny, who is dying in the Casterbridge workhouse just at the time her hair is being shown to Bathsheba in nearby Weatherbury. The hair relic's uncovering will lead to the uncovering of Fanny's corpse in her coffin (and that of her baby, born just at her death) because Bathsheba wants to confirm the color of her hair, to see if it matches the yellow lock in the watch.[41] The opening of the back of the timepiece and of the coffin lid become movements bound together inextricably, just as the tress works as a sort of stand-in for the corpse and the watch as a coffin.[42] As with many material objects in the novel, the hair drives the living to act – or even to die – an idea I will examine later. This relic signifies the larger movements in the plot that, taken together, speak of a particular brand of materialized death culture that affirms the death written in bodies while they are still animated. This is an idea found in Dickens and postmortem art, as was discussed in Chapter 3, but with Hardy the stop of death is a fuller stop, one that moves into retrospective plot rather than forward.

Hardy takes the title for his novel *Far From the Madding Crowd* from the Graveyard poet Thomas Gray's "Elegy Written in a Country Churchyard." The stanza describes the individuals buried in the cemetery who, because they were dwellers of rural places and not extraordinary people, lived:

> Far from the madding crowd's ignoble strife,
>   Their sober wishes never learned to stray;
> Along the cool sequestered vale of life
>   They kept the noiseless tenor of their way. (lines 53–56)

Thus these were people doubly buried.[43] The "purest ray serene" of their "gem" was hidden in "the dark unfathomed caves of ocean," just as they "will blush unseen" and waste their sweetness, like opening flowers, "on the desert air."[44] Their lives private, inconsequential, quiet, they have now become even more so – permanently – in death. Gray's elegy brings such people back into memory – as a class, though, rather than actual individuals – just as Hardy's representation of the preindustrial English town and country that was vanishing during his lifetime seeks to set time and place in the amber of prose.[45] In a preface to *Far From the Madding Crowd* written in the 1890s, Hardy laments the disappearance of the villages and houses on which Weatherbury was based, which "led to a break of continuity in local history, more fatal than any other thing to the preservation of legend, folk-lore, close inter-social relation and eccentric individualities" (34). The layering of place, the past, and human materiality becomes interrupted when the "attachment of the soil of one particular spot by generation after generation" (34) is ruptured. As glorifiers of the temporality of local place – Gray of rustic graves being lost to time, in particular the churchyard of St. Giles's Church, Stoke Poges, and Hardy of the Dorset area – they seem to want to recuperate these singular collections of things, bodies, and structures. Yet what they uncover is how these existences always had an inward, even secretive quality. Those "mute inglorious Miltons" of Gray's poem in some sense *never* fully spoke out, even premortem.[46] Dying and being buried continues the process started with birth of vanishing into the material landscape.

In *Far From the Madding Crowd* the unknowability – and unreadability – of the other, cemented in death, is expressed haptically. Meaning happens beneath a material surface and then might be imperfectly felt or seen through a sense of touch or through the feelings of the body.[47] Shapes pushing through an outer covering or skin is one of the most common figures in the novel. The possible revivification of the marriage between Bathsheba and Troy is expressed, for example, through her form distending the material of a tent from within, so that he can feel her with his body from without: "Bathsheba ... leant so idly upon the canvas that it was pressed to the shape of her shoulder, and she was, in fact, as good as in Troy's arms; and he was obliged to keep his breast carefully backward that she might not feel its warmth" (436).[48] Feeling the heat of a body through the thin skin of the canvas is to still remain apart, close but shapes rather than fully fleshed, speaking individuals. This idea saturates the story with the repeated emphasis on the sublimity of inwardness and silence, which appears throughout the narrative as privileged modes of expression. Virginia Woolf called this deliberate obscurity Hardy's "margin of the unexpressed."[49] Both Gabriel Oak and Farmer Boldwood have interiorities largely unavailable to the other characters in the novel and thus also to the reader. Oak's most vivid imaginings, for example, happen under his closed eyelids, where all was "full of movement, like a river flowing rapidly under its ice" (112). Through silence more is expressed than through sound because signals steeped in matter hold the most meaning. Farmer Boldwood is often described as a mute block of a man: "Those who have the power of reproaching in silence may find it a means more effective than words. There are accents in the eye which are not on the tongue, and more tales come from pale lips than can enter an ear. It is both grandeur and the pain of the remoter moods that they avoid the pathway of sound" (267).[50] Bodies "speak" more than anything else: "A man's body is as the shell, or the tablet, of his soul, as he is reserved or ingenuous, overflowing or self-contained" (173). Because of this emphasis, blushing becomes the standard means to express emotion. The many blushes that rise hotly on the countenances of Bathsheba, Gabriel, and others make the body into a book, one difficult to read because its language is personal and hidden. "But man, even to himself, is a palimpsest, having an ostensible writing, and another beneath the lines" (317). The main vehicle for knowledge, the flesh carries its many layers of writing, its meaning occluded.[51]

Bodies and other matter, such as the tress mentioned earlier, therefore have a subtle kind of influence on plots. Hardy's animism, which has been explored by many critics, gives objects the agency to "speak" or be motivating, especially when the body becomes a thing through dying.[52] In *The Mayor of Casterbridge*, for instance, when Elizabeth-Jane acts as a "waker" over her mother's corpse, she becomes philosophical about the ticking clock and other possessions around her. She asks "why things . . . stared at her so helplessly, as if waiting for the touch of some wand that should release them from terrestrial constraint; what that chaos called consciousness, which spun in her at this moment like a top, tended to, and began in."[53] Might things come alive just as the living become things? Where does consciousness end and inanimacy begin, she asks? Grace, in *The Woodlanders*, interrogates the objects in her room to a similar effect. "The world of little things therein gazed at her in helpless stationariness, as though they had tried and been unable to make any progress without her presence."[54] Objects communicate through mere presence, even a kind of animating magic, as they also do in *Far From the Madding Crowd*. Women's dress is a "part of her countenance" (117), just as women "can have eyes in their ribbons" (137). The old bible in Bathsheba's house speaks of its uses in the past through the pattern of wear made on its pages by long-gone fingers, and the ancient house's ready responsiveness expresses, through trembles, creaks, and grooves where many feet had walked, the bodies that have dwelled in it in the past. Bodies themselves pass their influence onto what surrounds them. Gabriel, when he meets Fanny for the first and last time, "fancied that he had felt himself in the penumbra of a very deep sadness when touching that slight and fragile creature" (92). Bathsheba feels Boldwood's desire like an odor he carries around with him: "She heard footsteps brushing the grass, and had a consciousness that love was encircling her like a perfume" (178). The things that Bathsheba has touched or worn – her clothing Gabriel loves, her handwriting on the valentine sent to Boldwood – not only hold her presence, but they are forces that move and change people and plots.[55] Tim Armstrong, in his analysis of Hardy's poetry, remarks on "the way in which material objects carry the traces of the dead."[56] We are now in the same territory as *Wuthering Heights* and *Great Expectations*, where the boundary between vital bodies and inanimate matter is fluid.

The substance that works as a key motivating force in *Far From the Madding Crowd* is "the coil of pale hair," which functions "as the fuze to this great explosion" (416). Like the blushing body, the heated form through a thin skin, and the silent block of a man, hair snippets push characters toward their fate. Hardy's plots are often propelled by relics, a point made by Brandon Bennett in his reading of melancholia in *The Woodlanders*, where he singles out the power of "a bit of severed hair or even flesh."[57] When Troy seductively takes a mold of Bathsheba's figure with the arc of light of his sword, itself "like a living thing" (426), he seals her fate by stealing away much of her power when he severs a "winding lock" and puts it in "the breast of his coat" (251). Swamped with emotion and desire, she finds that his power over her "eventually permeated and coloured her whole constitution" (251). Hardy uses the Samson-like force of hair in *The Woodlanders* when Marty South sells hers, knowing she has lost Giles Winterborne to Grace. Felice Charmond adds the tresses to her own and draws Edred Fitzpiers to her with its mass. Her power over him finally snaps when he reads the note from Marty, explaining that Felice wears a false supplement, a severed piece from Marty's authentic body. Hardy, drawing on effects used by writers like Wilkie Collins, Mary Elizabeth Braddon, and the Brontës, often uses the hair talisman to represent the potency of the body's leavings.[58]

Such an approach to body parts partook of old and pagan forms of faith. The sexualized lingering over remains – a *petite mort* fully realized, a *liebestod* with the *tod* reemphasized – goes back, as we have seen, to well before Donne, but its full flowering as a theme came in the nineteenth century. As mentioned already, with *Wuthering Heights*, Heathcliff imagines his earthly fulfillment in Catherine's remains; a lock of his hair will hopefully keep this promise for the future tangible, tactile. Rossetti, Brontë, and Hardy all call on an ancient fabric of belief – sympathetic magic. The folk wisdom behind the full force of synecdoche is at work here: the piece of the person can bring the presence of the whole.[59] Amorous exchanges of hair stand as a simple example: to give a lock is to give one's body in promise.[60] In Wilkie Collins's *No Name*, when Magdalen draws a morsel of hair out of a white silk bag from around her neck, she speaks to it:

> "I can sit and look at you sometimes, till I almost think I am looking at Frank. Oh, my darling! My darling!" Her voice faltered softly, and she put the lock of hair, with a languid gentleness, to her lips. It fell from her fingers into her bosom. A lovely tinge of color rose on her cheeks, and spread downward to her neck, as if it followed the falling hair. She closed her eyes, and let her fair head droop softly. The world passed from her; and, for one enchanted moment, Love opened the gates of Paradise to the daughter of Eve.[61]

No longer a memento or souvenir of a past time and an absent person, Magdalen's talisman almost abolishes time and space; the two bodies meet orgasmically.[62] In the scene referred to earlier in *Wuthering Heights*, when Heathcliff storms into Catherine's death chamber and replaces Linton's hair with his own in the locket, the bodily fragment expresses an erotic possession through synecdoche – Catherine belongs to Heathcliff because his body, a morsel of it, will go with her to the grave. After Heathcliff leaves, Nelly Dean, the constant meddler, comes into the room. She finds Edgar Linton's pale sliver of hair on the floor and twines it round Heathcliff's thick black one, placing them both in the locket. With her actions, she opens the possibility of a postmortem storm of jealousy. Intertwining the hair of two or more individuals made present, some believed, a relationship consigned in reality only to memory, or fantasy. The young Paulina in Charlotte Brontë's *Villette* takes locks of hair from her father and her future husband, Dr. Graham Bretton, and plaits them together with one of her own curls. "'Now,' said she, 'there is an amulet made, which has the virtue to keep you two always friends. You can never quarrel so long as I wear this.'"[63]

Other types of pagan faith in magic that persisted in the nineteenth century gave secular reliquary jewelry a potent aura. By placing hairwork within the larger history of jewelry in the Western world, we can trace it not only to early Christian reliquary jewelry, as explored already, but also to other types of amulets worn for their protective qualities. A practice that stretches back to antiquity, using certain materials or gems to guard against unhappy events such as illness, slander, or the "evil eye" continued to be common throughout the medieval and Renaissance periods and maintained a hold on smaller groups throughout the nineteenth century.[64] Rings holding "toadstones" (thought to be from the head of a toad, but actually the fossilized tooth of a now-extinct fish) kept the wearer free of poison and kidney disease, for example, and rubies were believed to aid one in holding onto land and status.[65] The jewel's effect increased when it was open backed, therefore touching the skin of the wearer directly. Some Victorian jewelry contained other relic fortifications, such as the caul mentioned earlier, supposed to guard the owner against drowning. But hairwork itself maintained the talismanic quality of earlier jewelry. To have a magical piece of that loved one on one's frame (and usually worn near to the heart), through that paring of hair in its ornamented encasement, was to hold close that foundational safeguard of deep caring. A similar type of faith invoked to describe the power of the relic, like sympathetic magic and folk remedies, was the pseudoscience of animal magnetism. If bodies and things could interact via a fluid that permeated the world, then certain objects might draw an absent individual's "fluid" or presence toward one. Hairwork had this capability for many. The narrator in M. E. Braddon's *The Lovels of Arden*, in reference to a locket inset with hair, remarks, "There are those among our disciples of modern magic who believe there is a subtle animal magnetism in such things; that the mere possession of such a token constitutes a kind of spiritual link between two beings."[66] The need to believe that bodies might be permanently intertwined increased when Christian faith in an afterlife waned. In hairwork was found these special powers to keep present the dead or absent, in a physical memory.

Hardy's novels are full of superstitions and magic ascribed to objects, part of his project of keeping alive the folklore of the Dorset countryside but also an extension of the animism the runs through much of his writing. A kind of sympathetic magic hangs about Fanny's coil of hair. As mentioned earlier, just as her lock of hair is seen for the first time by Bathsheba (and the reader) she dies. The lock of hair not only "carries" the narrative of a life and tells of the future (or past) death, it also seems to *cause* death. Fanny can't speak of her love and pregnancy; the only type of expression possible is the silence of her relic, which comes to mean, through synecdoche, the silence of her corpse. These are the same expressive silences carried by Oak and Boldwood, a telling of a story through material. The story told here, though, as I've already implied, is a sort of fatedness. The fate written in the objects' influence is foretold death, the buried quality that Hardy's characters already hold within them. Commonplace in Hardy's novels are prefigurations like this one in *Far From the Madding Crowd*: "The village of Weatherbury was quiet as the graveyard in its midst, and the living were lying well-nigh as still as the dead" (276). The hair relic, as has been discussed, is especially steeped in transience. By placing Fanny's coil in a timepiece, Hardy makes explicit hairwork's relationship to temporality.[67] When a lock cut from a living person is put in or made into a piece of jewelry, it evokes one of the central meanings of hairwork. Preserved from the source in the midst of an active love, the lock of hair's bodily warmth points to daily intimacies, yet its division from this activity equates it with the inanimate gem. A head of hair, alive with shimmering light, in motion with the gestures of the head and neck, symbolizes the body's movement through time. This movement is never more present, paradoxically, than in the silence of hairwork, in the fragment of corporeality made into a jewel. The "dead" curl strikes one as emblematic of the body in its most mysterious state: stillness. With this sense of frozen movement, hairwork reminds us of the moment, the sadness and elation of its singularity. Hardy evokes this fossilization in a poem written in 1913, "On a Discovered Curl of Hair," about a lock of his late wife's hair. In the first stanza he recalls the scene of its paring when it was "waving on your head" (line 2) and "brushed and clung about my face" (line 5). Finding it many years later, after her death, he asks "Where are its fellows now?" and finds a dual answer: "Ah they / For brightest brown have donned a gray, / And gone into a caverned ark, / Ever unopened, always dark!" (lines 9–12). First the hair became gray, then it went down into the grave. Its mystery is disclosed in the final stanza:

> Yet this one curl, untouched of time,
> Beams with live brown as in its prime,
> So that it seems I even could now
> Restore it to the living brow ... (lines 13–18)[68]

Cutting hair and offering it to a lover is an unrepeatable act, a sliver of time crystallized in the material object that is no longer able to grow and move with the life of the body. Placing the hair within a piece of jewelry marks the moment of love as contained, but also removed and never to be lived again.

Geoffrey Batchen, who writes of the meaning of photographs that are coupled with various types of material objects, explores such temporality. In a locket that contains a photograph along with hair, "at least five distinct moments intersect – the time of its manufacture, of the taking of a hair sample, the making of a photograph, their later combination, and its perception now, many years after it was made."[69] With hairwork, we might add here another layer of temporality – that of the wearer. These were portable materials of stopped time, worn on still-changing bodies. Inscriptions add a further stratum of time, one that involves, importantly, the reader. A Victorian-era locket at the Victoria and Albert, for instance, is inscribed on the outside with the initials L.B.F. Inside resides a curl under glass, along with a photograph of the deceased. Engraved on the reverse: "In remembrance of L.B.F. Oct. 7th 1871 from C.G.S.F. (see Fig. 16)"[70] The reader today functions as a sort of witness to the instances of congealed time (now made nearly unknowable) that make up this material object. The act of reading the inscription points to the possibility of "reading" the lock of hair itself. Like all relics – as discussed in previous chapters – hairwork, despite its placid muteness, holds truly narrative qualities. Marcia Pointon calls hair jewelry "textual artifacts," life stories themselves caught up in narrative.[71] Inscriptions work not, as one might think, to prove that the hair needs an accompanying narrative, but rather further indicates the way that stories come seemingly embedded in hair-work. Narrative emerges from the moments concealed in the thing. The "reader" wonders why and when the hair was cut: under what conditions? With what care or emotions? Who made it into a jewel, and who wore it? Was it passed down to other family members? A mute testifier, the curl glimmers with secret tales. Because of its silent "speech," hairwork pro-vided Hardy with a material representation of the larger philosophy of *Far From the Madding Crowd*: the embodied secret of the other.

The way that hairwork and other relics can seem to fossilize the instant and the organic life and growth of the body, thus turning it into an (almost) unchangeable thing, takes us back again to Barthes's theories of the photo-graph as a type of relic. Looking at a nineteenth-century photograph of a man who was been condemned to execution, Barthes suggests that:

> the punctum is: *he is going to die.* I read at the same time: *This will be* and *this has been*; I observe with horror an anterior future of which death is the stake. By giving me the absolute past of the pose (aorist), the photograph tells me death in the future. What *pricks* me is the discovery of this equivalence... Whether or not the subject is already dead, every photo-graph is this catastrophe.[72]

The lock of hair causes this "prick" of pain; it is this "catastrophe." It evokes the same anterior future of the old photograph. Gazing on any curl of hair, it is difficult to avoid thinking, with Barthes, *this person is going to die.* With nineteenth-century hairwork viewed today, one finds this tan-gible death sentence – not only, this person is going to die, but also, *this person has already died.* A clipping of hair works always as a synecdoche of that weight of flesh, that moment of death, preserved from its decay yet referring to it endlessly. The meaning of the detached fragment of a physical existence is, like the photograph, always in its referent. To pore over the relic is to fall into the reverie of memory, to call to mind the absent being. The object disappears and becomes pure symbol, pointing only outside itself. Yet the texture, its somewhat shocking substantiality as a thing, as an actual piece of that person, can call one back from reverie to feel its bluntness, its weighty, obstinate "thingness," its nonsymbolic quality, which refers to nothing but its own presence. The relic can startle in its defamiliarization: hair, teeth, and other body parts are everyday objects that one has become fully habituated to and thus hardly notices, and, as relics, divorced from their original contexts, they have been made strange as tactile, silent material.

To return to Hardy's plot, Fanny's coil has an even uncannier feel than most hairwork. It says not only that she is going to die, like any tress would, but also that she is dying *right now*. Hardy seems to be placing side-by-side, in an especially definitive manner, this temporality, this quality of such objects to have death written on them, whether it is future, past, or, in this case, present. Hardy makes concrete the little death in every instance of hair being cut, of every moment of being. In this way he gives the thing its apparently embedded narrative. Another element of the hair's storytelling force involves its metonymic qualities, which makes hairwork always clue-like, in its silent testimony to its referent. When Bathsheba sees Fanny's lock of hair, it becomes a kind of double clue. It might unlock Troy's past life, and Bathsheba uses it to pry open the secrets of her husband's sexual liaisons. The hair leads Bathsheba to Fanny's corpse, which is another "clue" to the story she seeks to uncover. When Bathsheba opens that coffin in order to trace the source of the yellow hair, she knows of the consummation of Fanny and Troy's love, made material in her hair and in the baby's body. Yet despite her "speaking" relics, Fanny's corpse represents, in the final analysis, the stillness of a story ended and disappeared. Because Hardy's use of hairwork never expresses a connection to an afterlife, as in *Wuthering Heights*, *In Memoriam*, and the object discourse that comes out of Evangelicalism and Spiritualism, it is rather a means to try to understand, through material and memory, the past, carried through and in bodies and what they've influenced. This is the second mystery the hairwork clue "solves": that all such clues lead eventually to the unknowability of death.

Because relics, in the secular world of Hardy, don't point to what is still to happen, they work as a kind of evidence of what happened in the past, similar to Tennyson's use of relics and the elegy discussed in Chapter 4. The need to authenticate identity, to say *that-has-been*, to use Barthes's phrase, became a central use of the relic, particularly of hair jewelry. Returning now to the problems with authenticity discussed in Chapter 1 in relation to Shelley's skull fragments and the long history of fake Catholic relics, anxieties emerged in the 1850s about unscrupulous makers of mourning ornaments. The fear was that if one sent a scrap of hair and instructions to the jeweler or hairworker through the mail, it might be replaced in the final product by an anonymous donor's hair with the same color – a swatch easier to work because it was coarser, thicker, and longer.[73] Thus the jewel returned would *not* attest to the presence in the past – the absence – of a wholly original being. In fact, perhaps the material trace of the loved one was now lost. The "false" locket or brooch took on the qualities of a disturbingly anonymous "grave" and could represent the full mystery of a disappeared and forgotten individual. This anxiety was stoked, perhaps even invented, by the women's craft journals and instructional manuals that provided step-by-step directions and patterns on hairwork. "Why should we confide to others the precious locks or tress we prize," the anonymous writer for *The Family Friend* asks, "risking its being lost, and the hair of some other person being substituted for it, when we may ourselves weave it into the ornament we desire?"[74] And *The English-woman's Domestic Magazine* remarks, "When we think of the imperishable nature of human hair, we can easily understand the anxiety with which a tress or lock cut from the forehead of a friend who is perhaps long among the dead ... is preserved."[75] The relic must be *the thing itself*, without mediation, otherwise its value is lost. The increased mass production of the relic, in its casings and in the anonymity of the worker and his or her division of labor, served to broaden the possibility that the bodily remnant might not be able to express directly and purely the truth of the singular being, something that the relic needed to emphatically repeat to do its work.[76]

The status of hairwork as a consumer good could, in certain instances, reflect that of all such goods during the era. As discussed in Chapter 2, the power of relics comes from their inalienability, their grounding in a unique set of people and sentiments, their rootedness in a singular time (or lifetimes) and in the local. Unmoored from such stability, relics make of the body just another saleable item, a thing among a mass of things that have a public, assignable value. In her history of hairwork in America, Helen Sheumaker explores at length the ambiguous status of such keepsakes (and they held a similar status in Britain). "On the one hand, hair jewelry was very much a commodity, buttressed as it was by marketing and salesmanship; on the other hand, it was exactly that which could not be completely commodified."[77] The handcraft of hair jewelry, made at home by those who had an indelible connection to the irreplaceable object, came to share ideas with anti-industrial, proto-Marxist craft communities. To work against such depredations of industrialization, thinkers and artists linked to the Pre-Raphaelites and their later groupings struggled to keep preindustrial forms of making alive. Critics like John Ruskin and artists like William Morris and his design firm (which included Rossetti, Edward Burne-Jones, Simeon Solomon, and others) promulgated a nostalgic, highly romanticized view of earlier production methods that, they felt, valued the individuality, the embodied creativity, of the craftsman.[78] Such objects (buildings, textiles, furniture, etc.), they argued, were handmade with a knowledge and care that would show in the beautiful irregularity (what Ruskin saw as a highly prized Gothic quality) of the piece. The material should be marked by the hand of that individual identity that shaped it (rather than a steam-powered machine that would merely spit it out). The object should express in its appearance – on its surface, so to speak – that it was touched by the craftsman's flesh, his warm and breathing body. Such a linkage to a singular person would then keep that object moored in the unique moment (and place) of its production, in a body that moved through time. Hardy, as a socialist and, in some ways, a medieval-revivalist, held a similar set of beliefs. In his autobiographical writings, he celebrates objects or marks "raised or made by man on a scene," such as "the wear on a threshold, or the print of a hand."[79] As an architect like Morris, Hardy especially privileged buildings whose ancient uses tied them to a local place and a craft that involved the workers' embodied production.[80] The medieval "great barn" used for sheep-shearing in *Far From the Madding Crowd* is one of the best examples of these "objects" that manage to be local, everlasting, and marked by many hands. The wood threshing-floor, for example, was "polished by the beating of flails for many generations, till it had grown as slippery and rich in hue as the state-room floors of an Elizabethan mansion" (200). The barn is a cathedral to Hardy, it attests to the "religion" of "the defense and salvation of the body by daily bread" (200). What these thinkers wanted, then, was to lend everyday things something of a relic status, to be certain they had been warmed by hands caught up in mortality. Keeping the object tied to singular identity might stay its depersonalization, its inter-changeability and dull disposability. Such objects contain the trace of the moment of making, but also the inevitable fleetingness of all embodiment.

In a related need to assuage such anxieties, many Victorian writers littered their plots, as we have seen, with relics – snatches of hair, creased gloves, monogrammed handkerchiefs, scraps of handwriting, death masks, lockets, mourning jewelry – often as a means to authenticate identity, like an autograph or handwriting, proving the subject and his or her body to be unrepeatable and nonreproducible. Hair, and to a lesser extent other types of relics, were thus recognized as a material original, like a fingerprint. Locks of hair are questioned for their ability to prove identity not only in *Far From the Madding Crowd* and *The Woodlanders*, but also in Dickens's *A Tale of Two Cities* and *Oliver Twist*, Wilkie Collins's *Queen of Hearts*, George Eliot's *Felix Holt*, M. E. Braddon's *Fenton's Quest*, and in many other Victorian novels.[81] In Collins's *Hide and Seek*, the story unfolds around the mystery of a hair bracelet – "made of two kinds of hair [one from her dead aunt and the other her still-alive father] ... And on the flat clasp of the bracelet there was cut in tiny letters, 'In memory of S.G.'" – the only clue to the identity of a deaf and dumb foundling girl, Mary (nicknamed Madonna).[82] Madonna, whose outcast (because unwed) mother, dying of inanition, gives up her baby to the kind wife of a circus clown, becomes herself a rare wonder – called "the Beloved Object" – an "irresistible," "innocent beauty" who "brought fresh life with her to all who lived in her new home."[83] The bracelet, which works as a secret cabinet of clues that needs to be unlocked using the unique hair that it contains, becomes the driving force of the plot.[84] But through association, or metonymy, Madonna herself comes to have the same qualities as the relic – a kind of holy unknown quantity. Her adoptive father, Valentine Blyth, often finds pleasure in watching her inward thoughts (not subsequently shared with him) cast shadows over her features. "It was one of Valentine's many eccentric fancies that she was not meditating only, at such times as these, but that, deaf and dumb as she was with the creatures of this world, she could talk with the angels, and could hear what the heavenly voices said to her in return."[85] Both the hair bracelet and Madonna take on this role of impenetrable cipher; her mystery makes her impossibly desirable to anyone who lays eyes on her.[86] As in *Far From the Madding Crowd*, many Victorian novels show that uncovering the secret narrative of the curl might reveal the *truth* of a life, its skein of narrative woven into the lives of others. The plot of the novel narrows down to a compact essence in hairwork; the fragment of the body becomes the site where the most important moment might be finally understood or remembered. The fact that so many sensation and detective novels need to retell the story of hairwork affirming unique identity mirrors the more general use of the tress as a site to reaffirm memory and love. And the need to repeat the affirmation again and again points to an encroaching gloom – the worry that the hair is all there is left, that the relic is just another useless possession to be discarded in short order.

Being toward death

In sum, it is in the relics found in Hardy's writing that we can "read" his complicated relationship to late-nineteenth-century death culture. Returning to two notions mentioned in the beginning of this chapter: first, Hardy's atheistic beliefs, developed in part from following closely the scientific rationalism of such thinkers as Darwin, informed his approach to death in his novels and poetry. And second, because of his celebration (not uncomplicated) of ancient, rural, attitudes, he mingled this sense of mortality being a full stop with an understanding of death as a familiar fact that, because it is congruent with the natural world, is to be accepted stoically. Gabriel Oak's "indifference to fate," for example, becomes the basis for his "sublimity" (77–8). Philippe Ariès locates this attitude toward death in the early Middle Ages, but it describes well what Hardy represents as his characters' beliefs. Yet there is a third thread to this death culture. He also carries into his plots this Victorian love of the preindustrial (again, not uncomplicated), of what shows the traces of the unique body. Similar to those who made, wore, and wrote about hairwork, Hardy cares about the singular individual and wants that singularity to not disappear with the various forces massing against it, such as consumerism and the proliferation of machine-produced objects. Yet in line with his atheism and what we'll call his early medievalism, he sees death as pulling singularity into the stream of natural rhythms and cosmic time frames. When Gabriel and Bathsheba fight to cover the wheat and barley ricks in the face of the terrible lightning and thunder, "love, life, everything human, seemed small and trifling in such close juxtaposition with an infuriated universe" (325). The impersonal, earthly force that death is in Hardy begins and ends with the materiality of the body. Matter has its day and then is buried, becoming part of the sedimentation of earthly layers. Although Hardy's complex beliefs were uniquely his own, many of their basic elements were, as we have seen with hairwork, a common part of relic culture toward the end of the nineteenth century: affirming singularity through material against annihilation and the inauthenticity of modernity. Furthermore, for those whose religious belief was waning or lost, consolation could be located in the dead's connectedness to nature rather than the spiritual. The unique matter of an individual could be carried back into the cycles of the seasons. In Hardy, we find both a need to savor the singularity of the self and also a sense of calm in the fact that the self's material will be subsumed eventually by other material. Therefore, the lock of hair can represent both comfort and grief, reminding us of the eternal in the finite.

Ariès describes the tame death thus: "Regret for life goes hand in hand with a simple acceptance of imminent death. It bespeaks a familiarity with death."[87] Hardy expresses this familiarity in his writings by a nonlinear temporality, represented through the body and its leavings. His means of showing death's penetration of all stages of life through materiality, something we have seen already in *Wuthering Heights* and *Great Expectations*, involves characters who die, in a sense, before they die. With Hardy, these little halts point to the full halt of the burial mound, rather than continued motion and vigor postdeath. The fluency between people and things noted earlier emerged not from the possibility of the corpse jumping up and dancing, as we see with Dickens, but rather from a faith that the material of the body is its final and its most important significance. Matter is meaning; it is what truly speaks. But it will eventually be silent, despite the possible magical properties it had once held. This is part of this "fatedness" of Hardy's narratives, their hidden, buried quality – he spreads the silence of the grave over the stretch of his tales. We might link this idea to Hardy's famous pessimism, but I want to suggest that it has a different tonal quality.[88] Because Hardy's death culture finds its roots in object-hood, it doesn't so much undo or unravel individual plots. Some charac-ters fall prey earlier and others later, but this preordained finale permeates all steps nevertheless. These facts are given not in a melodramatic or sentimental light, nor, of course, a religious one, but rather, as mentioned before, as the simple fate of all. Hotz also undercuts Hardy's pessimism; she eloquently points out that Hardy "believes that the apparently lost world of the dead has profound lessons to teach the living: the power of the corpse, for example, to transform the lives of individuals and commu-nities."[89] She finds that death, in Hardy's novels, works as a positive force for community cohesion, as expressive of lasting love. My argument about the power of corpses develops along different lines. Death doesn't so much have a givingness, but nor is it just a gloomy taking away. In Hardy's writing, the singularity of each individual can only be understood as part of the larger difficulty of knowing any individual. He expresses this diffi-culty – indeed, he locates this difficulty – in the material nature of bodies and in the death he finds inherent in these bodies. Little silences and impossibilities of knowledge end with the final quiet and closure of the grave.

With its scrap of hair at the center, the plot of *Far From the Madding Crowd* illustrates this "already deadness" and its materiality in a manner easy to trace, although many of Hardy's writings have this quality. The characters who exemplify most clearly this death before death are Frank Troy and Fanny, not surprisingly given that they die as part of the novel's plot. Fanny's death is prefossilized in her lock of hair, as we have seen. With Troy, Hardy gives so many foreshadowings of his death, it can feel a little ham-handed at times to readers. Troy is, first, thought to have drowned when swimming in the ocean near Casterbridge, based on the clue of his contact relics left behind on the beach: his clothing and his watch containing Fanny's hair. When he decides to return to Weatherbury to reclaim his place as husband and as a still-alive personage, he compares himself to Alonzo the Brave, a character from a ballad that appears in Matthew Lewis's *The Monk* (1796). Alonzo arrives as a corpse at the wedding feast of his former lover, and the guests watch as worms wriggle in and out of his skeletal head. A bald prefiguring of his murder at the moment he walks into Boldwood's party, this gothic image shows us Troy as a rotting corpse, which he will be very soon. Many characters appear as their dead selves in the midst of their narrative, such as Boldwood, who stalks nights "like an unhappy shade in the Mournful Fields by Acheron" (306). Corpses and other remains, as we have seen, have the capability to stir up the plot by their still presence, just as bodies that still move about carry nimbuses or auras that are felt by and drive others, as if their material itself exudes death's power. Fanny's corpse has the power to make temporarily apparent the death written in materiality more generally. As her body is carried toward Weatherbury, a creeping mist brings a sheet of silence and blindness to the natural landscape and the characters who wander through it. Bathsheba begins to take on some of Fanny's characteristics; she roams as if she is homeless on her land, as Fanny did before her. When she opens that coffin lid, Bathsheba becomes "like a corpse on end" (379), and her body seems for a brief time to be animated by "Fanny's own spirit" (382). After this, Bathsheba will think of herself for a time as "now a dead person" (417). She feels her eventual posthumousness in her body; she sees her corpse already laid out when she sees Fanny and her baby thus.

Tim Armstrong finds a similar convoluted temporality in Hardy's poetry and especially in Hardy's own writing about himself. As a way of thinking about Derrida's theories about death, he sees the "idea of being 'already dead'" as an "important part of Hardy's self-conception."[90] Many of Hardy's poems show a haunting sense of "retroactive meaning" and "prearranged drama," Armstrong contends.[91] Similar ideas crop up in much Hardy criticism. Beer calls this quality "an inevitable overthrow long foreseen" and a "doomed sense of weighted past."[92] J. Hillis Miller deems this prolepsis a "fatalizing perspective" where the future is intimated always in the present, and the characters' stories merely need to catch up to that of the narrative's preknowledge.[93] This sense of future death coloring all, an idea I've touched on throughout these chapters, has been understood by many as the basic structure of all stories, all existences. Peter Brooks, for example, sees narrative as caught up in Freud's death drive, with the aim of life being death and the little pleasures along the way as postponements or detours from the final end that all moves toward.[94] Martin Heidegger, in theories about the relationship between existence and temporality, finds that all being is structured by its relation to death. Only by looking first at the whole completion of a story can each moment of it be understood. Caught up in living our everyday lives, we cover over the certainty of death, concealing "that it is possible in every moment."[95] Heidegger explains that "as soon as a human being is born, he is old enough to die right away."[96] An existence is only an individuated whole in its realization of this finiteness, and living is always "running ahead" to the end. "The not-yet is already included in its own being, by no means as an arbitrary determination, but as a constituent" Heidegger explains, and existence "is always already its not-yet as long as it is."[97] As soon as there is nothing more "missing" then an existence will cease to be. With Hardy, stories have this kind of rounding off with their ending, which every moment is carved out of. He describes Troy's being-toward-death in this way: "A coral reef which just comes short of the ocean surface is no more to the horizon than if it had never been begun, and the mere finishing stroke is what often appears to create an event which has long been potentially an accomplished thing" (402). Death is the mere finishing stroke that makes the reef visible. This is, as I have been arguing throughout this chapter, the temporality of hairwork. The hair relic makes apparent the moment that the body becomes object; it is a figure for death but also a figure for the instant, for presentness, for beginnings and futures. The meaning that Hardy finds in matter is that the present moment and its fixedness in material contains all there is.[98]

Cherishing the relic could be a means to keep loss ever present, to see death as death. In hairwork we find made legible not only the fleeting time of an individual, but also the developing and disappearing history of a nation and era. As the Victorians struggled with an increasingly secular and scientific modernity, older forms of religious belief were vanishing. The anxieties that surfaced from these losses – the worry that a loved one might meld into a meaningless reproducibility – can be read in hair relics. The cherishing of these artifacts could represent a conventional looking back at a more conservative form of belief, or it could show a need to keep memory alive because it was becoming harder and harder to believe there was anything but memory. Secularization was one of the main reasons for the popularity of hairwork – for the transfer of love for saintly bodies to those of the ordinary individual. But it is also a central force that would lead to its decline, once it set in deeply and pervasively. The increase in skepticism in the afterlife – a slice of despair – came to replace the beatitude of Christian believers. Could the magic of that singular body, that selfhood, be brought back – felt – in the material trace? Could the talisman somehow prove that the desired being still had existence some-where? The creeping unbelief of modernity interwoven inextricably with the rise of humanism more generally made relic worship ever more personal, a means to recover individual memory or love. And if that past might not be retrievable, if that beloved body might be gone for good, then to focus all one's passion and desire on the trace made all the more sense. The secular relic culture of the Romantics and Victorians would, then, "speak" of a world perfect because it might be unrecoverable. But this was a delicate balance, and the tipping of the scales would eventually come to make the relish for the materials of death ever rarer in the first few decades of the twentieth century.

Afterword: death as death

> Form is henceforth divorced from matter. In fact, matter as a visible object is of no great use any longer, except as the mould on which form is shaped. Give us a few negatives of a thing worth seeing, taken from different points of view, and that is all we want of it. Pull it down or burn it up, if you please ... Matter in large masses must always be fixed and dear; form is cheap and transportable. We have got the fruit of creation now, and need not trouble ourselves with the core.
>
> —Oliver Wendell Holmes[1]

Hardy's heart also "wandered" after his death, yet the climate for this traveling had shifted significantly from the time when Mary Shelley lavished so much attention on her husband's fragmented remains. When Hardy died of a massive heart attack on January 11, 1928, at the age of 88, discord swiftly developed over his corpse and where it would rest. In his will Hardy expressed the desire to be buried in his hometown of Stinsford – in that Dorset so important to his writing – near his parents' burial place and in his first wife Emma's grave.[2] His friends Sydney Cockerell and Sir James Barrie began what would be a successful application to have him interred in Westminster Abbey's Poet's Corner. This would mean the alienation of his corpse from his native landscape and a Christian entombment for this outspoken atheist. It also meant cremation, a practice becoming increasingly common, yet for his traditional brother and sister, and many of the local people, it – and all of the problems surrounding an Abbey interment – were reason for outrage and protest. Despite the strong objection to it, Westminster won out, with the backing of Hardy's most powerful friends. A sort of compromise was developed, however. Out of a conversation between Hardy's second wife Florence, the Rector of Stinsford, and his wife emerged the idea of inhuming Hardy's heart at Stinsford and then cremating the rest of him for Westminster. Michael Millgate suggests that this notion may have been gleaned from a recent lecture by a local historian on heart-burial in Dorset in the Middle Ages.[3] Hardy's physician, a Dr. Mann, and the local surgeon removed the organ in Hardy's bedroom on the evening of the 13th, wrapped it in a towel, and placed it in a biscuit tin brought up from the kitchen.[4] Dr. Mann carried it to his home for the evening. The sealed tin was then put in a burial casket the next morning. Three funeral ceremonies happened simultaneously on January 16th – one for the heart, another for the ashes, and a civic observance in St. Peter's, Dorchester. Many of Hardy's contemporaries found this "dismemberment" to be macabre; Edmund Gosse called it "medieval butchery."[5] Some found it poignantly fitting given Hardy's twin interests: his fervent localism and his relish for fame. The editor of *Punch*, Sir Owen Seaman, printed some lines of verse he penned on the matter:

> The Nation's Temple claims her noblest Dead,
>   So to its care his ashes we confide,
> But where his heart would choose a lowlier bed
>   There lay it, in his own loved countryside.

There were some who took it as an occasion for dark humor. A rumor was spread that when Dr. Mann took the heart home with him, his cat got into the tin and ate it, requiring an enterprising servant to substitute a pig's heart.[6] What Hardy would have made of these manipulations of his corpse and the reactions to them is, of course, impossible to know. With his attention to "life's little ironies," he may have found it all rather appropriate.

Hardy's heart was not a grave good, such as the hair bracelet in Donne's poems or the hair that goes down into the grave with Catherine in *Wuthering Heights*. It is not imagined as useful for anyone in a postlife place, nor does it represent an embodied love in some heaven, to be handled and reverenced by others in an immortal sphere. No one thought of keeping his heart above ground, in a book, box, or any other container. A major shift in attitudes toward dying and the dead body that had begun earlier had gained a critical momentum by the 1920s. Indeed, as early as the end of the nineteenth century the death of the other had not only become less of a shared experience among a community, but also last things such as final words and remains were increasingly to be pushed to the back of consciousness and hence to the lumber room of meaning and importance. The broadening secularization of the time was a key factor, of course, as has been discussed in previous chapters.[7] The secularization of relic culture in Britain had been developing and deepening since the Reformation, and with the Enlightenment and Romanticism, as has been explored, it became pervasive. The religious revivalism in Victorian England can be seen as part of this long shadow of unbelief. As J. Hillis Miller maintains: "In nineteenth-century England, Evangelicalism and the Catholic revival are belated attempts to stop the 'melancholy, long, withdrawing roar' of the sea of faith."[8] Secularization even influenced the religious in the decades after the 1870s, Jose Harris demonstrates, as Christianity became more of a nebulous, undogmatic, social organization.[9] As we have seen, relic culture had its place in opposing movements: agnosticism and atheism, and forms of religious regeneration. Yet the transfer of fetishistic qualities from saints' remains to those of any body was, ultimately, the beginning of the end. The personal devotion to familial groups that opened the practice would lead eventually to its attenuation. Placing so much meaning in one individual, and being convinced that death is the final goodbye, led to remains signifying pain and ultimate loss.

Along with this "withdrawing roar" and the concomitant waning of belief in an afterlife, medical advances created a change in the understanding of the dying process. Patricia Jalland indicates that uncertainties about faith coincided, in the late nineteenth century, with revised views about bacteria, germ theory, and disease. Death was attributed to specific diseases rather than divine influence.[10] Doctors focused increasingly on keeping patients free of pain, which often meant that they were unconscious when they died, thus undercutting the significance of the "happy" death that evangelicals had championed, when last words might crown a deserving life. If God had not called the dying, then it was more difficult to believe that their countenances indicated their entrance into heaven. Body parts no longer served as windows to divinity, as evidence that the loved one had transformed into another existence. Death began to have more of a flavor of failure than of triumph – a defeat of the doctors' skill, a collapse of will on the part of the patient. As Philippe Ariès asserts, death is denied "by masking it with disease."[11] Detailed accounts of a loved one's last days fell out of favor. Consolation letters became shorter and less frequent. Mourners increasingly withdrew into isolation and silence rather than joining a grieving community. Corpses were less commonly seen as things of value, beauty, and poignancy – worthy as art or keepsakes. Relics that had the closest connection to the body became ever rarer means to remember the dead.

As significant as the ebbing of faith and the medicalization of death, the Great War caused a radical rupture in the Victorian Christian way of death.[12] With the tragic deaths of hundreds of thousands of young men (over 400,000 British soldiers died in the battle of the Somme alone), the desire to distance the physicality of death intensified. As the war worsened, mass graves replaced personal ones. Many were buried where they fell or, worse, couldn't be buried at all because they lay in No Man's Land or because the grave diggers were overwhelmed by the thousands of corpses. Some had been blasted into bits, their bodies simply disappearing in a moment. Nearly half of the bodies of the British dead were never located.[13] Cadavers rotting on the ground became part of the texture of the trench warfare experience; they were trod on or their parts became fodder for the building of more trenches.[14] This catastrophe changed mourning customs for good. Joanna Bourke explains that grieving rituals of all sorts became muted and attenuated. The Great War "shattered Victorian customs of deathbed farewells, burial, and mourning ritual."[15] Death's corporeality marked little except for pain, humiliation, and, to many, meaningless sacrifice. It was difficult to see these demises as in any way Evangelical "good deaths," nor were they Romantic "beautiful deaths." This proof of the fragility of existence was not a rich joy, as it was for Keats in many of his poems. These locales were not shrines to be savored because the deaths that occurred there sanctified them. A rumor that was believed by many British soldiers serves to illustrate the radical alteration in thinking about the body that had occurred since the mid-Victorian era. Fats were in such short supply in Germany due to blockades, it was reported, that corpses from the battlefield were taken to rendering factories. The "Corpse-Rendering Works" turned the bodies of British soldiers into candles and other goods.[16] Compare such imagined atrocities with Dickens's midcentury jocularity about the corpse as a thing that might be eaten, recycled, aestheticized. The reuse of death's matter had lost its comfort or whimsy. Now it signaled a tragic anonymity, a carelessness for the life of the singular individual.

The changed conception of the corpse became especially legible with the rise of cremation, newly satisfying to a significant number of Britons as an alternative to burial after the First World War. Bourke posits that the ugly nature of the deaths of the Great War brought an urge to envision an "immaculate counterpart" to rotting remains on the battlefield.[17] A need to purify and sanitize death gained momentum, as a way to contain the remembrance of the ghastly mess of decay and putrefaction and, if possible, to make meaning out of the general meaninglessness of war deaths and those after, contaminated as they had become by its frightening chaos. This desire to forget the capability of the body to be a thing that smelled and leaked led to the spread of the destruction of the corpse by fire. Cremationists capitalized on this general revulsion, Bourke argues, by claiming that the flames rendered bodies into "pearly white" and "delicate" ashes. The body disappeared in a cleansing fire, transformed into an "intact and pure" substance.[18] Crematoria were designed as majestic, clean-lined spaces to reject "'the old conception that the great passing over [should] be surrounded by signs of decay.'"[19] The distance between this type of aestheticization of death and the Victorian practice of venerating remains – recording them through death masks and holding onto them synecdochically through hair jewelry – is stark. Here aestheticization annihilates the body as a mortal object. In a flash of heat, flesh disappears into ash, a trace lacking individuality: the body and yet not the body. Ashes, unlike hair mementos or death masks, remove reminders of the ongoingness of being. Memories of tresses as part of the minutiae of workaday being, of the lines of the face and what put them there, are obliterated, and ashes become a substance that doesn't recall the body's vital existence as mortal matter. Lost is the deep need that existed for much of the nineteenth century to keep whole death's embodiment for a future reunion in heaven. Gone are grave goods, and cemetery meanderings lost much of their poetic power when there wasn't a body to mull over.

Even before the Great War, however, the aestheticization of the dead, of their memory, had begun its progression toward disembodiment. In addition to the factors already explored, technology played a pivotal role in the shift in representation and reproduction of the dead. The most important technology for this process, as has been signaled in previous pages, was photography. The rise of photography coincided with the height of popularity of secular relic veneration, which would seem to contradict the argument that it would come to replace the use of relics as recorders of memory. One way of understanding this coexistence of the two for decades is through Benjamin's theory of the aura, discussed in the introduction. The value of the relic was only fully recognized when its uses would begin to disappear. The love for relics flamed up before it flamed out. Yet there is a less abstract way of thinking about this transitional time. The efficacy of photographs to serve as representations of the dead, as holders of memory, was unstable in the first decades of its invention, not to mention too expensive for all but the wealthiest (photography didn't become widely available to the lower classes until 1900, when Kodak brought out the inexpensive Brownie camera). A widespread doubt about what photography meant in relation to death and the body can be found up until at least the 1870s (and continued, in a much diminished form and mostly among theoreticians, into the twentieth century and beyond). The questions that arose for those yearning to keep a trace of their perished included the problem that the photograph didn't have an intimacy with the tactile body, had not been a part of the individual's daily, haptic round. As a representation, could it "speak" so fruitfully of, and for, the body now gone? Could it replace the thing itself, the residue of that flesh? Might it serve as the same type of proof?

One of the first photographs to appear in a publication was a calotype of a postmortem bust of one Catherine Mary Walter.[20] The 1844 English commemorative booklet, entitled *Record of the Death Bed of C.M.W.*, establishes, from the beginning of its history, photography's memorial function and its close connectedness to postmortem art. Early photography was used to "reproduce" postmortem paintings, death masks, effigies, marble busts, miniatures, and tombstones so that family members might have copies, or so that some could see the memorial for the first time if they lived too far away to travel to these often immobile and otherwise difficult to reproduce objects.[21] Occasionally, relics themselves were photographed, as a way to multiply them, or, in certain situations, to make them more permanent. Audrey Linkman reproduces an 1860s albumen silver print, made by the London Studio of Augustus Lupson, of a straw hat that had belonged to a child. The hat has a paper band around it, which reads, "In affectionate remembrance Richard Nicholls Milliken Born Feb 11 1857 Died Dec 23 1861." The photograph is inscribed: "3rd Boy in Milliken Family (U[ncle] Fred.) died when 5 years old. Having no photo A[unt] Anne had his hat photographed with an inscription."[22] The hat serves as a replacement for the body, making the photograph a representation of a representation (and the writing in and on the photograph becomes a further layer of representation). We can speculate that photography, for these individuals, wasn't enough in itself to act as a memory saver; rather, it had the less important function of making "real" relics more readily accessible. It was merely a mechanical means to spread the power of objects that had more sensuous immediacy.

Photography, however, quickly became its own form of postmortem art. Daguerreotypes of corpses first began to be produced in the early 1840s.[23] Their uses had some affinities with paintings, drawings, and castings of the just-dead body. They could work as another means to record the evangelical "happy death" and thus to find consolation in expressions that seemed tranquil. Queen Victoria, for instance, had one commissioned of Prince Albert after his death in 1861. A viewer of this now-lost photograph reported that "the beautiful face" looked "so calm and peaceful."[24] After Lord Frederick Cavendish's brutal murder in 1882 by Irish rebels, a postmortem photo was taken (and officials snipped a ringlet for his wife

Lucy). Earl Spencer remarked when he saw it that "the horror [was] all stilled by that heavenly look of peace."[25] In Victorian Britain – as opposed to nineteenth-century America, where postmortem photography was more widespread and had a more lasting popularity – photographs of dead children, especially infants, were the most common type of postmortem photography. The bodies of babies appeared especially attractive since their innocence assured them, many believed, of a direct entrance to a paradisiacal afterworld. Images of consolation, of faith in an angelic future, these records of death, and this subset of photography's uses – postmortem photography – would fall out of favor by the early twentieth century, thus following on the footsteps of the receding of relic culture and therefore another victim of the distancing of the corporeality of death.

Yet the relationship between photography and the remembered body is more complicated than a study of postmortem photography would lead us to believe. Can the photograph work as a relic, provide the same degree and amount of consolation? As we have seen, Roland Barthes argues, in his influential writings on death and photography, that the photograph *is* a contact relic. This is what moves him so much about the "winter garden photograph" of his dead mother: it provides material proof that she did once exist, that she had a place in time and space. Barthes writes that the photograph is "literally an emanation of the referent. From a real body, which was there, proceed radiations which ultimately touch me, who am here."[26] The light that touched her body also touched the sensitive instrument, as if the body had directly pressed against the plate. Her form seared the apparatus; she effigized like the tomb sculptures of earlier eras. Barthes exclaims, in this deep need to reassert repeatedly that his mother did exist, "someone has seen the referent" of a photograph " . . . in *flesh and blood*."[27] Historians of photography influenced by Barthes call photos "something directly stenciled off the real" and "a kind of deposit of the real itself." Furthermore, they can "claim to be a kind of chemical fingerprint."[28] The question of the corporeality of photography, of its use as evidence of embodiment, also concerned the Victorians. Some had little trouble with the photograph as an intimate memory saver, much akin to relics. Elizabeth Barrett Browning wrote to her friend Mary Russell Mitford in 1843 about a postmortem daguerreotype she had recently seen. She was charmed by the "sense of nearness involved in the thing . . . the fact of the *very shadow of the person* lying there fixed forever! . . . I would rather have such a memorial of one dearly loved, than the noblest artist's work ever produced."[29] Still, Barrett Browning was a relic lover of the first water; she especially collected locks of hair from those close to her. We might argue that the "shadow" would never be enough for her; she needed the substance as well.

Photography was, in many ways, at its most relic-like in its beginnings. Nonreproducible, hard-plate photos, such as daguerreotypes, tintypes, and ambrotypes, can be understood as the congealing of a moment – as the only representation of a moment in time – not so different from hair jewelry. Rather than purely visual mementos, these photos assert their objecthood. Geoffrey Batchen notes that daguerreotypes "made of metal, glass, timber, and leather, have a distinctive heft, a feature that adds the gravitas of gravity to their characteristics."[30] They partake of the nature of the "this-ness" of relics. As with remains, these photos were usually placed in cases – essentially little boxes, with lids that closed. Framing or encasing a photo gives it three-dimensionality, Batchen observes, which privileges its thingness and "requires our hands as well as our eyes."[31] This palpable nature of their materiality lends them a uniqueness, a strong relation to touch, reminiscent of the immediacy of relics. The possessor of a daguerreotype in its case could "hide" the dead or display them, as she might make hairwork visible or hidden. Into these "reliquaries" were sometimes added other representations of the dead, just as saints' reliquaries held, for instance, a sliver of touched wood, a fragment of worn clothing, and a segment of bone. Curls of hair were sewn into the fabric of the case, or secreted behind the photo itself. Swatches of clothing that had belonged to the dead, small toys that had given pleasure to the dead child pictured, and coffin plates – metal labels, usually inscribed with the names and dates of the dead, that were displayed in the lid of the coffin during the viewing of the body and then removed before burial – were all supplements that turned these photos into artifacts.[32] Placing relics next to or inside photos brought in conjunction, for a brief span in history, an ancient technology with the new one that would largely take its place.

Daguerreotype cases can be understood as small shrines or memory boxes (or spaces, to return to an idea from Chapter 4), yet their designs were most closely modeled on leather-bound books, with tooled or stamped covers. They often contained text within their covers, making them, in effect, bound books (with illustration more prominent than text). Poems were occasionally placed in the case, or affixed to the interior, sometimes original productions or well-known verse (Tennyson was a favorite) copied by the hand of the possessor of the photo or the one pictured. Texts integral to these assemblages were often epitaph-like, with birth and death dates and commonplace tomb sentiments, similar to inscription on hairwork, and thus another means to bring the dead and the "grave" into the home. Daguerreotypes within their "bindings" and with their added matter had narrative qualities – the "reader" opened the covers, and their eyes roamed from image to object, each with their stories. Shelley's *Last Days*, with locks of hair and his ashes held in cavities inside the front and back covers and the texts consisting of letters and other handwritten manuscripts relating to his death, is an example within the historical trajectory of such memory assemblages. In this case, manuscripts describing and attesting to his last days were not enough. Further proof of his singular existence, and of the love Mary and his devoted readers had for him, was required in the form of bodily matter. Language was needed, but so was a more concrete representation. Adding photography to hybrid reliquaries was another way to layer one technology for representing the past onto another, to add one materialized story to another. Touch, vision, and text came together in an attempt to stave off forgetting. Personal books and books of personhood, these artifacts celebrate the poetics of one body.

This history continued even when photography became easily reproducible, losing some of its particularity and thingness in the possibility of copies that held the same status as the original. In fact, assemblages made one photograph unique, with an authenticity that could not be copied. Photos were hung in shadow boxes, for instance, and then embellished with keepsakes like hair wreaths, wedding veils and bouquets (when the box commemorated a wedding), feathers, coffin plates, or other effects, giving a thickness to memory.[33] Painting was sometimes added to photographs, which carried the machine-made representation into the present, through the tactility of the brushstroke. Many British photos of the dead, for example, were touched up with little strokes of color, especially to the dress. Cheeks were reddened to give them a life-like blush.[34] In considering painted photos, Batchen explores their capacity to make the "image that remains look less situated in a specific moment, more ageless, less mortal." The image is "slowed down," and is "no longer just the remnant of an instant's exposure to light," but rather its "elaborated surface" must be read.[35] That is, paint makes the photo more like the relic: opaque with a surface to be decoded. Photographic albums, especially those of the nineteenth and early twentieth centuries, also had these narrative, mixed-media qualities. Like daguerreotype cases, their cover material and designs were replicas of expensively bound books, decorated so that they were objects to be touched and handled as well as gazed on. Elizabeth Edwards and Janice Hart explain that many Victorian albums were made to look, specifically, like precious religious texts, "with heavy embossed covers and gold edged pages that are closed with metal clasps, clearly a reference to medieval devotional books, the *carte de visite* album becoming a form of secular Bible."³⁶ Text written under or near photos added inscription and handwriting – an extra bit of corporeal character – to these remembrance "books." Batchen observes that when the album's pages are turned, then "we put the photograph in motion, literally in an arc through space and metaphorically in a sequential narrative."³⁷ Albums were further framed and personalized through building them into stands and incorporating them into home altars. Photo-artifacts took on the qualities of secular shrines, affirmations of singularity and the caring of the still-living for the dead. Their relationship to the earlier history of sacred and secular materiality and texts was made manifest in their surfaces.

Why did photographs need such additions? It is clear from these manipulated images that, for many, the photograph required an extra warmth, an additional layer of the dead one's felt being – or the possessor's – to increase its power as a technology for memory (see Fig. 16). Helen Groth, in surveying Victorian-era writing on photography, finds discussions of its "destabilizing effects." "For never far from the surface was a profound sense of epistemic unease," she explains.³⁸ For a time, then, photography wasn't enough for many. Despite Barthes's poignant assertions, ultimately photographs are visual representations, not material ones.

Figure 16.   A locket inscribed on the back: "In remembrance of L.B.F. Oct 7th 1871, from C.G.S.F." M. 11-1972, c. 1871.

They are designed to be looked "through," like a transparent window, to a memory, be it embodied or not.[39] When it is most successful, the photo as a thing is forgotten, and it becomes a pure referent, pointing to the memory of that captured moment and its contexts that lie outside its frame. A relic also signals its referent, of course, but it stops such reverie with its sensuous *thisness*. Most important, however, photographs are not, in most cases, touched by the body pictured in them. They record a body without contact with its fleshly chaos. There is something essentially ethereal about a photograph; it is a supplement to the real rather than a sample of it. In other words, a photograph is a remembrance technology that archives a moment but doesn't subtract anything from it, whereas a relic takes a bit of the real with it, whether it is a portion of hair or a contact relic that has a residue of embodiment in or on it, even if only in the imagination.[40] Photos, including daguerreotypes, dematerialize memory as part of their representation of it.

To braid photos with relics was to interrupt this disembodiment, to call the memory back to the tangible. Such "hybrid-objects," Batchen posits, "constitute a skeptical commentary on the capacity of photography by itself to provide a compelling memorial experience. They suggest that something creative must be done to a photograph, some addition has to be made to its form, if it is to function as an effective memory object."[41] Incorporating a haptic portion of the existence of the pictured dead into a photograph contaminates "visibility with touch."[42] As with the mass-production of hair jewelry during the mid- to late nineteenth century, the easy reproducibility of photographs encroached on their inalienability, their irreplaceable thing-in-itself-ness. Saving the photo as a unique, incommensurable object by turning it into an artifact became a popular domestic handcraft, one that women were especially encouraged to practice in the home. The means of their production was an integral part of their history, of their aesthetic, keeping them tethered to the place and time of their creation, to the warm body – the fingers – that made them. They were a means to halt, as much as possible, the commodification of memories, to keep legible and palpable all stages of their existence. According to Batchen, photography was problematic because it participated in the reification of memory, the commercialization of keepsakes and personal souvenirs. The photograph can thus be a hollowed out memory, "disconnected from the social realities of its own production and also from those who are doing the remembering."[43] Relic supplementation localized photography; moored it in place, time, and corpus; and kept it from being just another exchangeable good.

Hand-in-hand with the distancing of the material nature of death after the Great War came the general loss of this skepticism about photography and other uncorporeal technologies. Photographs were increasingly used on their own, without a need for augmentation or material mediation. The scopic became sufficient for memory; the corpse fell away. A return to Hardy provides a useful illustration of this change. Hardy not only lived through the First World War, but his writing also played an important role in and after the war, especially in relation to literature. Paul Fussell sees Hardy's book of poems, *Satires of Circumstance*, published in November 1914, as a kind of "medium for perceiving the events of the war just beginning," full as they are of death, irony, and general bleakness.[44] Many wartime writers read Hardy and found his work helpful for their own fiction and nonfiction. For example, Siegfried Sassoon, whose satirical poems about the war were heavily influenced by *Satires of Circumstance*, writes about being huddled in his little dugout, just before the attack on the Somme, reading *Tess of the D'Urbervilles*.[45] Hardy also wrote numerous poems about photography's memorial function. In "The Son's Portrait" (written in 1924), both themes come together: the Great War's reconfiguration of attitudes toward the dead body and the uses of photography. A grieving father rifles through odds and ends at a junk shop. He lights upon a "fly-specked" photo of his own son, who was "sent to the front-trench-line, / And fell there fighting" (lines 18–19). The son's widow, now remarried, sold it to the shop. The father buys "the gift she had held so light, / And buried it – as 'twere he. – " (lines 21–22). Not having the corpse, the father buries the photograph as a replacement for the missing body. Erecting graves or memorial tombs without bodies became a common practice during the Great War. Building cenotaphs as memorials for lost soldiers began as a ritual during, and because of, World War I. Photographs, Hardy seems to be saying with his poem, were themselves cenotaphs. Eduardo Cadava remarks that the photograph is "its own grave ... It is what remains of what passes into history."[46] Yet photos can only ever be empty graves.[47]

This spectral quality of photography was recognized early on – its place in calling up a yearning for what is gone. Spirit photographers capitalized on its ghostly effect by tricking mourners into believing the sensitive apparatus could "catch" the hovering dead, wafting by in ectoplasmic draperies. Produced in large numbers from 1880–1920, spirit photographs can be seen as another transitional-period flourishing – a final flaring up on the edge of extinction.[48] Photos of "ghosts" were, to those who believed they were real, an attempt to harness these new technologies to finally prove that there was an afterlife, that dead loved ones were never gone for good, during a time when such beliefs were in widespread doubt. The fraudulent nature of the photos was fairly easy to prove, however, making them, in this instance, unlike those of relics, which were difficult to authenticate before twentieth-century methods. Other new technologies were seen as having a haunting quality, a capacity to record something of the dead, if not the body. In 1900, W. T. Stead celebrated the phonograph as a means to carry "the very sound and accent of the living words of the dead whose bodies are in the dust" and which "have become the common inheritance of mankind." Paraphrasing Tennyson, he remarks that "countless generations mourning the dead have cried with vain longings to hear the sound of the voice that is still. But in dreams alone in those rare visions vouchsafed to finer souls was the prayer now granted."[49] Tim Armstrong comments that the radio was linked to the supernatural in the imaginations of its inventors and for writers like W. B. Yeats and Ezra Pound.[50] Many technologies that came into use in rapid succession during the late nineteenth and early twentieth centuries similarly served as relic replacements. In addition to aural technology "embalming" the voice, the typewriter replaced the holographic – the fingers pressing the writing implement into the page replaced by a metal letter stamping a clamped page. The telegraph, telephone, film: all recorded or transmitted the person but in such a way that needn't include the nearness or touch of the body.

The proliferation of these "empty graves" can be seen as part of the expanding consumer culture of the late nineteenth and the early twentieth centuries, which destabilized the rooted and fixed and distanced the material object from the bodily personality, especially of the dead. As with relics more generally, photographic artifacts fell victim to this culture in flux. As Jonathan Crary defines it, this modernization is "the process by which capitalism uproots and makes mobile that which is grounded, clears away or obliterates that which impedes circulation, and makes exchangeable that which is singular."[51] This is what Marx lamented about capitalism, of course: the way its objects became sites of exchange rather than themselves material for immanent and localized meaning. In his exploration of Marx's ideas about materiality, Peter Stallybrass points to the "radically dematerialized" opposition between individuals and their objects that is part of consumer societies.[52] Mobilization and ungroundedness, coupled with the secularization and medicalization of death, caused the embodied keepsakes of Victorians to be relegated to the periphery, to become the practice of eccentrics or the religious minority.

Tim Armstrong explores the anxiety that many had, at the end of the nineteenth century and the start of the twentieth, that the embodied self was disappearing into scientific and technological systems. The body was itself seen as a machine – a producing and consuming motor or apparatus – just as bodies were thought of as more powerful when technology was used in conjunction with them, such as prostheses, organ-replacement, sensory-extension.[53] Many of these new technologies had been modeled on the deficient body, Armstrong notes: "the telephone emerging from research on the mechanism of the ear; the typewriter from a desire to let the blind write by touch; film from persistence of vision."[54] Therefore, machine technology emphasized the inadequate body, one needing extensions or replacements, which mirrored the discourse about death during the turn of the century and the war years. As a sort of failed machine, the body and its leavings could be replaced by sleeker machines and their creations, such as the motion picture camera and its productions. The body as a thing that breaks down, that crumbles and fragments, that works as a center for the understanding of the mortality of all things, had been set aside as somehow unglorified and no long beautiful. Relics lost their unruly, wild nature. They could no longer be spots of infinity or eternity. As such, objects of all sorts lost a bit of enchantment, their sense of touching or partaking of an unknown world.[55]

Notes

Introduction

1 George Eliot wrote this in a condolence letter to John Walter Cross, December 13, 1877. *The George Eliot Letters*, ed. Gordon S. Haight, vol. 6 (New Haven: Yale University Press, 1955), 433.

2 Elaine Freedgood, *The Ideas in Things* (Chicago: Chicago University Press, 2006), 12.

3 This aspect of my argument will, at times, dovetail with Samantha Matthews's exploration of poets' graves and bodies as coming to "represent" their texts: "Nineteenth-century writers and readers had a heightened awareness of the significant relationship between the materiality of death and the materiality of books." *Poetical Remains: Poets' Graves, Bodies, and Books in the Nineteenth Century* (New York: Oxford University Press, 2004), 11. Carol Christ also remarks that "the value that Victorian culture placed upon the representation of the dead carried important implications for literary representation. . . . Much as Victorians created material objects that were effigies for the dead, Victorian writers often sought to substitute the literary work for the dead body. A reversal of divine incarnation, the flesh becomes word, and the art object presents itself as the auto-icon" (392). "Browning's Corpses," *Victorian Poetry* 33 (1995), 391–401. Yet I aim to make a broader and more historical point than the conflation by Romantic and Victorian readers of a famous poet's grave and corpse with his books of poetry and written words. In fact, I am making a case for a new philosophical approach to nineteenth-century materiality and death.

4 Bill Brown, *A Sense of Things: The Object Matter of American Literature* (Chicago: University of Chicago Press, 2003), 18.

5 This etymology is from the OED.

6 Caroline Walker Bynum, *Christian Materiality: An Essay on Religion in Late Medieval Europe* (New York: Zone, 2011), 233.

7 Diana Fuss, "Corpse Poem," *Critical Inquiry* 30 (2003), 1–30. Fuss remarks, in a paraphrase of Joseph Jacobs, "The Dying of Death," *Fortnightly Review* 72 (July–Dec. 1899), that the "moribund state of death came because of increased life expectancies, the decline of belief in resurrection and eternal life, the disappearance of hell from popular theology, and the shift in clerical focus from preparing for the afterlife to living better in this one . . . [For these reasons] death loses its power or influence" (6).

8 Thomas Hardy, *The Well-Beloved* (London: Macmillan, 1975), 216. All subsequent references will be to this edition and will be cited parenthetically.

9 Benjamin's writing on the aura was originally published in 1936. Walter Benjamin, "The Work of Art in the Age of Mechanical Reproduction," *Illuminations*, ed. Hannah Arendt (New York: Schocken, 1968), 220.

10 Ibid., 221.

11 Although my argument is closely related to Benjamin's conception of the aura, I define the aura of relics differently. Their aura comes with the corporeal touch, something Benjamin doesn't take up. Our arguments also diverge with the result of this decay of the aura. I find reasons to lament it, whereas Benjamin finds much that is positive for the masses in the loss of the aura.

12 Benjamin, "The Storyteller," *Illuminations*, 94.

13 Elisabeth Bronfen puts this in another way: "Death emerges as that moment in a person's life where individuality and absolute rarity could finally be attained, in a singular and unique severment from common or collective affiliation" (77). *Over Her Dead Body: Death, Femininity and the Aesthetic* (Manchester, UK: Manchester University Press, 1992).

14 My project shares a basic philosophical foundation with Samantha Matthews's *Poetical Remains*. As she eloquently remarks, "Rather than see the nineteenth-century fetishization of material memorials as a 'barbaric' survival or superstitious aberration, I suggest that we read these relics sympathetically, as emotionally and spiritually resonant embodied texts, circulating in a culture attempting to come to terms with the march of materialism and secularization" (29). Similarly, Mary Elizabeth Hotz comments that "individual contact with death engenders an understanding of the human condition that transcends class boundaries" (41). *Literary Remains: Representations of Death and Burial in Victorian England* (New York: SUNY, 2009).

15 One of my central arguments is that the Victorians generally held onto an intimacy with death and the corpse that had existed, in slightly different forms, in previous centuries. This was certainly beginning to change, but a celebration of relics remained strong until the end of the century, a point that Patricia Jalland (*Death in the Victorian Family* [New York: Oxford University Press, 1996]); Samantha Matthews (*Poetical Remains*); Philippe Ariès (*The Hour of Our Death* [New York: Knopf, 1981]); and others take up. For this reason, my argument moves away from Mary Elizabeth Hotz's assertion, in *Literary Remains*, that a sweeping movement among the middle classes in the Victorian period existed to distance the living from the "disease-ridden" dead. There was some evidence for such a distancing – due to a desire to professionalize and centralize the practice of undertaking and burial – from burial reformers like Edwin Chadwick. Yet there is insufficient evidence to see this as a widespread movement until, at the earliest, the 1880s. Many of Hotz's other arguments inform the ones made in this study, however, such as her point that the working classes did have a closer connection to the corpse and her idea that "Victorian novelists located corpses at the center of a surprisingly extensive range of contemporary concerns" (2).

Chapter 1

1 The bone fragments are fixed in a plastic frame along with two authentication letters. Despite the letters, it is doubtful that these shavings were actually part of Shelley. The authentication rests on the famously unreliable testimony of Edward Trelawny, who claims to have gathered them, along with ashes and the famous heart, from the cremated remains of Shelley on the beach of the Gulf of Spezio. The letters trace the relics back to Trelawny's niece, a Miss Taylor.

2 These artifacts are all at the Pforzheimer.

3 Also at the Bodleian are locks of Mary and Percy Bysshe Shelley's hair, his spyglass, watch and chain, his left glove, and a water-damaged, pocket-sized copy of Sophocles that he, supposedly, had on him when he drowned. Keats House, London, holds a few pieces of jewelry containing his hair. Many Victorians plucked flowers from Keats's grave, such as Hardy, who, most notably for this book, visited both Shelley's and Keats's graves when in Rome with Emma, in 1887. He picked some violets growing out of Keats's plot. See Claire Tomalin, *Thomas Hardy* (New York: Penguin, 2006), 235. For more information about the taking of souvenirs from Keats's burial place, see Matthews, *Poetical Remains*, 12 and Chapter 4.

4 The longer title is *Percy Bysshe Shelley, His Last Days Told by His Wife, with Locks of Hair and Some of the Poet's Ashes.* Ashley MS 5022. As with the skull fragments, it is doubtful that these ashes are genuine, especially given the fact that the producer of this book was the forger Thomas J. Wise. The British Library also holds locks from Leigh Hunt, Byron, and Keats (kept with a tress from Fanny Brawne).

5 When I wished to see the Shelley skull fragments at the Pforzheimer, in February 2011, and could not locate them using the finding aids, one of the curators of the collection admitted to me that they were uncataloged. She promised to remedy the situation shortly. Some exceptions to this difficulty of locating relics exist, such as with the British Museum and their published list of "human remains."

6 Hermione Lee, *Virginia Woolf's Nose: Essays on Biography* (Princeton, NJ: Princeton University Press, 2007). In her exploration of the activity surrounding the remains of Cromwell and Milton, Lorna Clymer makes a similar point: "In order to receive any type of treatment, a corpse and its parts must be reconstituted in narrative; that is, they must be made literary. Appearing to offer a rationale for treatment, the narrative actually constructs the identity and meaning of the corpse. Such narratives have obvious political possibilities since they can be used to demonstrate veneration of a hero or to effect an ultimate punishment on an enemy. The corpse's ambivalent status as an object, by which it becomes its own image, prevents it from carrying meaning outside of a narrative. Or, we might say that the material nature of human remains extinguishes a body's meaning unless narrative encases a corpse" (92). She calls this "corpse theory": "a method of interpreting the nexus of meaning bestowed upon human remains" (91). "Cromwell's Head and Milton's Hair: Corpse

Theory in Spectacular Bodies of the Interregnum," *Eighteenth Century: Theory and Interpretation* 40.2 (Summer 1999). Although her argument is true for the remains of historical or famous bodies, I will argue in this chapter that the relics of ordinary people needed no such narrative encasement.

7 For a detailed discussion of the many stories of Shelley's death and the activities around and with his remains, see Matthews, *Poetical Remains*, Chapter 4. See also Judith Pascoe, *The Hummingbird Cabinet: A Rare and Curious History of Romantic Collectors* (Ithaca, NY: Cornell University Press, 2006), 1–11. Matthews describes the cremation as "a scene that is now so layered in narrative that its original outlines are hard to discern" (128).

8 Edward Trelawny, *Records of Shelley, Byron, and the Author* (New York: New York Review of Books, 2000), 145.

9 The heart and other internal organs were often buried separately in the case of important people, as a means to spread the "magic" the body parts were thought to exude. Some of Byron's organs, for example, were buried in Greece, where he died and was adored as a hero. A more plebeian occurrence was the need to remove the organs for embalmment, thus resulting in a separate "viscera box" being buried. During the excavation of the tombs underneath Christ Church in Spitalfields, such boxes were found in a vault dating from the early nineteenth century. See Margaret Cox, *Life and Death in Spitalfields* (London: Council for British Archaeology, 1996).

10 Bodleian, Shelley adds. D.6.

11 The authentication letters accompanying the Shelley skull fragments in the Pforzheimer collection, for instance, mention a series of owners with the final giving an act of deep friendship. One of the letters reads: "given by me to my friend Wilfred Maynell, as the greatest proof of our friendship in my power."

12 For a history of relic collecting, see Susan Pearce, *On Collecting: An Investigation into Collecting in the European Tradition* (London: Routledge, 1995), especially 98–107. Various parts of the long history of the cult of saints can be found in David Sox, *Relics and Shrines* (London: Allen and Unwin, 1985); Peter Brown, *The Cult of Saints* (Chicago: University of Chicago Press, 1981); and *Treasures of Heaven: Saints, Relics, and Devotion in Medieval Europe*, Martina Bagnoli, Holger A. Klein, C. Griffith Mann and James Robinson, eds. (New Haven, CT: Yale University Press, 2010).

13 Brown, *The Cult of Saints*, 3.

14 Quoted in Brown, *The Cult of Saints*, 11.

15 Quoted in Brown, *The Cult of Saints*, 4.

16 Quoted in Brown, *The Cult of Saints*, 78.

17 Joan Carroll Cruz, *Relics* (Huntington, IN: Our Sunday Visitor, 1984), 188–189, 182.

18 David Sox notes that because many believed that these saints were present in their corpses, the dead saints themselves had agency in their movements, or "kidnappings." Many stories tell of the saint either refusing to be stolen (by becoming suddenly heavy, for instance) or "blessing" the translation by a sign, such as pervading the air with perfume. See *Relics and Shrines*, 47–53.

19 Bertram Puckle, in *Funeral Customs: Their Origin and Development* (London: T. Werner Laurie, 1926), tells a number of wandering heart stories, such as that of Robert Bruce. In another story, the heart of James, the Marquis of Montrose (executed in 1650), was put in a steel box and sent to the exiled Duke of Montrose. But it was stolen en route and eventually "discovered in an obscure shop in Flanders" (194). The organ was later taken to India by a family member and there was stolen, once again, by an Indian. It somehow made it back to Europe and disappeared, probably for good, during the French Revolution. See Puckle, 193–195. Ariès, in *The Hour of Our Death*, also retails a number of these stories. Marat's heart, after his death in 1793, did not remain in his tomb but became "a domestic and transportable object" (388). Ariès also tells the story of one Charles Maurras, who wanted his heart to be kept in his mother's sewing basket. See 387.

20 Reliquaries come in all sorts and sizes, and many of them are gorgeous art objects in their own right. Examples are arm and hand reliquaries that sit as if the hand is being held up by an invisible body. The gold or silver fingers (which sometimes contain the real fingers, hidden inside) often wear rings, and the hand has some characteristic gesture. Generally there is a little window or door in the reliquary, so the bone (and sometimes mummified flesh) inside can be either seen and/or touched. In some ceremonies, the priest touched the congregation with the hand or arm reliquary to perform acts of healing. Cynthia Hahn explains that "speaking reliquaries" often only had part of the body part represented, or even a collection of relics unrelated to the shape of the container. See "The Spectacle of the Charismatic Body: Patrons, Artists, and Body-Part Reliquaries," *Treasures of Heaven*, 165–166. "Speaking reliquaries" can be found today in the British Museum, the treasury of the Basil Cathedral, the treasury of St. Mark's Basilica, Venice, and in the Berlin Kunstgewerbemuseum, among many other places.

21 See *Treasures of Heaven*, 46–47.

22 Bynum, *Christian Materiality*, 21.

23 Quoted in Bynum, *Christian Materiality*, 113–116.

24 Bynum, *Christian Materiality*, 89.

25 See, for instance, H. Milman, *A History of Latin Christianity* (New York: Armstrong, 1903) and Ronald C. Finucane, *Miracles and Pilgrims: Popular Beliefs in Medieval England* (London: Dent, 1977).

26 Quoted in Arnold Angenendt, "Relics and Their Veneration," *Treasures of Heaven*, 26.

27 Brown, *The Cult of Saints*, 55. He also explains that the saints were "invisible beings who were fellow humans and whom they could invest with the precise and palpable features of beloved and powerful figures in their own society" (50).

28 Eamon Duffy, *The Stripping of the Altars: Traditional Religion in England 1400–1580* (New Haven, CT: Yale University Press, 1992), 160–161.

29 Ibid., 164.

30 Ibid., 381–384.

31 Quoted in Duffy, 415.

32 For example, in the inventories for the parishes of Bedfordshire, created for the royal visitations, the Rayleigh parish still had, in 1552, marble altars containing relics. See H. W. King, "Inventories of Church Goods 6th Edw. VI," *Transactions of the Essex Archaeological Society*, v (1873), 118, and Duffy, 485.

33 Alexander Nagel, "The Afterlife of the Reliquary," *Treasures of Heaven*, 212. British relics that survived include a reliquary pendant (ca. 1200) set with numerous saints' relics (British Museum, PE 1946, 9497.1). Some believe that Saint Thomas Becket's remains were saved when Henry VIII's commissioners destroyed his shrine in 1538, despite reports that they were burned and the ashes scattered to the winds. For this debate and the evidence on both sides, see John Butler, *The Quest for Becket's Bones: The Mystery of the Relics of St. Thomas Becket of Canterbury* (New Haven, CT: Yale University Press, 1995).

34 See Kenneth Fincham and Nicholas Tyacke, *Altars Restored: The Changing Face of English Religious Worship, 1547–c.1700* (Oxford: Oxford University Press, 2007), Chapter 1 and Duffy, 517.

35 Even with the rise of Laudianism in the 1630s and the beautification of churches, the veneration of relics did not return. See Fincham and Tyacke, Chapter 6.

36 In Medieval England and France, the touch of a monarch was thought to heal an illness called the "King's Evil," or scrofula, probably a form of tuberculosis. Touchpieces would be presented at such healing ceremonies—metal pieces that "held" the touch—and were pierced so they could be worn around the neck. The Wellcome has one: A641045. Queen Anne didn't enjoy touching her subjects, so she would use a loadstone instead: Wellcome A641031.

37 Carson I. A. Ritchie, *The British Dog: Its History from Earliest Times* (London: Robert Hale, 1981), 103.

38 See Clymer, "Cromwell's Head and Milton's Hair." Patricia Fumerton, in *Cultural Aesthetics: Renaissance Literature and the Practice of Social Ornament* (Chicago: University of Chicago Press, 1991), lists the mementoes made on the death of Charles I, many of them including various objects soaked in his blood. She quotes a witness, Sir Roger Manley: "His hair and blood were sold by parcels. Their hands and sticks were tinged by his blood and the block, now cut into chips, as also the sand sprinkled with his sacred gore, were exposed for sale. Which were greedily bought, but for different ends, by some as trophies of their slain enemy, and by others as precious reliques of their beloved prince" (9). At least one reliquary holding his blood still exists, in a private collection, and the gloves he wore when executed are at the Lambeth Palace Library.

39 Alexander Nagel comments, "[S]ecular reliquaries had become an established category by the eighteenth century." See "The Afterlife of the Reliquary," *Treasures of Heaven*, 215.

40 Another way to think of this history is through biography. Richard D. Altick sees the saints' lives as the early history of literary biography. See *Lives and Letters* (New York: Knopf, 1965).

41 A conversation in letters to the London *Times*, in 1879, took up the case of the mummified head of Henry Grey, Duke of Suffolk, who was executed in 1554. Kept at the church of the Holy Trinity of the Minories, the head, some citizens worried, wasn't being properly cared for. (A few, probably facetious, letters urged that it be deposited at the National Portrait Gallery.) See the *Times*, Oct. 10, 1879, p. 10, col. A for initial letter. Later responses, Oct. 11–16.

42 The Victorians sometimes complained of this relic love as having too much of a Catholic flavor. An 1870 article in the London *Times* complains of "Protestant Relic Worship": "Among the articles deposited beneath the foundation-stone, laid a few days ago, of a new façade to the Wesleyan Chapel Burslem, were a bit of the coffin, a piece of the shroud, and a lock of the hair of John Wesley. The announcement of the deposit of these articles by the resident minister was greeted with great applause by the spectators of the ceremony" (March 11, p. 4, col. F). On this topic, see Susan M. Griffin, *Anti-Catholicism and Nineteenth-Century Fiction* (Cambridge: Cambridge University Press, 2004); Dominic Janes, *Victorian Reformation: The Fight over Idolatry in the Church of England, 1840–60* (New York: Oxford University Press, 2009); and D. G. Paz, *Popular Anti-Catholicism in Mid-Victorian England* (Stanford, CA: Stanford University Press, 1992).

43 Péter Dávidházi, *The Romantic Cult of Shakespeare* (New York: Palgrave, 1998), 15–16. He goes on to explore anthropological accounts of secular pilgrimages being modeled closely on sacred ones.

44 Ibid., 70.

45 Clymer, "Cromwell's Head and Milton's Hair," 99. Matthews, in *Poetical Remains*, describes this "violation" in great detail, and she also notes various poems written in response to the "stealing" of his relics.

46 Susan Stewart, *On Longing: Narratives of the Miniature, the Gigantic, the Souvenir, the Collection* (Durham, NC: Duke University Press, 1993), 135.

47 Pearce, in *On Collecting*, explores Scott's importance to the history of collecting. See page 131 especially. Also see Nicola Watson, *The Literary Tourist: Readers and Places in Romantic and Victorian Britain* (New York: Palgrave, 2008), especially pages 91–105.

48 Pearce, *On Collecting*, 116.

49 Ian Ousby, in *The Englishman's England: Taste, Travel and the Rise of Tourism* (New York: Cambridge University Press, 1990), explores how the Romantic cult of personality grew into the Victorian cult of hero worship. See especially 180. Some Victorian writers who worshiped the Byron personality when young were Anthony Trollope, Emily and Charlotte Brontë, Edward Bulwer-Lytton, and Benjamin Disraeli. See Andrew Elfenbein, *Byron and the Victorians* (Cambridge: Cambridge University Press, 1996).

50 Pascoe, in *Hummingbird Cabinet*, discusses Napoleon's penis, see 100–101, as does Hermione Lee, in *Virginia Woolf's Nose*. Another national figure around which a relic and souvenir cult grew was Nelson. The National Maritime Museum displays the pocket watch he wore when he was killed (JEW 0248), jewelry with his hair, and much more. A snuffbox at the Victoria and Albert

reproduces his death mask in miniature. It is also partly made of the oak from Nelson's ship, the H.M.S Bellerophon. The British Library holds a similar item: a wooden box made from a fragment of the H.M.S. Victory shot off during the battle of Trafalgar. It contains Nelson's hair, taken at the same battle. The box has a small brass plate on the lid, inscribed "Victory Trafalgar. Octr 21 1805." Add MSS 56226. The Wellcome owns his razor, A650921, and at Westminster Abbey they have a suit of his clothes, in the Museum.

51 Both Matthews, in *Poetical Remains*, and Pascoe, in *Hummingbird Cabinet*, discuss the Romantic poets' interest in the posthumous at great length.

52 Andrew Bennett, *Romantic Poets and the Culture of Posterity* (Cambridge: Cambridge University Press, 1999), 200.

53 Ibid., 16.

54 Andrew Bennett, *Keats, Narrative and Audience: The Posthumous Life of Writing* (Cambridge: Cambridge University Press, 1994), 11.

55 Shelley, *The Complete Poems of Percy Bysshe Shelley* (New York: Modern Library, 1994), 617, line 54. All subsequent citations of Shelley's poems will be from this edition with line numbers cited parenthetically.

56 Matthews, *Poetical Remains*, 44.

57 Ibid., 11.

58 Quoted in Matthews, *Poetical Remains*, 70.

59 For more on the Burns cult, see Watson, *The Literary Tourist*.

60 The phrase "materialized secret" comes from Stewart, *On Longing*, in reference to dollhouses. Christian Holm describes mourning jewelry as "exhibited secrets" (140) and remarks on their narrative qualities. "Sentimental Cuts: Eighteenth-Century Mourning Jewelry with Hair," *Eighteenth-Century Studies* 38.1 (2004), 139–143.

61 By "ordinary" here, I refer to middle-class individuals who were not famous. For discussions of working-class attitudes to death, see Julie-Marie Strange, *Death, Grief and Poverty in Britain, 1870–1914* (Cambridge: Cambridge University Press, 2005); Ruth Richardson, *Death, Dissection and the Destitute* (Chicago: University of Chicago Press, 2000); and Hotz, *Literary Remains*. For explorations of gender, mourning, and death culture, see Lou Taylor, *Mourning Dress: A Costume and Social History* (London: Allen and Unwin, 1983); Bronfen, *Over Her Dead Body*; and Jalland, *Death in the Victorian Family*.

62 See Hallam and Hockey, *Death, Memory and Material Culture*, 8.

63 The Victoria and Albert Museum has a couple of examples of these, such as T.44–1962, a band of hair lace, probably worn as a bracelet, dating from 1625–1675.

64 Hallam and Hockey, *Death, Memory, and Material Culture*, 136.

65 An example of a jewel containing a caul is held at the British Museum, Cat. 229–30, 577. Dating from the early nineteenth century, this English gold pendent has, in addition to plaited hair, a caul set in the back. In addition to the teeth jewelry pictured here, there is a gold and enamel brooch representing a thistle that holds, as its flower, a milk tooth of Princess Victoria.

An inscription on the back states that it was pulled by her father, Prince Albert, on September 13, 1847. Balmoral Castle, RNIN 13517. Evans, in *A History of Jewellery*, mentions teeth jewelry as does Taylor, *Mourning Dress*. These teeth "relics" can be interestingly compared to a relic, kept at the abbey of Saint-Médard in Soissons, that is claimed to be the milk tooth of Christ.

66 Pascoe, *The Hummingbird Cabinet*, 4.

67 The anthropologists Hallam and Hockey, in *Death, Memory and Material Culture*, discuss a related history, that of the materialization of memory, or the belief that "material objects can hold and preserve memories" (49).

68 See, for instance, Ian Ousby, *The Englishman's England*, who discusses the opening of the country house and how it expressed the person. Emily Jane Cohen elaborates on this creation of "the analogy between people and their property" (894) in "Museums of the Mind: The Gothic and the Art of Memory," *ELH* 62.4 (1995), 883–905. See also Pascoe, *The Hummingbird Cabinet*, and Pearce, *On Collecting*.

69 Elizabeth Fay, *Fashioning Faces: The Portraitive Mode in British Romanticism* (Lebanon: University of New Hampshire Press, 2010), 145.

70 Ibid., 178.

71 In his discussion of royal deaths and the attitudes around them, John Wolffe, *Great Deaths: Grieving, Religion, and Nationhood in Victorian and Edwardian Britain* (Oxford: Oxford University Press, 2000), makes a related argument about the increased sympathy for the pain of others characteristic of the Romantic and Victorian eras. "The very consciousness of individual human frailty that appears to have lessened the impact of royal deaths in the eighteenth century was, with enhanced sympathetic identification with the sufferings of others, to become a key factor in their widespread emotional resonance in the changing cultural context of late Georgian and Victorian Britain" (18). This was why, he points out, the details of the deaths of the royals were discussed in the press like never before. For instance, Princess Charlotte's "last agony was narrated in detail in commemorative pamphlets" and on George IV's death in 1830 "the somewhat gruesome details of the post-mortem were published in the newspapers" (19).

72 Pascoe, *The Hummingbird Cabinet*, 3.

73 William Godwin, *Essay on Sepulchres: Or, Proposal for Erecting Some Memorial of the Illustrious Dead* (London: W. Miller, 1809), 25.

74 Shelley, *The Complete Works of Percy Bysshe Shelley*, vol. 7, ed. Roger Ingpen and Walter E. Peck (London: Ernest Benn, 1965), 117.

75 Bennett, *Romantic Poets*, 176.

76 Quoted in Stephen Gill, *William Wordsworth: A Life* (New York: Oxford University Press, 1990), 180.

77 See Kurt Fosso, *Buried Communities: Wordsworth and the Bonds of Mourning* (Albany: State University of New York, 2004), for a tracing of the idea of the "social powers of grief" through Wordsworth's writing. Fosso observes that Wordsworth creates a spiritual community between the living and the dead in his poetry and that mourning founds collectives.

78 William Wordsworth to Samuel Rogers, April 5, 1835. *The Letters of William and Dorothy Wordsworth*, 2nd edn., vol. VI, ed. Alan G. Hill (London: Oxford, 1982), 41.

79 Wordsworth, *The Poetical Works of William Wordsworth*, ed. E. De Selincourt (London: Oxford, 1940), "Lines Written in Early Spring," line 1. All subsequent quotations of Wordsworth's poetry are from this edition and will be cited by line numbers parenthetically. Wordsworth profoundly influenced many of the most important Victorian writers, and this poem was especially important. Stephen Gill, in *Wordsworth and the Victorians*, traces this influence, especially on Elizabeth Gaskell, George Eliot, John Ruskin, Matthew Arnold, and Tennyson.

80 Elizabeth Fay, in *Fashioning Faces*, lists some of these objects the Romantics meditated on in their poetry: "Fragmented objects or funerary urns during the Romantic period were particular foci for such meditations ... Wordsworth considered nature's reclamation of ruins and memory in 'Tintern Abbey,' Byron mused on ancient Rome in Childe Harold IV, and Keats rearticulated semiotically dead vase figures in 'Ode on a Grecian Urn.'" She goes on to point out that "meditation on object attitude encourages an emotional attachment to things that might not have economic value but that retain a psychic investment through their speculative or scopophliac value. Their aura of interiority lends them an expressive connection to their past and present owners" (147).

81 Peter Brown calls this "inverted magnitudes," or their miniature quality being, paradoxically, the very thing that makes them doors to an infinite space.

82 On a less material but related note, Karen Sánchez-Eppler argues that Wordsworth uses death as a means of generating poetry: "throughout his writings the grave appears as the source of language ... the tombstone ... stands at the origin of writing – the first inscription, the primal poem." "Decomposing: Wordsworth's Poetry of Epitaph and English Burial Reform," *Nineteenth-Century Literature* 42.4 (1988), 418–421.

83 Mary Shelley also wanted her husband's heart for political reasons; it added to her authority as the executor of his literary legacy.

84 See Esther Schor, *Bearing the Dead: the British Culture of Mourning from the Enlightenment to Victoria* (Princeton, NJ: Princeton University Press, 1994) for a history of the elegy in the eighteenth and early nineteenth centuries and its relationship to the Graveyard School.

85 See Ian Ousby, *The Englishman's England*, for a further discussion of the Romantic love of ruins, graveyards, and tombs.

86 Mario Praz, *The Romantic Agony* (New York: Oxford, 1978) is one history, of many, of the gothic and Romantic interest in the morbid and "evil." He comments, "The very objects which should induce a shudder – the livid face of the severed head, the squirming mass of vipers, the rigidity of death, the sinister light, the repulsive animals, the lizard, the bat – all these give rise to a new sense of beauty, a beauty imperiled and contaminated, a new thrill" (26).

87 Ariès, *The Hour of Our Death*, 15.

88 Ibid., 109.

89 Ibid., 332.

90 Ibid., 405.

91 Ibid., 471.

92 There are some important dissenters from Ariès's version of this history. Patricia Jalland in particular disagrees with his dating of the "beautiful death" to the Victorian period, where she finds, rather, the evangelical "good death" (an idea I discuss more fully in Chapter 2). Ariès's remarks about death culture are, however, certainly supported by much of the literature (and sculpture, architecture, and historical documents such as wills and religious texts) of the periods he explores. Yet one of my central arguments in this book will be that more than one of these views of death can be found existing simultaneously during the Romantic and Victorian eras, especially when different groups are studied, such as those divided by class, education level, gender, race, and even age. As I will suggest, in nineteenth-century Britain many varied ideas about death coexisted. This does not lead to Ariès's history being discounted, however, but rather it gives it further layers and complications. For other histories of attitudes toward death, see especially Bronfen, *Over Her Dead Body*; Schor, *Bearing the Dead*; and James Curl, *The Victorian Celebration of Death* (Stroud, Gloucestershire: Sutton, 2000).

93 Ariès, *The Hour of Our Death*, 415.

94 Quoted in Jalland, *Death in the Victorian Family*, 41.

95 Robert Douglas-Fairhurst, *Victorian Afterlives: The Shaping of Influence in Nineteenth-Century Literature* (London: Oxford University Press, 2004), 14.

96 Quoted in Andrew Motion, *Keats* (London: Faber and Faber, 1975), 499.

97 Andrew Motion's discussions of beliefs about consumption and Keats's place in them can be found in *Keats*, 498–501. He also points out that masturbation was another activity linked to consumption, again as both a cause of the disease and a result.

98 Quoted in Douglas-Fairhurst, *Victorian Afterlives*, 13.

99 John Keats to Fanny Brawne, July 25, 1819. *The Poetical Works and Other Writings of John Keats*, vol. 8, ed. H. Buxton Forman (New York: Phaeton, 1970), 16–17.

100 Paul H. Fry, *The Poet's Calling in the English Ode* (New Haven, CT: Yale University Press, 1980), 84.

101 *Ibid.*, 86.

102 Keats, *The Poems of John Keats*, ed. Jack Stillinger (Cambridge, MA: Harvard University Press, 1978), "Ode on a Grecian Urn," lines 21–22. All subsequent citations of Keats's poems will be from this edition, with line numbers cited parenthetically.

103 Fay, *Fashioning Faces*, 153.

104 Stuart A. Ende, *Keats and the Sublime* (New Haven, CT: Yale University Press, 1976), 71.

105 *Ibid.*, 70.

106 Quoted in Motion, *Keats*, 228.

107 Ende, *Keats and the Sublime*, 72.

108 John Barnard, *John Keats* (Cambridge: Cambridge University Press, 1987), 77.

109 John Keats to Benjamin Bailey, November 22, 1817. *Poetical Works and Other Writings*, vol. 6, Forman, 97.
110 Barnard, *John Keats*, 111.
111 John Keats to John Hamilton Reynolds, May 3, 1818. *Poetical Works and Other Writings*, vol. 7, Forman, 7.
112 John Keats to George and Georgiana Keats, September 17–27, 1819. *Poetical Works and Other Writings*, vol. 8, Forman, 101.
113 Bennett, *Romantic Poets*, 151.
114 Brooke Hopkins, "Keats and the Uncanny: 'This Living Hand,'" *The Kenyon Review* 11.4 (1989), 35–6.
115 Ibid., 35.
116 Bennett, *Romantic Poets*, 154.
117 See James Pope-Hennessy, *Monckton Milnes: The Years of Promise, 1809–1851* (New York: Farrar, Straus and Cudahy, 1955).
118 See Jan Marsh, *Dante Gabriel Rossetti: Painter and Poet* (London: Orion, 2006), Chapter 3.
119 Bennett, *Romantic Poets*, 148.
120 This sonnet and the two that follow on Blake and Shelley are quoted from Rossetti, *Poems*, ed. Oswald Doughty (London: Dent, 1957), 252–4.
121 For details on Rossetti's burial and exhumation of his manuscript, see Jan Marsh, *Dante Gabriel Rossetti*; Bronfen, *Over Her Dead Body*, 168–177; and Matthews, *Poetical Remains*, Chapter 1.
122 Quoted in "Painters Behind the Scenes," *The Edinburgh Review* 185 (April 1897), 499.
123 Samantha Matthews, in *Poetical Remains*, makes a similar point about Rossetti's gesture: "In wrapping her gold hair around the book of poems, Rossetti posited a posthumous marriage between her corporal and his textual body – to be consummated in the grave. Metaphorically, it represented a pledge that his poems died with her; in physical terms, the book substituted for the husband's still-living body" (23).
124 Letter from D. G. Rossetti to Charles Augustus Howell, August 16, 1869. William Fredeman, ed., *The Correspondence of Dante Gabriel Rossetti*, vol. 4 (Cambridge: Brewer, 2002), 235.
125 Letter from D. G. Rossetti to W. M. Rossetti, October 13, 1869. Fredeman, vol. 4, *The Correspondence*, 303.
126 Letter from D. G. Rossetti to Ford Madox Brown, October 14, 1869. Fredeman, vol. 4, *The Correspondence*, 304.
127 Letter from D. G. Rossetti to W. M. Rossetti, October 13, 1869. Fredeman, vol. 4, *The Correspondence*, 302.
128 This detail comes from Carol Christ, "Painting the Dead: Portraiture and Necrophilia in Victorian Art and Poetry," *Death and Representation*, ed. Sarah Webster Goodwin and Elisabeth Bronfen (Baltimore: Johns Hopkins University Press, 1993), 133.
129 According to Ariès (*The Hour of Our Death*), Michael Wheeler (*Death and the Future Life in Victorian Literature and Theology* [New York: Cambridge

University Press, 1990]), and Elisabeth Bronfen (*Over Her Dead Body*), death culture had become more private, personal, and secularized by the end of the nineteenth century. Jalland (*Death in the Victorian Family*), who focuses on Victorian Britain and often explicitly disagrees with Ariès's statements about the Victorian period, dates this movement to beginning around 1870, as do Peter Jupp and C. Gittings, *Death in England: An Illustrated History* (New Brunswick, NJ: Rutgers University Press, 2000). For a further discussion of the waning of religious belief and its effect on relic culture, see Chapter 5 and the afterword.

130 Walter Pater, *The Renaissance: Studies in Art and Poetry* (New York: Dover, 2005), 154.

131 For a longer meditation on this Victorian subgenre, see Christ, "Painting the Dead."

132 Bronfen (*Over Her Dead Body*) discusses (and reproduces) many nineteenth-century European examples of paintings of beautiful corpses or deaths, including the ones just discussed in the body of this chapter. She also analyzes Gabriel von Max's *Der Anatom* of 1869, Heinrich Mücke's *Übertragung des Leichnams der Heiligen Katharina zum Berge Sinai* of 1836, Anne-Lois Girodet de Roucy-Trioson's *Atala au tombeau* of 1808, Baron Pierre Guérin's *Le retour de Marcus-Sextus* of 1808, and Paul Delaroche's *La jeune martyre* of 1855.

133 For details about his work on the sketch and then the oil, see Marsh, *Dante Gabriel Rossetti*, and Edwin Becker and Julian Treuherz, eds., *Dante Gabriel Rossetti* (London: Thames and Hudson, 2003).

134 Quoted in William Sharp, *Dante Gabriel Rossetti: A Record and a Study* (London: Macmillan, 1882), 184.

135 Dante Gabriel Rossetti, *Collected Poetry and Prose*, ed. Jerome McGann (New Haven, CT: Yale University Press, 2003), 150, line 1. All subsequent references to Rossetti's poems will be from this edition, with line numbers cited parenthetically.

136 McGann, *Dante Gabriel Rossetti: Collected Poetry and Prose*, 382.

137 Locks of hair with amorous connotations are prominent in Rossetti's work. In his poem *Rose Mary*, a lock of hair on a dead man's body provides evidence he has cheated on his wife. In his watercolor *The Wedding of St. George and the Princess Sabra*, the Princess cuts a tress for him, as an erotic act. In a different register, Rossetti's illustration for his sister Christina's "*Goblin Market*", of the scene when Lizzie has her "fall," shows her cutting off a lock for the goblins.

138 In sonnet 18 of E. B. Browning's *Sonnets from the Portuguese*, the amorous lock is compared to the death one. As the speaker gives a lover a curl, she imagines, in a melancholy way, that "I thought the funeral shears / Would take this first" (lines 11–12).

Chapter 2

1 Emily's writing desk: Bonnell 1; Keeper's collar: H110.

2 The quote is from the museum wall text. Other secondary relics at the museum include Emily's paper knife, H136, and her artist's box, E. 2010.2.

3 Elizabeth Gaskell, *The Life of Charlotte Brontë* (New York: Penguin, 1997), 13–14.

4 Quoted in Marsh, *Dante Gabriel Rossetti*, 131.

5 Mrs. Humphry Ward dramatizes late Victorian-era pilgrimages to the Brontë house in *The History of David Grieve*. See also Kathleen Tillotson, "'Haworth Churchyard': The Making of Arnold's Elegy," *Brontë Society Transactions* 15 (1967), 105–122 and Amanda J. Collins, "Forging an Afterlife: Mrs. Humphry Ward and the Relics of the Brontës," *Australasian Victorian Studies Journal* 7 (2001), 12–25. Lucasta Miller, *The Brontë Myth* (London: Jonathon Cape, 2001), writes about the cult following that developed around Charlotte, starting even before her death: "One reason why Charlotte Brontë became such an appealing popular saint in the first six decades after her death was the fact that in Haworth she had an easily identifiable shrine. The almost religious awe in which she was held soon came to be focused on the place where she had spent nearly all her life, and a full-fledged cult developed complete with pilgrims and relics. Although literary cults were not confined to the Brontës in the latter half of the nineteenth century, Charlotte inspired a uniquely intense devotion. As one newspaper put it, 'Miss Austen and Thackeray have admirers; Charlotte Brontë has worshippers'" (98). Nicola Watson (*The Literary Tourist*) has a section on mid-to-late-Victorian pilgrimages to the Brontë parsonage. She describes souvenir hunters who carried away such things as, in 1861, a "fair amount" of the house when it was being renovated, including "the whole lower sash of the window of the bedroom of Charlotte" (114).

6 Writing of the jacket of a dead friend, Stallybrass laments, "he was there in the wrinkles of the elbows, wrinkles which in the technical jargon of sewing are called 'memory.'" "Worn Worlds: Clothes, Mourning, and the Life of Things," *Cultural Memory and the Construction of Identity*, ed. Dan Ben-Amos and Liliane Weissberg (Detroit, MI: Wayne State University Press, 1999), 39.

7 Brown, *Things*, 7.

8 Instruments that were part of Jesus's Passion, however, count as primary, or first-class, relics. These include the "Scourging Post," where Jesus was supposedly flagellated on that same fateful evening; the "Crown of Thorns," worn by him during the crucifixion; the "True Cross," on which he was crucified; and the "Holy Nails" that pierced his hands. See Cruz, *Relics*.

9 Acts 19:11–12.

10 Pascoe, *The Hummingbird Cabinet*, 95. A chapter or even a book could be written on trees as relics.

11 Pascoe explores Napoleon relics, in Chapter 3. Many can still be seen in London, at the Wellcome Collection, the British Museum, the Sir John Soane Museum, and Apsley house. Charlotte Brontë owned a piece of Napoleon's coffin: Brontë Parsonage Museum BS20a. See also Stuart Semmel, "Reading the Tangible Past: British Tourism, Collecting, and Memory after Waterloo," *Representations* 69 (2000), 9–37.

12 Christopher Hibbert, *Queen Victoria: A Personal History* (London: Harper Collins, 2000), 286–287. There was some worry about the idolatrous (and hence Catholic) nature of the Queen's mourning when her Prince died,

especially the anniversary services she arranged that some construed as prayers for the dead. See Wolffe, *Great Deaths*, 77.

13 Shirley Bury, *Jewellery, 1789–1910: The International Era* (Woodbridge, UK: Antique Collector's Club, 1991), 322. When Queen Victoria herself died, a certain cult developed around her remains. A contemporary remarked that "she had become a sort of fetish and was surrounded with a sort of sacred halo" (quoted in Wolffe, *Great Deaths*, 225). Wolffe also compares her role, after her death, to that of the Virgin Mary in Catholic countries, as a "super-human sympathizer with suffering" (229).

14 Lytton Strachey, *Queen Victoria* (London: Chatto and Windus, 1921), 400.

15 Quoted in Pascoe, *The Hummingbird Cabinet*, 9.

16 Wolffe, *Great Deaths*, 145. Wolffe also discusses John Gordon's death in Khartoum in 1884 and the way many Englishmen saw him as a Christian martyr. See 148. See also Justin D. Livingstone, "A 'Body' of Evidence: The Posthumous Presentation of David Livingstone," *Victorian Literature and Culture* 40 (2012), 1–24.

17 Wolffe, *Great Deaths*, 173.

18 *Times*, Oct. 25, 1837, p. 2, col. F.

19 *Times*, June 17, 1844, p. 6, col. G. This piece of jewelry is now part of the Royal Collection, Windsor Castle.

20 *Times*, July 9, 1845, p. 4, col. E. This coat (and other clothing) are now at the National Maritime Museum, London. UN 10024, UN 10031, UN 10032.

21 Jalland, *Death in the Victorian Family*, 297.

22 Ibid., 298.

23 To bring in a Romantic-era example, in Keats's "Isabella: or, the Pot of Basil," when Isabella digs up the corpse of her dead lover, the first thing she uncovers is "a soiled glove . . . She kiss'd it with a lip more chill than stone, / And put it in her bosom where it dries / And freezes utterly onto the bone" (47: lines 1, 3–5).

24 For studies on Victorian mourning culture, see especially Curl, *The Victorian Celebration of Death*; Schor, *Bearing the Dead*; and Taylor, *Mourning Dress*. Ariès also has a chapter on the Victorian period in his *The Hour of Our Death*. For an excellent general introduction to Victorian death culture, see Gerhard Joseph and Herbert Tucker, "Passing On: Death," *A Companion to Victorian Literature and Culture*, ed. Herbert Tucker (Malden, MA: Blackwell, 1999), 110–124.

25 Freedgood, *The Ideas in Things*, 8.

26 Other important books about Victorian material culture, in addition to the ones mentioned in the body of this chapter, include Asa Briggs, *Victorian Things* (London: B. T. Batsford, 1988); Deborah Cohen, *Household Gods: The British and Their Possessions* (New Haven, CT: Yale University Press, 2006); and Thad Logan, *The Victorian Parlour* (New York: Cambridge University Press, 2001).

27 See Peter Logan, *Victorian Fetishism: Intellectuals and Primitives* (Albany: SUNY, 2009).

28 Herbert Spencer, *Principles of Sociology*, vol. 1 (New York: Appleton, 1898), 326.

29 Ibid., 336. He continues, tellingly for the argument I will make in this chapter, to explain that "all the evidence goes to show that adoration of inanimate objects thus possessed by ghosts, is really adoration of the indwelling ghosts" (338).

30 Tim Armstrong surveys some of the philosophical and scientific beliefs behind Victorian fetishism and animism. See *Haunted Hardy: Poetry, History, Memory* (New York: Palgrave, 2000), especially Chapter 2.

31 John Plotz, *Portable Property: Victorian Culture on the Move* (Princeton, NJ: Princeton University Press, 2009), goes on, "'Things,' then, are limit cases at which our ordinary categories for classifying signs and substances, meaning and materiality, appear to break down" (25). The anthropologists Hallam and Hockey (*Death, Memory and Material Culture*) call such category-crossing things, "hybrid objects" (116).

32 These are all notions discussed by Bill Brown in *A Sense of Things*.

33 Plotz, *Portable Property*, 2.

34 Annette Weiner, *Inalienable Possessions: The Paradox of Keeping-While-Giving* (Berkeley: University of California Press, 1992), 6–7.

35 Richardson, *Death, Dissection, and the Destitute*, 7.

36 Ibid., 27.

37 In Jewish tradition, however, covering mirrors and not bathing during a wake are means to honor the dead by putting aside all considerations of personal appearance.

38 Richardson, *Death, Dissection, and the Destitute*, 27.

39 David Cecil, *Early Victorian Novelists; Essays in Revaluation* (Indianapolis, IN: Bobbs-Merrill, 1935), 161.

40 J. Hillis Miller, *The Disappearance of God: Five Nineteenth-Century Writers* (Cambridge, MA: Harvard University Press, 1963), 175. Robert Polhemus more recently uses "the erotic calling in *Wuthering Heights*" to represent the "involuntary vocation of being human." *Erotic Faith: Being in Love from Jane Austen to D. H. Lawrence* (Chicago: University of Chicago Press, 1990), 95. In addition, Daniel Cottom recently observed that the book shows "Gothic art coming alive in love and so giving the experience of love the place traditionally occupied in the Gothic novel by that of dramatic uncertainty." "I Think; Therefore, I Am Heathcliff," *English Literary History* 70:4 (2003), 50.

41 Emily Brontë, *Wuthering Heights*, ed. Beth Newman (Peterborough, Ontario: Broadview, 2000), 51, 140. Hereafter cited parenthetically by page number.

42 These ideas have become critical commonplaces. For instance, Terry Eagleton believes that their love works as "a revolutionary refusal of the given language of social roles and values" (108) and therefore remains an "unhistorical essence which fails to enter into concrete existence" (109). He also points to "the curious impersonality of the relation between Catherine and Heathcliff" (107). *Myths of Power: A Marxist Study of the Brontës* (Basingstoke: Macmillan Press,

1975). Sandra Gilbert and Susan Gubar argue that "happiness has few of the variations of despair," and thus Catherine's "earthly paradise" of childhood and love is "easy to summarize" (267). *The Madwoman in the Attic; The Woman Writer and the Nineteenth-Century Literary Imagination* (New Haven, CT: Yale University Press, 2000).

43 Margaret Homans, "Repression and Sublimation of Nature in *Wuthering Heights*," *PMLA* 93.1 (1978), 19. Stevie Davies writes in a similar vein when she remarks of the moors in the novel: "The very absence of description is a secret of the mysterious sense of adjacent presence or being which the novel sets up," *Emily Brontë: Heretic* (London: Women's Press, 1994), 181.

44 See Steven Vine, *Emily Brontë* (New York: Twayne, 1998), 132.

45 Bronfen, *Over Her Dead Body*, 308. Philippe Ariès uses *Wuthering Heights* as his central source text to tell the history of nineteenth-century British attitudes toward death. See *The Hour of Our Death*. Also, Georges Bataille remarks of the novel, "death seems to be the truth of love, just as love is the truth of death." *Literature and Evil: Essays* (London: Boyars, 1997), 16.

46 That Brontë crafts her novel using some aspects of her contemporary death culture challenges a common thread in Brontë scholarship: that *Wuthering Heights* is a heretical text of rebellion against all contemporary religious dictates. The most influential proponents of this argument were Gilbert and Gubar, in their chapter on *Wuthering Heights* in *The Madwoman in the Attic*. Brontë, they believe, inverts heaven and hell, making the Satanic Heathcliff into a hero, and converting the moors, a pagan, androgynous place, into an anti-Christian heaven. They see Brontë as committed "to the belief that the state of being patriarchal Christianity calls 'hell' is eternally, energetically delightful, whereas the state called 'heaven' is rigidly hierarchical" (255). This point is repeated or developed by many later scholars, such as Steven Vine, who believes Brontë rejects "orthodox Christian immortality in favor of the heretical creed that 'the disembodied soul continues to be active in this life'" (129). Certainly Brontë does challenge general Christian morals with the brutal savagery and amorality of her Heathcliff. Yet to understand the ways she pulls her belief from her own era tells us something about a Victorian understanding of experiencing death through its materials. See also Marianne Thormählen, *The Brontës and Religion* (Cambridge: Cambridge University Press, 1999).

47 Daniel Cottom, in his book *Unhuman Culture* (Philadelphia: University of Pennsylvania Press, 2006), uses Heathcliff to explore art as (quoting Baude-laire) "'a permanent protest against morality'" (4). His misanthropy makes him "unhuman," Cottom believes, and thus very different from the other characters in the novel. Although Brontë distinguishes Heathcliff as someone who loves more profoundly than most, I would argue that his means of loving the dead makes him very much like, not only the other characters in the book, but Victorians more generally.

48 These many sudden deaths compare to Dickens's late novels. *Our Mutual Friend, Great Expectations,* and *Bleak House* in particular pack in a surprising

number of deaths. For instance, in *Bleak House* eleven people die. For a discussion of deathbed scenes in Victorian novels, see Garrett Stewart, *Death Sentences: Styles of Dying in British Fiction* (Cambridge, MA: Harvard University Press, 1984) and Margarete Holubetz, "Death-Bed Scenes in Victorian Fiction," *English Studies* 67.1 (1986), 14–34.

49 Laura Inman enumerates the many deaths in the novel, exploring the characters' presentiments of death coming and the quality of their grief after death. She also links the deaths in Brontë's own life to the characters' deaths in the novel. "'The Awful Event,' in *Wuthering Heights*," *Brontë Studies: The Journal of the Brontë Society* 33 (2008), 192–202.

50 In addition to the more momentous deaths of Catherine and Heathcliff, there are nine. Before the action begins, the Earnshaw's first son has already gone. Both the Earnshaw parents are done away with by Chapter 6, and then the Lintons' father and mother slip away. Hindley's wife Frances makes a brief appearance, exiting in the fever of consumption. Hindley knocks himself out of the world with drink; Edgar Linton slides off calmly, as does his sickly nephew, Heathcliff's son Linton.

51 Brontë pictures such immensity in numerous poems, for instance, in the famous "I'm happiest when most away," the speaker is happiest when she "can bear my soul from its home of clay" (line 1), "when I am not and none beside . . . But only spirit wandering wide/Through infinite immensity" (lines 5, 7–8).

52 Inscribing one's name on something is a secondary relic of a special type. The hand has touched the thing, but also the unique personality is, to some extent, transferred into the scratched signature.

53 Catherine Gallagher and Stephen Greenblatt, *Practicing New Historicism* (Chicago: University of Chicago Press, 2000), 189.

54 Ibid., 193.

55 Brown, *Things*, 4.

56 Not only did John and Charles Wesley often preach in the district in the eighteenth century, but also William Grimshaw had previously held Patrick's curacy. For a further discussion of Brontë's religious background, see Juliet Barker, *The Brontës* (New York: St. Martin's, 1994) and Winifred Gérin, *Emily Brontë: A Biography* (Oxford: Clarendon Press, 1971).

57 As children, Emily's sister Charlotte and her brother Branwell wrote comic stories that parodied the language of low-church preachers. Emily composed school essays that think about theological issues, ruminating about the nature of sin and its punishment by God's law. See her two Brussels essays "Filial Love" and "Letter from One Brother to Another," *The Belgian Essays*, ed. Sue Lonoff (New Haven, CT: Yale University Press, 1996). Some of her poems express a musing about God's nature and existence and a questioning about the realm of the afterlife. In her poem "The winter wind is loud and wild," for instance, the speaker describes her "fervent hope . . . To reach, at last, the eternal home— / The steadfast, changeless shore!" (lines 67, 70). In her poem "Death," when the speaker loses her beloved, she wishes death will strike her

down, so that other "boughs may flourish" (line 29). "Thus, at least, its mouldering corpse will nourish / That from which it sprung—Eternity" (lines 31–32). And "No coward soul is mine" expresses a belief that the dead are taken into an eternity. See Janet Gezari, *Last Things: Emily Brontë's Poems* (Oxford: Oxford University Press, 2007), especially Chapter 6.

58 For evangelicalism's pervasiveness throughout Victorian culture, see G. M. Young, *Victorian England: Portrait of an Age* (London: Oxford University Press, 1936).

59 Jalland, *Death in the Victorian Family*.

60 Ian Bradley discusses these tracts and their popularity. See *The Call to Seriousness: The Evangelical Impact on the Victorians* (New York: Macmillan, 1976).

61 Charles Wesley, "Hymn XXII: On the Corpse of a Believer," *Hymns on the great festivals, and other occasions*, music by John Frederick Lampe (London: Cooper, 1746), 56, lines 1–8.

62 From Emily Leakey, *Clear Shining Light: A Memoir of Caroline W. Leakey*. Quoted in Jalland, *Death in the Victorian Family*, 22. The beauty of the calm mien of death was usually described as Anne Blunt (the wife of the artist and poet Wilfrid Scawen Blunt) does in her diary, when she and her husband were making sketches of her just-dead brother-in-law's countenance: "His face was beautiful like the face of a saint as I imagine it to be." The painter John Horsley made a drawing of his father, just after his death in 1858. His mother remarked on this drawing, "The peace and beauty of his expression is not to be described" (quoted in Jalland, 289).

63 For a discussion of Romanticism's influence on Evangelicalism, see D. W. Bebbington, *Evangelicalism in Modern Britain: A History from the 1730s to the 1980s* (London: Unwin Hyman, 1989) and Jalland, *Death in the Victorian Family*.

64 Daniela Garofalo observes that Heathcliff represents a particular kind of Victorian collector in his need to reach Catherine through materiality. His "collecting" of Catherine memorabilia, she asserts, is a form of participating in a commodity culture that requires "a desire for the lost object" (826). She sees him as the type of Victorian capitalist who dedicates him or herself to accumulation rather than consumption, to a delay of pleasure rather than a wallowing in it. While the broad sweep of his brutal acts of collecting houses and capital as a form of revenge certainly does fall under this definition of consumption, I argue that relics resist modern forms of commodity culture. "Impossible Love and Commodity Culture in Emily Brontë's *Wuthering Heights*," *ELH* 75.4 (2008). Other critics who note that the love between Heathcliff and Catherine is constituted by its deferral read it psychoanalytic-ally. See Robin DeRosa, "'To Save the Life of the Novel': Sadomasochism and Representation in 'Wuthering Heights,'" *Rocky Mountain Review of Language and Literature* 52.1 (1998), 27–43 and Elisabeth Bronfen, *Over Her Dead Body*.

65 Ingrid Geerken, "'The Dead are Not Annihilated': Mortal Regret in *Wuthering Heights*," *Journal of Narrative Theory* 34 (2004), 376.

66 There is another lock of hair in the book that works synecdochically. Isabella
sends some of her son's hair to Edgar, and Cathy keeps it in a box.

67 Keats also had Fanny's letters and a purse made by his sister buried with him.
Motion, *Keats*, 564. When Tennyson died, he was buried with a laurel wreath
made from leaves picked from trees that grew on Virgil's grave.

68 Jalland recounts this tale and discusses the practice generally; see especially
214. According to Bertram Puckle, *Funeral Customs: Their Origins and Development* (London: T. Werner Laurie, 1926), 269, the ancient Greeks would cut
the hair of a child whose parent had died, as a token of grief, and then bury a
lock with the parent.

69 Brontë probably had in mind here the belief that the saints' dead bodies would
remain free from corruption, further linking Catherine to sainthood. It is
likely she was familiar with the many tales of the opening of saints' tombs and
the reports that the corpses looked freshly dead, after decades or more of
interment.

70 Anthropologists have found in many cultures the belief that death brings a
renewal. Maurice Bloch and Jonathan Parry, in *Death and the Regeneration of
Life* (Cambridge: Cambridge University Press, 1982), find this idea linked, in
Christian culture, to relics. Golgotha is the site of Christ's crucifixion, "but
also the center of the world where Adam was created and buried. The blood of
the Saviour falls on the skull of Adam interred at the foot of the Cross, and
redeems him and mankind" (14). Mary Elizabeth Hotz expands on the idea
that death can bring renewal in her discussion of Victorian working-class
communities, in *Literary Remains*.

71 The eroticism of meeting in the grave can be found in other Victorian writing,
such as Tennyson's "Locksley Hall":

> He will answer to the purpose, easy things to understand—
> Better thou wert dead before me, tho' I slew thee with my hand!
> Better thou and I were lying, hidden from the heart's disgrace,
> Roll'd in one another's arms, and silent in a last embrace. (lines 55–58)

And Swinburne's "Triumph of Time":

> I wish we were dead together to-day,
>   Lost sight of, hidden away out of sight,
> Clasped and clothed in the cloven clay,
>   Out of the world's way, out of the light,
> Out of the ages of worldly weather,
> Forgotten of all men altogether,
> As the world's first dead, taken wholly away,
>   Made one with death, filled full of the night.
>
> How we should slumber, how we should sleep,
>   Far in the dark with the dreams and the dews!
> And dreaming, grow to each other, and weep,
>   Laugh low, live softly, murmur and muse;

Yea, and it may be, struck through by the dream,
Feel the dust quicken and quiver, and seem
Alive as of old to the lips, and leap
    Spirit to spirit as lovers use. (lines 114–129).

I thank Terry Meyers for these two references.

72 Ruth Richardson explains that in the popular folklore of death during the early nineteenth century there existed a prevailing belief that the personality and soul clung to the body well after death. See *Death, Dissection, and the Destitute*, 7. Nigel Llewellyn also points out that, in post-Reformation England, the belief that the body and soul were still connected after death maintained a place in the popular imagination. *The Art of Death: Visual Culture in the English Death Ritual c. 1500–c. 1800* (London: Reaktion Books, 1991), 57.

73 In *Dombey and Son* (London: Oxford, 1974), for instance, Dickens has little Paul see, as he is dying, his mother, who predeceased him, standing on the shores of a beautiful river ready to welcome him. See 224–225.

74 Wheeler, *Death and the Future Life*, 122.

75 Wolffe, *Great Deaths*, 63. He also finds a popular idealizing of heaven as a perfect domesticity.

76 Quoted in Jalland, *Death in the Victorian Family*, 275.

77 Examining the hundreds of consolation letters sent to Gladstone's family after his death, John Wolffe found many that "wondered about Gladstone's location in the geography of heaven, or speculated on the work he would be undertaking in his new sphere of existence," *Great Deaths*, 179. Other consolation letters imagined him looking down on the living and giving them comfort, and the writers looked forward to being reunited again with him in heaven.

78 Quoted in Jane Jordan, *Josephine Butler* (London: John Murray, 2001), 56.

79 Puckle, *Funeral Customs*, 206. Ruth Richardson tells of a woman who had promised a close friend to bury with her letters from her dead son. When her friend died, the woman forgot to include the letters in the coffin. When a local postman died soon after, she buried the letters with him, thinking that he would also deliver letters in the afterlife. See *Death, Dissection and the Destitute*, 4.

80 Many examples of this can be found, such as John Horsley placing in his wife's coffin a pine box containing his letters to her. See Jalland, *Death in the Victorian Family*, 214. Numerous such artifacts were found among Margaret Cox's excavations of eighteenth- to nineteenth-century burial vaults underneath Christ Church, Spitalfields, such as jewelry, pennies, combs, medicine bottles, and a small wooden barrel containing two molars. See *Life and Death in Spitalfields*. A slightly different type of "grave good" is the coffin Nelson was buried in, partially made from a piece of *L'Orient's* mainmast, the French ship Nelson and his crew blew up during the Battle of the Nile. The coffin was a gift from his friend Benjamin Hallowell, who played a part in the battle.

81 Margaret Cox discusses the popular belief in resurrection, which "demanded complete mortal remains" (101). She explains the proliferation of lead coffins in this way, found among her excavations. See *Life and Death in Spitalfields*.

82 As Richardson, in *Death, Dissection and the Destitute*, puts it: "dissection represented ... the deliberate mutilation or destruction of identity, perhaps for eternity" (29).

83 Leo Bersani, *A Future for Astyanax: Character and Desire in Literature* (Boston: Little Brown, 1976), 211.

84 Bataille, *Literature and Evil*, 21.

85 Davies, *Emily Brontë*, 174.

86 Miller, *The Disappearance of God*, 186–7.

87 Ibid., 209.

88 Philippe Ariès, *Images of Man and Death* (Cambridge, MA: Harvard University Press, 1985), 241.

Chapter 3

1 Quoted in Peter Ackroyd, *Dickens* (New York: Harper Perennial, 1990), xii.

2 Frederic George Kitton, *Charles Dickens by Pen and Pencil* (London: F. T. Sabin, 1890), 97.

3 The Millais pencil sketch and a plaster cast of the marble bust by Woolner can be viewed today at the Dickens Museum, London, along with many other relics, such as his "commode," the china monkey that sat on his desk, and a clock from Gad's Hill. There is also a table with a brass plaque nailed to it that reads, "Table (from the Chalet) upon which Charles Dickens penned his last words." A small window hangs on a wall, with a plaque affixed to it: "A genuine Dickens relic. The window of the little attic in 141, Bayham Street, Camden Town, occupied by Charles Dickens as a boy of 11 years of age in 1832, when the Dickens family came to London from Chatham."

4 Charles Dickens to John Forster, December 11, 1837. *The Letters of Charles Dickens: The Pilgrim Edition*, vol. 1, ed. Madeline House and Graham Storey (New York: Oxford, 1981), 341.

5 An attendee of séances and practitioner of table-spinning, although also critical of the practices, Dickens wrote of haunting: "I have always had a strong interest in the subject, and never knowingly lost an opportunity of pursuing it." Charles Dickens to William Howitt, September 6, 1859. *The Letters of Charles Dickens*, House, vol. 9, 116.

6 Charles Dickens to William Bradbury, March 3, 1839. *The Letters of Charles Dickens*, House, vol. 1, 516.

7 See Ariès, *Images of Man and Death*.

8 A second step complicates this direct contact. A cast was a "negative" image (to compare the process to that of photography) of the face and made direct contact with it. But then the mask itself, made from this cast, would be a "positive" image, which would have touched the cast but not the flesh itself.

9 Ariès points out that making death masks became standard practice around the sixteenth century. See *Images of Man and Death*, 128. The tradition of taking a cast for the sake of love and desire – in order to document and remember the person – wasn't established until the end of the eighteenth century.

10 Llewellyn, *The Art of Death*, 31.

11 Ibid., 33.

12 Keats's death mask was made by Gherardi, the day after Keats's death, along with casts of his hands and feet. One of the masks made from this cast can be found at the Keats-Shelley Museum, in Rome, another at the Keats House Museum, London, and a third at the National Portrait Gallery, London.

13 The Scott mask was made by George Bullock and loaned to Edwin Landseer when he was painting his full-length portrait. See Laurence Hutton, "A Collection of Death Masks," *Harper's New Monthly Magazine* 85.509 (Oct. 1892), 792.

14 Thackeray's mask was made by Domenico Brucciani (as was D. G. Rossetti's), along with the cast of his right hand (because it was the hand he wrote with). The death mask and cast of his hand are now at the National Portrait Gallery, London. London is full of death masks that can still be viewed. These include the Duke of Wellington's, at Apsley, along with a bronze of his hands and a postmortem sketch; and Benjamin Disraeli's, at the Wellcome (A 652234).

15 Quoted in Jordan, *Josephine Butler*, 59.

16 Jalland, *Death in the Victorian Family*, 290.

17 Quoted in Jalland, *Death in the Victorian Family*, 290. She gives many more examples of postmortem art.

18 *Aurora Leigh* (London: Chapman and Hall, 1857), 6. E. B. Browning was both a relic collector (especially locks of hair and mourning jewelry) and a spiritualist.

19 Some idealizing in these death masks was fairly common. Philippe Ariès explains that an early realism in death masks gave way, by the nineteenth century, to some cleaning up to show serenity. See *Images of Man and Death*, 128.

20 Quoted in Jordan, *Josephine Butler*, 56.

21 Frederick Tennyson in a letter to John Frere, March 23, 1831. *The Letters of Alfred Lord Tennyson*. vol. 1, ed. Cecil Y. Lang and Edgar F. Shannon (Cambridge, MA, 1981), 56.

22 *Dombey and Son* (New York: Penguin, 2002), 297.

23 Cruz, *Relics*, 283.

24 Dickens discussed Catholic practices in *A Child's History of England* and *Pictures from Italy*. Michael Schiefelbein makes a case for Dickens's sympathy with Catholicism, in "Little Nell, Catholicism, and Dickens's Investigation of Death," *Dickens Quarterly* 9.3 (1992), 115–125. See also David Parker, "Dickens and the Death of Mary Hogarth," *Dickens Quarterly* 13.2 (1996), 67–75. Dickens was always curious about the doings of saints. Dickens adored, as a child, the illustrations from Foxe's *Book of Martyrs*, pictures of saints being flayed, boiled, roasted – meeting all manner of horrid deaths. See Harry Stone,

The Night Side of Dickens: Cannibalism, Passion, Necessity (Columbus: Ohio State University Press, 1994).

25 Not only do Dickens's novels attest to this, but so also do the many consolation letters he wrote to grieving friends. After Mary Hogarth's death, for instance, he wrote that her sister, his wife Catherine, "looks forward to being mercifully permitted one day to rejoin her sister in that happy World for which God adapted her better than for this." Dickens to Richard Johns, May 31, 1837. *The Letters of Charles Dickens*, vol. 1, 264.

26 *Old Curiosity Shop* (New York: Penguin, 2001), 522.

27 For a different understanding of the art of the death mask, see the short story "The Death Mask" by Ella D'Arcy, published in *The Yellow Book* in 1896. The death mask of a famous man, when seen in a certain light, shows clearly the worst characteristics of his personality, never seen so clearly in life. But when the mask is seen from a different angle and with another type of lighting, the lofty sweetness of his soul can be seen, also never so obviously apparent during his life.

28 In his history of Victorian Evangelicalism, Bradley, in *The Call to Seriousness*, remarks that "the Evangelicals believed that there were important moral lessons to be learned from witnessing and studying the manner of death of both sinners and the saved" (187). Lee Anne Gallaway-Mitchell explores such sentiments in women's consolation letters of the time. For instance, in a letter written to a friend after the death of Joanna Baillie, Sara Coleridge wrote, "You were privileged, dear friend, to have the sight of the dear face after death, and to see that 'friendly look,' so consolatory to survivors, and so precious a treasure for memory" (68). Writing a consolation letter to a friend who had recently experienced the death of his father, Coleridge pointed out the comfort in remembering a "good death": "those dying hours of our dearest ones can never be far out of mind, it is a blessing, indeed, when they have more of the rest of heaven in them than the sting of the grave" (75). See " 'Words Survive': Death and Dying in Women's Letters," Dissertation, University of Texas, Austin, 2008. For discussions about the way evangelicalism influenced the depiction of deathbed scenes in Victorian novels, see Holubetz, "Death-Bed Scenes in Victorian Fiction."

29 Ariès, *Images of Man and Death*, 247.

30 Charles Dickens, *Oliver Twist* (London: Penguin, 2002), 162. All subsequent references will be to this edition, and page numbers will be cited in the text.

31 *The Old Curiosity Shop*, 522. The death of Little Nell was considered one of the most famous deathbed scenes of the period, and it is not too much to say that the whole nation mourned when Dickens published this scene. Critics praised the passage for its "moral sublimity" (quoted in Holubetz, "Death-Bed Scenes in Victorian Fiction," 14). See also Stewart, *Death Sentences*. When the pure-living, hard-working old woman Betty Higden dies, in *Our Mutual Friend* (New York: Penguin, 1998), Lizzie Hexam "raised the weather-stained grey head, and lifted her as high as Heaven" (506).

32 Hotz, *Literary Remains*, 67.

33 Ariès, *Images of Man and Death*, 199.
34 There has been a good deal of writing on the theme of death in Dickens's novels. These include the chapters in Catherine Gallagher's two books, *Practicing New Historicism* (written with Stephen Greenblatt) and *The Body Economic: Life, Death, and Sensation in Political Economy and the Victorian Novel* (Princeton, NJ: Princeton University Press, 2006) on *Great Expectations* and *Our Mutual Friend*, respectively. In her chapter on *Our Mutual Friend*, Mary Elizabeth Hotz (*Literary Remains*) examines burial politics of the period and discusses Dickens's critique of the commodification of human beings. Rodney Stenning Edgecombe explores Dickens's use of "violent farce" in *Great Expectations* in "Violence, Death and Euphemism in *Great Expectations*," *VIJ: Victorians Institute Journal* 22 (1994), 85–98. Albert Hutter sees Dickens's novels, especially *A Tale of Two Cities*, as presenting a subversive view of death, a kind of nihilistic emptiness exemplified in the character Jerry Cruncher. He focuses on the image of the empty grave, without a body, as calling to mind the impossibility we all have of imagining our own deaths, when our consciousnesses will no longer exist. He explores Dickens's fiction as a form of "resurrecting" himself, his characters, his society. See "The Novelist as Resurrectionist: Dickens and the Dilemma of Death," *Dickens Studies Annual* 12 (1983), 1–39. See also Goldie Morgentaler, "Executing Beauty: Dickens and the Aesthetics of Death" *Dickens Studies Annual* 30 (2001) 45–57. George Levine remarks of Dickens's late fiction that "he had long since made a living out of death." See *Dying to Know: Scientific Epistemology and Narrative in Victorian England* (Chicago: University of Chicago Press, 2002), 152.
35 On death as rebirth and resurrection, see Andrew Sanders, *Charles Dickens: Resurrectionist* (London: Macmillan, 1982) and Gallagher, *The Body Economic*.
36 Charles Dickens, *Great Expectations* (London: Penguin, 1996), 7. All subsequent references will be to this edition, and page numbers will be cited in the text.
37 Poor little Oliver Twist is called "the item of mortality" (3) and "young gallows" (79).
38 Are they going to have him bound as an apprentice, Pip wonders on his way to the Town Hall, or are they just looking "in on our way to the scaffold?" (105).
39 Pip "smooths his face with his sleeve" (63) as a means to hide his hurt from Estella, just after their first meeting when she expresses her contempt for him.
40 For a discussion of class and materiality in relation to hands and gloves, see Ariel Beaujot, "'The Beauty of her Hands': The Glove and the Making of the Middle-Class Body," *Material Women, 1750–1950: Consuming Desires and Collecting Practices*, eds. Maureen Daly Goggin and Beth Fowkes Tobin (London: Ashgate, 2009).
41 John Carey, *The Violent Effigy: A Study of Dickens's Imagination* (London: Faber and Faber, 1973), 94.
42 What Pip worries about most, when he is apprenticed to Joe, is that Estella will see him "with a black face and hands" (108).

43 Conversely, like a nourishing covering, tears overlay "our hard hearts" like "rain upon the blinding dust of earth" (160).

44 Krook spontaneously combusts, transforming completely into a sooty fat that coats walls and hangs heavily in the London fog.

45 Dickens, *The Uncommercial Traveller* (London: Chapman and Hall, 1861), 64–65. See also Britta Martens, who compares the Victorians' visits to the morgue as similar to their attraction and repulsion to/from sensationalism in general. She in addition connects the display at the morgue to contemporary department stores. "Death as Spectacle: The Paris Morgue in Dickens and Browning," *Dickens Studies Annual* 39 (2008), 223–248. See also Alan Mitchell, "The Paris Morgue as a Social Institution in the Nineteenth Century," *Francia* 3 (1976), 581–596.

46 Carey, *The Violent Effigy*, 81.

47 As recounted in an early biography: John Camden Hotten, *Charles Dickens: The Story of his Life* (London: J. C. Hotten, 1872), 37.

48 *Our Mutual Friend* (New York: Penguin, 1997), 279.

49 Little Oliver Twist, just born, seems to want to slip back into the preborn state, rather than have to make his way in the fallen world. He "lay gasping on a little flock mattress, rather unequally poised between this world and the next, the balance being decidedly in favour of the latter" (4). As a child forced to work for an undertaker, Oliver wishes, "as he crept into his narrow bed, that that were his coffin, and that he could be laid in a calm and lasting sleep in the churchyard ground, with the tall grass waving gently above his head, and the sound of the old deep bell to soothe him in his sleep" (35).

50 Ariès, *Images of Man and Death*. The word *cemetery* comes from the Greek word for *dormitory*, which can also mean "burial place."

51 Ackroyd, *Dickens*, 390.

52 Puckle, *Funeral Customs*, 264–265. One such effigy of a knight (of the De Lacey family) with crossed legs can be found at the Victoria and Albert museum. Dating from around 1320–1340, the statue was formerly in the Lady Chapel, Lesnes Abbey, Kent. At the foot of its crossed legs reclines a little lion.

53 My reading of the opening scene of *Great Expectations* is informed by Peter Brooks's now classic interpretation of these passages, in Chapter 5 of his *Reading for the Plot: Design and Intention in Narrative* (Cambridge, MA: Harvard University Press, 1984).

54 Dickens makes the epitaph into a kind of postdeath art when he compares it to the photograph. Pip has only these tombstones to remember his family by, since "their days were long before the days of photographs" (3).

55 J. Hillis Miller, *Versions of Pygmalion* (Cambridge, MA: Harvard University Press, 1990), 186.

56 Ariès gives this history in *Images of Man and Death*, 52–85. He remarks, "The tomb was now used to display in a lasting fashion the subject's features as recorded at the moment of death" (84). See also his *The Hour of Our Death*, Chapter 5.

57 Ariès, *Images of Man and Death*, 52.

58 Charles Dickens, *Martin Chuzzlewit* (New York: Penguin, 2000), 446.

59 Herbert Spencer draws a direct connection between the use of these effigies of kings and queens and the idol worship of "primitive cultures," such as the Javanese, who use a man-shaped figure in rituals during their death festivals. He understands them both as part of the same continuum of "fetich [*sic*] worship." *Principles of Sociology*, 329.

60 See Anthony Harvey and Richard Mortimer, *The Funeral Effigies of Westminster Abbey* (Woodbridge: Boydell, 1994) and Llewellyn, *The Art of Death*, 55.

61 Richard Davey, *A History of Mourning* (London: Jay's, 1889). Modeled after the many made of saints and displayed in holy places, such effigies work as another signal of the move from the religious to the secular in mourning and death culture.

62 Some of the many recumbent figures at Westminster Abbey have countenances based on death masks, such as that of King Henry VII, Elizabeth I, and Elizabeth of York.

63 Wolffe, *Great Deaths*. Wolffe also remarks that Oliver Cromwell, in 1658, had an effigy procession, as did General Monk, Duke of Albemarle, in 1670. Puckle (*Funeral Customs*) recounts that Cromwell's effigy was exhibited to the public while his body was being embalmed.

64 Llewellyn, *The Art of Death*, 53.

65 Cruz, *Relics*, 225. Her hands were amputated from her corpse to be displayed elsewhere.

66 Catherine Gallagher, in her exploration of the way the dead become "reanimated" (and how many "inhabit states of suspended animation" [187]) in *Great Expectations*, remarks on those who straddle "the zones of life and death" (186) such as Miss Havisham. See *Practicing New Historicism*.

67 Bronfen, *Over Her Dead Body*, 349.

68 Ibid., 349.

69 Gallagher, *The Body Economic*, 95.

70 These were all common motifs in nineteenth-century mourning jewelry and tomb sculpture, especially a woman (sometimes meant to represent a personified Virtue) weeping over an urn.

71 In a related but differently framed argument, John Plotz, in *Portable Property*, remarks that Wemmick's keepsakes are not only "cash equivalents" but also a "domestic retreat" that he can carry around with him (xv).

72 Catherine Gallagher (*Practicing New Historicism*) describes Estella as the missing *corpus delicti* revived since she is the child thought to be murdered by her mother, Molly.

73 Gazing one night on her "awful figure," Pip sees her reflection "thrown large by the fire upon the ceiling and the wall," and he "saw in everything the construction that my mind had come to, repeated and thrown back at me" (303). The ways Miss Havisham "brandishes" her broken heart reminds us of those saints whose hearts not only are, reputedly, incorrupt years after death and displayed in various holy places, but also those whose hearts were supposedly carved with evidence of their holiness, such as St. Clare of

Montefalco's "in which are clearly imprinted the symbols of the Redeemer's Passion." The heart of the dead St. Francis de Sales is believed to exude a clear oil and to periodically bleed. Cruz, *Relics*, 230.

74 Gallagher, *Practicing New Historicism*, 197.

75 For an extended discussion of Dickens's interest in criminals, see Philip Collins, *Dickens and Crime* (London: Macmillan, 1962).

76 Dickens, "Visit to Newgate," *Sketches by Boz* (London: Penguin, 1995). Stanley Tick believes that these are the masks that become the models for the ones in Jaggers's office. "Cruncher on Resurrection: A Tale of Charles Dickens," *Renascence* 33 (1981), 98.

77 See Michael Slater, *Charles Dickens* (New York: Yale University Press, 2009), 153, 283. Dickens has Oliver Twist do what he himself had, on many an occasion: read "a history of the lives and trials of great criminals." The bodies of the murdered, in these stories, would work their way out of the ground to confront their murderers, who would be so maddened by the sight, they would confess their guilt and yell "for the gibbet to end their agony" (164).

78 *The Old Curiosity Shop*, 282.

79 Thomas de Quincey, for instance, bought a plaster cast of John Williams, an early nineteenth-century murderer. See de Quincey, *On Murder Considered as One of the Fine Arts* (New York: Putnam, n.d.). At the Hunterian Museum, London, the death mask of one Richard Parker (1767–1797) can be still be viewed. He was hanged for mutiny, and after he was buried, his wife exhumed his corpse. For a time it was on public display at the Hoop and Horseshoe tavern near Tower Hill, in London. Also at the Hunterian is displayed the skeleton of Jonathan Wild, hanged at Tyburn, London, in 1725, for being a receiver of stolen goods.

80 See Stanley Burns, *Sleeping Beauty: Memorial Photography in America* (Altadena, CA: Twelvetrees Press, 1990).

81 After 1835, the public could view lifelike representations of famous criminals done in wax at Madame Tussaud's.

82 Dickens, "Visit to Newgate," *Sketches by Boz*, 202–203.

83 John Forster, *The Life of Charles Dickens* (Philadelphia: Lippincott, 1873), 567.

84 See Sarah Goodwin, *Kitsch and Culture: The Dance of Death in Nineteenth-Century Literature and Graphic Arts* (London: Garland, 1988), for more on the popularity of the "dance of death" in images and texts during the nineteenth century (in Hardy and Baudelaire, for example).

85 Dickens, *The Uncommercial Traveller*, 64–65. Dickens goes on to write of an old man he saw in the morgue, in a letter to John Forster, January 1847: "It seemed the strangest thing in the world that it should have been necessary to take any trouble to stop such a feeble, spent, exhausted morsel of life." *The Letters of Charles Dickens: The Pilgrim Edition*, vol. 5 (New York: Oxford, 1981), 3.

86 Ariès, *The Hour of Our Death*, 116.

87 Goodwin (*Kitsch and Culture*) sees this suppleness in a different way, arguing that "death in the danse macabre exposes the fiction of identity, even as it grants the occasion for life's parade" (12).

88 For an extended discussion of Dickens's interest in and writings on the subject of cannibalism, see Part I of Stone, *The Night Side of Dickens*.

89 Mr. Grimwig, in a comical reference to autocannibalism, surely an impossible activity, often claims that, if he's wrong, he'll "be content to eat my own head, sir!" (110).

90 The residents of the ancient cathedral town in *The Mystery of Edwin Drood* can't help but ingest the "dust" of the many long-buried cadavers, giving their bodies "the attention which the Ogre in the story-book desired to render to his unbidden visitor, and grinds their bones to make his bread" (210).

91 Because of his disdain for the elaborate and expensive rituals that his contemporaries felt were needed when a loved one died, Dickens stipulated in his will that he wanted a simple funeral: ". . . I emphatically direct that I be buried in an inexpensive, unostentatious and strictly private manner . . ." He desired a simple epitaph: "I direct that my name be inscribed in plain English letters on my tomb" (quoted in Sanders, *Charles Dickens*, 38). He was also angry about the packed state of the city graveyards, expressed in *Bleak House* when "Nemo" is buried in a particularly fetid, rat-infested one, and in numerous other texts.

92 See Richardson, *Death, Dissection and the Destitute*, and Puckle, *Funeral Customs*.

93 See Puckle, *Funeral Customs*, and Richardson, *Death, Dissection and the Destitute*, for more about funeral feasts and the practice of "sin eating."

94 Dickens, *The Uncommercial Traveller*, 196.

95 George Levine, writing of *Our Mutual Friend*, makes a related point: "Death would be perfect if one could be alive in it." See *Dying to Know*, 159.

96 Gallagher, *The Body Economic*, 93.

97 Ibid., 96.

98 Quoted in Richardson, *Death, Dissection and the Destitute*, 168–9.

99 Patricia Fumerton, in *Cultural Aesthetics: Renaissance Literature and the Practice of Social Ornament* (Chicago: University of Chicago Press, 1991), relates an earlier example of using the body to bind books. When Charles I was executed, a poem "upon the King's Book (the Eikon Basilike) bound up in a cover," was "coloured with his blood" (9).

100 "Books Bound in Human Skins," *New York Times* (Jan. 25, 1886). This rumor obviously contained a political agenda, and a *Blackwoods* lampoon of 1838 that recommended the use of pauper's skin for leather also referenced class injustice, similar to Swift's "A Modest Proposal."

101 This edition dates from 1816, but was rebound by Zaehnsdorf in 1893 and is now at the John Hay Library, Brown University.

102 A copy of Vesalius's anatomy book, *De Humani Corporis Fabrica*, bound anthropodermically in the nineteenth century, can be found at the John Hay Library, and several medical books (to give an American example) at The College of Physicians, Philadelphia, are trimmed with the same material. A particularly strange example of binding mirroring content is a copy of

Thomas à Kempis's *Imitation of Christ* bound in human skin, which the late Victorian pornographer Leonard Smithers claimed to own. For Hankey, see the journals of Edmond and Jules Goncourt, *Pages from the Goncourt Journals*, ed. Robert Baldick (New York: NYRB, 2006) and Ian Gibson, *The Erotomaniac: The Secret Life of Henry Spencer Ashbee* (New York: De Capo, 2001).

103 "Human Skin as Binding," *Bookworm: An Illustrated Treasury of Old-Time Literature* (Jan. 1, 1891), 148.

104 The account of Corder's trial is written by the journalist James Curtis, and the surgeon who dissected him, George Creed, tanned the skin. The *Bookworm* reported in 1893 that the library of the Prince of Wales at Marlborough House contained two volumes made from the skin of Mary Patman (sometimes called Bateman), a Yorkshire witch hanged for murder in the early nineteenth century. "Human Skin as a Binding," *Bookworm: An Illustrated Treasury of Old-Time Literature* (Jan. 1, 1893), 103. Other examples include a book bound with the skin of George Cudmore, who poisoned his wife and was executed for it in 1830; an edition of Samuel Johnson's dictionary bound in the skin of James Johnson (relation unknown), hanged in Norwich in 1818; and a pocketbook made from the skin of William Burke, after he was hanged in 1829 for murder (now at the Museum of the Royal College of Surgeons, Edinburgh).

105 Dickens, "Visit to Newgate," *Sketches by Boz*, 76.

106 The full title of the volumes are *Narrative of the life of James Allen: alias George Walton, alias Jonas Pierce, alias James H. York, alias Burley Grove, the highwayman: being his death-bed confession, to the warden of the Massachusetts State Prison*. See Oliver Robinson, "Bound for Glory: The Macabre Practice of Book Bindings Made of Human Skin," *Rare Book Review* 33 (2006), 29–31.

107 Gallagher, *The Body Economic*, 111.

108 Ibid., 117.

109 Matthews, *Poetical Remains*, 3. She goes on to make the fascinating observation about a poet's book of poetry when she was recently deceased: "In such a memorial context the title-page became legible as a headstone inscription—name, epigraph, date of publication as compared with name, epitaph, and dates of birth and death: the poet's death invited the reader to respond to the book as he or she would read and contemplate the poet's grave" (5).

110 Quoted in Sanders, *Charles Dickens*, 38.

111 Dickens, *A Tale of Two Cities*, 10.

112 I Corinthians 15:31.

Chapter 4

1 A Catholic relic that relates poetically to devotion to a space linked to the absent is that of Jesus's breath, claimed to have been caught in a little vial.

2 Christ, "Browning's Corpses," 392.

3 Howard Colvin, in *Architecture and the Afterlife* (New Haven, CT: Yale University Press, 1991), remarks that "architecture in Western Europe begins with tombs. The earliest surviving structures that we can recognize were funerary monuments" (1).

4 Gaston Bachelard, in *The Poetics of Space* (Boston: Beacon Press, 1964), has this to say about caskets: "The casket contains the things that are *unforgettable*, unforgettable for us, but also unforgettable for those to whom we are giving our treasures. Here the past, the present and a future are condensed. Thus the casket is memory of what is immemorial" (84).

5 Colvin, *Architecture and the Afterlife*, 106.

6 See Sox, *Relics and Shrines*, 8 and Éric Palazzo, "Relics, Liturgical Space, and the Theology of the Church," *Treasures of Heaven*, 99–102. The 787 AD Second Council of Nicaea, in modern-day Turkey, decreed that every altar must contain the relics of a saint to be consecrated.

7 Colvin, *Architecture and the Afterlife*, 125.

8 Ariès, *The Hour of Our Death*, 41.

9 Ibid., 63.

10 An alternate history of the house or church-shaped shrine comes from the ancient Roman tradition of burying the dead in coffins resembling houses, with sloping roofs and gabled ends. Early Christians followed this practice, which then influenced saints' shrines. See also Arnold Angenendt, "Relics and Their Veneration," *Treasures of Heaven*, who argues that house-shaped shrines and reliquaries referenced the golden houses in heaven that the faithful believed they would inhabit when they arrived (25).

11 According to the museum catalogue, this piece is thought to have been made in the nineteenth century and passed off as a medieval work, partially because there is no means to access the relic. Other examples of building-shaped reliquaries include the now-destroyed shrine of St. Edmund at Bury St. Edmund's and the Spanish reliquary, from the early 1100s, fashioned like a dwelling place with "roof" tiles to hold the remains of Saints Adrian and Natalia (Art Institute of Chicago, 1843.65).

12 The British Museum has a collection of these tokens or badges, including ones from the Holy Land, Windsor, and Walsingham. Some of the Holy Land tokens were made from compacted earth from various sites. The pilgrims scraped a little dust from these tokens into water and then drank it as a form of miraculous "medicine." They were also often worn on the body to increase the blessings they brought for the wearer. See *Treasures of Heaven*, 43–44, 57.

13 Quoted in Sox, *Relics and Shrines*, 25. For the story about the finger-biting bishop, see Peter Manseau, *Rag and Bone* (New York: Henry Holt, 2009), 5. Sometimes stones, earth, and other materials from places like Calvary and the Holy Sepulcher were set into reliquaries, such as the one held at the Katholisches Münsterpfarramt, Zwiefalten, Germany, with stones from these sites behind gems, along with fragments of the True Cross.

14 See Watson, *The Literary Tourist*.

15 See ibid., 56.

16 Watson (*The Literary Tourist*) discusses the relationship between religious and literary pilgrimage, as does Dávidházi, *The Romantic Cult of Shakespeare*. Watson's argument about why literary pilgrimage became popular in the Romantic and Victorian periods follows the historical trajectory of relic culture more generally. She remarks that the pilgrimages came from a new "fixation upon the author's body ... fuelled by the rise in the importance of a newly topographicalized biography as an explanatory mechanism... along with the new 'romantic' sense of the author's subject matter as primarily personal and strongly subjective" (13). See also Paul Westover, *Necromanticism: Traveling to Meet the Dead, 1750–1860* (New York: Palgrave Macmillan, 2012).

17 As discussed in previous chapters, all relics are souvenirs of a sort. In the Musée Carnavalet, Paris, a box is labeled "souvenirs of Louis XVI's family," and it includes hair, bits of clothing, a razor belonging to the King, and other secondary relics. In French, "souvenir" means "remembrance."

18 For more about such studies, see Watson, *The Literary Tourist*, especially 9. T. P. Grinsted describes his project, in the Preface to *The Last Homes of Departed Genius* (London: Routledge, 1867): "Our plan is, first, to sketch the edifice or locality; then, to glance at the busy lives of those who there lie sleeping, and thus to present to the reader their *first and last*" (vi).

19 This history comes from both Ariès, *The Hour of Our Death* and Sox, *Relics and Shrines*.

20 Quoted in Pearce, *On Collecting*, 109.

21 See Colvin, *Architecture and the Afterlife*, Chapter 14, for this history.

22 From Ariès, *The Hour of Our Death*, 526. Visiting the grave of a loved one in order to feel his or her presence was not a common practice during certain spans of Western history. During the tenth century, for example, graves were not often marked, unless the personage was especially important. See Colvin, *Architecture and the Afterlife*.

23 Colvin, *Architecture and the Afterlife*, 331.

24 Ibid., 360. At Sir John Soane's house, in London (now a museum), Soane brought the funerary inside, with the various basement spaces he created called the "Monk's Parlour," "Monk's Cell," and the "Crypt." Here he displayed death masks, a skeleton, a sarcophagus, and memorials for his dead son and wife. He also created an enclosed yard ("Monk's Yard"), seen from many of the house windows, which contained what he called a "ruined cloister" and a grave (with an ostentatious tombstone) for his wife's dog Fanny. There was a certain amount of whimsical satirizing of the fad for Gothicism in these flourishes, although also a love of death-inflected things used as ornament.

25 See Ariès, *The Hour of Our Death*, 153.

26 Hallam and Hockey, *Death, Memory and Material Culture*, 29.

27 Bachelard, *The Poetics of Space*, 8.

28 Giorgio Agamben, *The End of the Poem: Studies in Poetics* (Stanford, CA: Stanford University Press, 1999), 74. J. Hillis Miller expands the definition of the word *prosopopoeia* to give it the larger sense that language has a

connectedness with death. He calls it the "imaginative gesture whereby someone who is absent or dead is brought back to life through an act of language" (47). He continues: "The gesture of prosopopoeia . . . is the projection of a human figure into the emptiness of ultimate loss. This gesture is eternally unsatisfactory. It contains the seed of its own undoing and must continually be done again" (127). See *Versions of Pygmalion*.

29 See Gerald Bruns, *The Material of Poetry* (Athens: University of Georgia Press, 2005).

30 Ariès, *The Hour of Our Death*, 232.

31 Watson, *The Literary Tourist*, 29.

32 From Ariès, *The Hour of Our Death*, 524.

33 In a strange twist of this relation between the elegy and the grave, a memorial at the churchyard of St. Giles's Church, Stoke Poges, the graveyard where Thomas Gray was thought to have written his "Elegy Written in a Country Churchyard," has been erected to commemorate the elegy itself.

34 Tim Armstrong, in his exploration of Hardy's poetry and its relationship to the dead, sees poems as themselves fetishes, "never able to give full reign to the disembodied spirit" (51). See *Haunted Hardy: Poetry, History, Memory* (London: Palgrave, 2000).

35 Matthews, *Poetical Remains*, 261.

36 Robert Bernard Martin, *Tennyson: The Unquiet Heart* (New York: Oxford University Press, 1980), 252. Watson (*The Literary Tourist*) discusses other similar acts of graffiti, especially in Robert Burns's house.

37 See Jalland (*Death in the Victorian Family*), who reports that *In Memoriam* was read widely as consolation literature by the bereaved.

38 There is a long history of scholarship exploring religious faith and doubt in *In Memoriam*. See, for example, Eugene R. August, "Tennyson and Teilhard: The Faith of 'In Memoriam,' " *PMLA* 84.2 (1969), 217–226; Alan Sinfield, *Alfred Tennyson* (Oxford: Blackwell, 1986); Carlisle Moore, "Faith, Doubt, and Mystical Experience in 'In Memoriam,'" *Victorian Studies* 7.2 (1963), 155–169); and Douglas-Fairhurst, *Victorian Afterlives*.

39 James Anthony Froude, *Thomas Carlyle: A History of His Life in London 1834–1881*, vol. 1 (New York: Scribner, 1884), 248. See also Gill, *Wordsworth and the Victorians*, 196.

40 Quoted in Martin, *Tennyson*, 203.

41 See, for instance, James Kissane, "Tennyson: The Passion of the Past and the Curse of Time," *ELH* 32.1 (1965), 85–109.

42 Quoted in Christopher Ricks, *Tennyson* (New York: Macmillan, 1972), 14.

43 Quoted in Martin, *Tennyson*, 557.

44 From a letter Tennyson wrote to Princess Alice (of December 23, 1861), to be passed on to Queen Victoria, as a form of solace after Prince Albert's death. Tennyson is remembering how he felt just after Hallam died. He goes on, "And the record of my grief I put into a book; and I continually receive letters from those who suffer telling me how great a solace this book has been to them." *The Letters of Alfred Lord Tennyson*, Lang, vol. 2, 290.

45 I, lines 9–12. *The Poems of Tennyson*, ed. Christopher Ricks (London: Longman, 1987), 2nd ed. All subsequent references to *In Memoriam* and other Tennyson poems will be from this volume and will be cited parenthetically in the text.

46 For a longer investigation into Tennyson's elegies as epitaph-like, see W. David Shaw, "Tennyson's Late Elegies," *Victorian Poetry* 12:1 (1974), 1–12.

47 Darrel Mansell, "Displacing Hallam's Tomb in Tennyson's *In Memoriam*," *Victorian Poetry* 36.1 (1998), 97–111.

48 Quoted in Gill, *Wordsworth and the Victorians*, 195.

49 Gerhard Joseph remarks that the sword Excalibur, in *The Passing of Arthur*, is a "noncommodifiable object/sign, one that is incommensurable and inalienable," thus making it similar to a relic, as I define it. See "Commodifying Tennyson: The Historical Transformation of 'Brand Loyalty,'" *Victorian Poetry* 34.2 (1996), 134.

50 Tennyson affirms belief in a Christian afterlife repeatedly (although he also affirms doubt). One example of many: "'They do not die / Nor lose their mortal sympathy, / Nor change to us, although they change" (30, lines 22–24).

51 Mansell, "Displacing Hallam's Tomb in Tennyson's *In Memoriam*," 100. Michael Tomko argues that Tennyson's stanzas that deal with geology free him from this dependence on the bodily. "Varieties of Geological Experience: Religion, Body, and Spirit in Tennyson's *In Memoriam* and Lyell's *Principles of Geology*," *Victorian Poetry* 42.2 (2004), 126. Donald Hair's careful and intricately wrought study of Tennyson's delving into ideas about the spirit and soul in *In Memoriam* comes to a sort of middle ground, which is neither materialist nor utterly disembodied. He sees Tennyson wanting to affirm "the particular and substantive nature of everything," which is also "one with the general soul." "Soul and Spirit in *In Memoriam*," *Victorian Poetry* 34.2 (1996), 189. For an argument about Tennyson's ambivalent stance toward the material world's capability to hold onto the past, to be "spiritualized material," see Allison Adler Kroll, "Tennyson and the Metaphysics of Material Culture: The Early Poetry," *Victorian Poetry* 47.3 (2009), 463.

52 Peter Sacks, *The English Elegy: Studies in the Genre from Spenser to Yeats* (Baltimore: Johns Hopkins University Press, 1985), 172.

53 Another important reference to Hallam's hands comes in poem 80: " . . . from the grave / Reach out dead hands to comfort me" (lines 15–16). John Rosenberg also sees this house as a body, a grave, and "an empty tomb." He finds the word "hand" in 42 places. "Stopping for Death: Tennyson's 'In Memoriam,'" *Victorian Poetry* 30.3/4 (1992), 297.

54 Samantha Matthews (*Poetical Remains*) also discusses the importance of Hallam's body to and in the poem.

55 John Rosenberg, "Stopping for Death: Tennyson's 'In Memoriam,' " 295.

56 For discussions of Milton and Tennyson, see especially Mansell, "Displacing Hallam's Tomb in Tennyson's *In Memoriam*" and Joseph Sendry, "*In Memoriam* and *Lycidas*," *PMLA* 82.5 (1967), 440.

57 Milton, *The Complete Poems*, vol. 4 (New York: Collier, 1909), 74, lines 154–158, 163–164.

58 For an exploration of the errors Tennyson made about Hallam's death and funeral, see Mansell, "Displacing Hallam's Tomb in Tennyson's *In Memoriam.*"

59 Patrick Scott, "Tennyson, Lincolnshire, and Provinciality: The Topographical Narrative of *In Memoriam*," *Victorian Poetry* 34.1 (1996), 39–51.

60 Sacks, *The English Elegy*, 191.

61 In a different argument, Sacks discusses the "materiality" of the language of the poem, the "'earthly' nature of language." *The English Elegy*, 193.

62 Rosenberg, "Stopping for Death: Tennyson's 'In Memoriam,'" 313.

63 For discussions of the materiality of Spiritualism and its general history, see Janet Oppenheim, *The Other World: Spiritualism and Psychical Research in England, 1850–1914* (New York: Cambridge University Press, 1985); Alex Owen, *The Darkened Room: Women, Power, and Spiritualism* (Philadelphia: University of Pennsylvania Press, 1990); and Marlene Tromp, *Altered States: Sex, Nation, Drugs, and Self-Transformation in Victorian Spiritualism* (Albany: SUNY Press, 2006).

64 Tim Armstrong discusses Leslie Stephen's idea that animism was part of the Spiritualists' belief in the material embodiment of ghosts. He also explores other philosophical ideas that influenced a Victorian belief in ghosts. See *Haunted Hardy*, especially Chapter 2.

65 Another Spiritualist belief, according to the late-Victorian scholar of folklore Bertram Puckle (*Funeral Customs*), is "that the soul is attached to the body by an elastic cord of unlimited tension to the various parts of the body, and we are told that for a period lasting for days, or weeks . . . the soul is not severed from the body, even if burial has taken place in the meantime" (26–27).

66 Owen, *The Darkened Room*, 55.

67 Quoted in ibid., 53.

68 Quoted in Hibbert, *Queen Victoria*, 293.

69 Quoted in Wolffe, *Great Deaths*, 204–205.

70 Zuzanna Shonfield, *The Precariously Privileged: A Professional Family in Victorian London* (Oxford: Oxford University Press, 1987), 112.

71 Ariès (*The Hour of Our Death*) links the Romantic beautiful death with Spiritualism: "In the beautiful death of the nineteenth and twentieth centuries, the room of the dying man is filled with disembodied friends and relatives who have come from the other world to assist and guide him in this first migration" (460).

72 W. E. Fredeman, "The Letters of Pictor Ignotus: William Bell Scott's Correspondence with Alice Boyd 1859–1884," *Bulletin of the John Rylands Library* 58.2 (1976), 92.

73 Patricia Jalland (*Death in the Victorian Family*) is one; she remarks that many of the members of the Society of Psychical Research, founded in 1882 by Cambridge scientists for the serious study of spiritualist claims, were Christians "haunted by religious doubt . . . seeking empirical evidence of immortality" (366).

74 See Oppenheim, *The Other World*.

75 Christ, "Browning's Corpses," 392.
76 James Kincaid, "Forgetting to Remember: Tennyson's Happy Losses," *Victorian Poetry* 30.3/4 (1992), 201.
77 Timothy Peltason, *Reading In Memoriam* (Princeton, NJ: Princeton University Press, 1985), 48.
78 See Susan Gates, "Poetics, Metaphysics, Genre: The Stanza Form of *In Memoriam*," *Victorian Poetry* 37 (1999), 508.
79 Ricks, *Tennyson*, 228. He also quotes Henry James: "the phrase always seems to me to pause and slowly pivot upon itself, or at most to move backward" (228). And Charles Kingsley, who notes that "the mournful minor rhyme of each first and fourth line always leads the ear to expect something beyond" (228).
80 Sacks, *The English Elegy*, 167.
81 Roland Barthes, *Camera Lucida* (New York: Hill and Wang, 1981), 49.
82 Ibid., 77.
83 Ibid., 71.
84 Ibid., 75.
85 Peltason, *Reading In Memoriam*, 21–22.
86 Fuss, "Corpse Poem," 27.
87 Sacks, *The English Elegy*, 168–169.
88 Still, as mentioned in Chapter 1, Victorian elegies (and shrines) generally have a less triumphant, sublime air; they are, for the most part, more gentle and—in certain cases—shot through with doubt. Stephen Gill (*Wordsworth and the Victorians*) comments that, unlike the Romantics, Tennyson did not have the same kind of confidence or affirmation. The speaker is "acutely aware of his inadequacy to deal with the whole compass of the universe. Vulnerable, hesitant, and doubting, the speaker registers through much of the poem the fragility of his sense of sense" (203). He continues: "What emerges most strongly is a sense that consolation has been wrested from loss, not, as in 'Tintern Abbey,' that loss is fundamental to growth and to Nature's power" (204).

Chapter 5

1 Lines 5, 2. *The Complete Poems of Thomas Hardy*, ed. James Gibson (London: Macmillan, 1976), 62. All of Hardy's poems will be from this edition with in-text citations.
2 Tim Armstrong explores Hardy's attempts, in these elegies to Emma, to "engage with memory-traces" and to seek her voice. See *Haunted Hardy*, especially Chapter 6.
3 Hardy, *Woodlanders* (London: Penguin, 1994), 125.
4 In *The Mayor of Casterbridge*, he describes the inhabitants occasionally uncovering Roman graves, something Hardy himself did when building his home Max Gate, just outside of Dorchester.
5 Hotz, *Literary Remains*, 119.

6 Gillian Beer, *Darwin's Plots: Evolutionary Narrative in Darwin, George Eliot and Nineteenth-Century Fiction* (New York: Cambridge University Press, 2009), 224.

7 Claire Tomalin, *Thomas Hardy* (New York: Penguin, 2006), 281.

8 See ibid.

9 Hardy, *Far From the Madding Crowd* (London: Macmillan, 1975), 434. All subsequent citations will be from this edition and will be indicated in the text parenthetically.

10 Most of Hardy's works contain locks of hair and secondary relics (objects that have touched the beloved body). In the short story "An Imaginative Woman," a lock of hair from a dead man represents unrequited passion. Ella falls for a young poet, but never meets him. When he dies, she pines over a lock of his hair. The prosperous Mayor of Casterbridge must give up all his possessions when he becomes a bankrupt, but when he hands over his watch, he keeps back the hair chain his lover Lucetta wove him.

11 Of Saint Thérèse of Lisieux, called "the Little Flower," we still have a cascade of hair cut when she entered the convent as well as a lily made from a lock of her hair. These and other relics of the saint are on display at the Carmelite Convent of Lisieux, France. See Cruz, *Relics*, 298.

12 According to Joan Evans, this amulet was buried with Charlemagne at Aix-la-Chapelle in 814 and rediscovered when the tomb was opened by Otto III in 1000. Preserved in the treasury of the Cathedral, it was given by the canons to Empress Josephine in 1804, who wore it at her coronation, set into her crown. See Evans, *A History of Jewellery*, 42. See also James Robinson, "From Altar to Amulet: Relics, Portability, and Devotion," *Treasures of Heaven*, 113.

13 Both the Victoria and Albert and the British Museum have numerous examples of reliquary jewelry containing saints' remains (and churches and museums throughout Europe contain hundreds more). For examples of enkolpia and phylacteries, see Derek Krueger, "The Religion of Relics in Late Antiquity and Byzantium," and James Robinson, "From Altar to Amulet: Relics, Portability, and Devotion," *Treasures of Heaven*, 14–15; 44–51; and 112–115.

14 The information about this jewel (and a picture of it) comes from Diana Scarisbrick, *Ancestral Jewels* (London: Deutsch, 1989). See also Scarisbrick, "The Aberdeen Jewel," *Burlington Magazine* 130 (1988), 427–428.

15 Scarisbrick, *Ancestral Jewels*, 67–68. One of these hair rings can be seen at the Victoria and Albert Museum.

16 See Patricia Fumerton, *Cultural Aesthetics*, 9.

17 Quoted in Pascoe, *The Hummingbird Cabinet*, 59.

18 Frank Herrmann, *The English as Collectors: A Documentary Chrestomathy* (New York: Norton, 1972), tells some interesting stories of other royal or noble locks. For pictures of some royal reliquary jewelry, see Geoffrey Munn, *The Triumph of Love: Jewelry 1530–1930* (London: Thames and Hudson, 1993).

19 See Scarisbrick (*Ancestral Jewels*) for a picture of this piece, 122. Another example of the popularity of inscribing jewelry to mark an important event

can be found in the *Illustrated London News* in 1868. They report that "it is the fashion this year for ladies to wear lockets on black velvet ribbons round their necks – the more lockets you can collect and wear the finer you are. Each locket represents an event such as a birthday or anniversary, a bet – any excuse serves as the pretext for giving a locket." Scarisbrick points out that the majority of these lockets held hair.

20 Quoted in Bury, *Jewellery*, 664. Irene Guggenheim Navarro ("Hairwork of the 19th Century") discusses the many hair jewels given by Queen Victoria as well as those she received.

21 See Bury (*Sentimental Jewelry*) and Evans (*A History of Jewellery 1100–1870*). For the most brilliant writing on the history of hair jewelry and its meanings, see Marcia Pointon, "Materializing Mourning: Hair, Jewellery and the Body," *Material Memories: Design and Evocation*, ed. Marius Kwint et al. (New York: Oxford University Press, 1999); "Wearing Memory: Mourning, Jewellery and the Body," *Trauer Tragen—Trauer Zeigen: Inszenierungen der Geschlechter*, ed. Gisela Ecker (Munich: Fink, 1999); and *Brilliant Effects: A Cultural History of Gem Stones and Jewellery* (New Haven, CT: Yale University Press, 2009).

22 The famous line, "Bracelet of bright haire about the bone" (line 6) comes from "The Relique." In "The Funerall," it is "That subtle wreath of hair which crowns my arm" (line 3). Donne based his idea for "The Relique" on a Latin poem by the Augustan Propertius, showing his awareness of a much longer history of secular hair jewelry. Another example from the same period is a poem attributed to Shakespeare (convincing scholarly work has been done recently arguing that this poem is not by Shakespeare), called "A Lover's Complaint":

> And, lo, behold these talents of their hair,
> With twisted metal amorously impleached,
> I have received from many a several fair,
> Their kind acceptance weepingly beseeched
> With the annexions of fair gems enriched,
> And deep-brained sonnets that did amplify
> Each stone's dear nature, worth, and quality. (lines 204–210, from
> *William Shakespeare: The Complete Sonnets and Poems*)

I thank James Bednarz for this reference.

23 The growth of the Victorian hair jewelry industry midcentury is discussed in Holm, "Sentimental Cuts: Eighteenth–Century Mourning Jewelry with Hair"; Pamela Miller, "Hair Jewelry as Fetish," *Objects of Special Devotion: Fetishes and Fetishism in Popular Culture*, ed. Ray B. Browne (Bowling Green, OH: Bowling Green University Press, n.d.); Diana Cooper and Norman Battershill, *Victorian Sentimental Jewellery* (London: Newton Abbot, 1972); and Bury, *Jewellery: 1789–1910*.

24 Navarro, "Hairwork of the 19th Century." Bury (*Jewellery: 1789–1910*) also mentions Forrer and Garrard as the best-known hairworkers midcentury.

25 See the *Official Descriptive and Illustrated Catalogue of the Great Exhibition of 1851* (London: Spicer Brothers, 1851), which lists 11 displays of hair art. Navarro, "Hairwork of the 19th Century" and Bury (*Jewellery: 1789–1910*) also discuss the hair at the Great Exhibition and the medals won by Forrer. For a French example of a hair portrait, see Flaubert's *Madame Bovary* (New York: Penguin, 2002), 36. Emma has a memorial card for her mother made out of the dead woman's hair.

26 *Catalogue of the Great Exhibition of 1851*, 1223.

27 For a discussion of hairwork and gender, see Beverly Gordon, "Woman's Domestic Body," *Winterhur Portfolio* 31.4 (1996) and Talia Schaffer, *Novel Craft: Victorian Domestic Handicraft and Nineteenth-Century Fiction* (New York: Oxford University Press, 2011), Chapter 5. Elisabeth Gitter calls up the long history and mythology of women spinning in her discussion of hair during the Victorian period. "The Power of Women's Hair in the Victorian Imagination," *PMLA* 99 (1984), 936–954.

28 One might simply hold onto a lock of hair, kept in an envelope, a diary or book, or even a desk drawer. A particularly poignant instance of an unworked, unbejewelled lock is kept at Cannon Hall in Yorkshire, labeled "My dear little Catherine's hair cut off the morning I lost her, Nov. 20, 1795."

29 This amethyst bracelet is at the Brontë Parsonage Museum, J14, where there are around 30 curls of hair or pieces of hair jewelry, either from the heads of the Brontë family or from friends and relatives. Helen Sheumaker history of hairwork in America describes different types of hairwork and how these pieces were made (and by whom). *Love Entwined: The Curious History of Hairwork in America* (Philadelphia: University of Pennsylvania Press, 2007). Although the American use and history of hairwork was different from the British one, the patterns and manufacture were similar.

30 Victoria and Albert Museum, M.21–1972. To return to an idea put forth in Chapter 1, the hair jewelry at the Victoria and Albert is positively "ghettoized." The major pieces of the museum's jewelry collection are openly displayed on the first floor. Up some rickety spiral stairs is the mezzanine section, where few of the normal museum goers venture. Here are kept the "minor" or leftover pieces. But even here one has a difficult time finding the hair jewelry. They are stored in the drawers of a black cabinet that doesn't at first seem to have drawers, so well are they hidden. This is presumably because of their light-sensitive nature, but they are so successfully secreted that there must be something else at stake.

31 Wilkie Collins, *Hide and Seek* (Oxford: Oxford, 1993), 256.

32 *Our Mutual Friend* (New York: Penguin, 1997), 218. Miss Peecher, the tidy schoolmistress who is in love with Headstone, wishes she could be his hair-guard. "The decent hair-guard that went round his neck and took care of his decent silver watch was an object of envy to her. So would Miss Peecher have gone round his neck and taken care of him" (219). Helen Huntingdon in Anne Brontë's *Tenant of Wildfell Hall* (New York: Barnes and Noble, 2006) also wears a hair-chain.

33 Edward, in love with Elinor Dashwood, initially lies, claiming the hair to be that of his sister Fanny. Both Elinor and Marianne believe the hair is Elinor's, but as the plot unfolds, they discover it belongs to the love of Edward's youth, the horrid Lucy Steele.

34 Male womanizers sometimes collected the locks of their many lovers. In a cynical rendering of what had become so commonplace it was ripe for parody, Flaubert describes the oversentimental love between Madame Bovary and her rake Rudolphe by remarking, "great handfuls of hair had been cut off" (157). Later, Rudolphe opens a box where he keeps the mementos of his past lovers: "he began to hunt through this mound of papers and things, turning up haphazard bunches of flowers, a garter . . . and locks of hair – what hair! Brown and blonde; some, even, caught in the hinges of the tin, broke when he opened it" (187). When George IV died, his large collection of women's hair was found, with "some locks with the powder and pomatum still sticking to them" (quoted in Pascoe, *The Hummingbird Cabinet*, 59–60).

35 Jalland (*Death in the Victorian Family*) also discusses how sometimes hair for mourning jewels would be collected well before death, and then divvied up among family members postmortem. Women's informal wills (informal since they couldn't, by law, have formal ones) often included instructions as to whom was to receive snippets of their hair, or premade hair jewelry.

36 Quoted in Jalland, *Death in the Victorian Family*, 298.

37 *Cassell's Household Guide*, 4, 337.

38 *The Family Friend*, 5 (1853), 55.

39 Pointon, "Materializing Mourning: Hair, Jewellery and the Body," 45.

40 Rhoda Broughton, *Cometh Up as a Flower: An Autobiography* (London: Richard Bentley and Son, 1878), 345.

41 Susan Beegel sees this scene's "morbidity" as further proof of Troy's "brand of death-dealing passion" (for Bathsheba as well as Fanny). "Bathsheba's Lovers: Male Sexuality in *Far From the Madding Crowd*," *Sexuality and Victorian Literature*, ed. Don Richard Cox (Knoxville: University of Tennessee Press, 1984), 210. Rosemarie Morgan helpfully details how this passage was severely shortened by Leslie Stephen's editing, due to his squeamishness about the illegitimate baby. The original passage emphasizes more fully the materiality of the two corpses, especially the baby, whose little hands are compared to "mushrooms on a dewy morning." *Cancelled Words: Rediscovering Thomas Hardy* (London: Routledge, 1992), 144.

42 For a fascinating reading of clocks and watches and how, in *Far From the Madding Crowd* and other Hardy novels, they generate comparisons to the human body, see Marjorie Garson, *Hardy's Fables of Integrity: Woman, Body, Text* (New York: Oxford, 1992). This comparison leads her to an argument about gender: Hardy invests his male bodies with a wholeness borrowed from the female ones, expressing an anxiety about bodily integrity.

43 For an exploration of the burial mound and graves more generally in Hardy's poetry and in *Far From the Madding Crowd*, see Catherine Robson, "'Where

Heaves the Turf': Thomas Hardy and the Boundaries of the Earth," *Victorian Literature and Culture* 32.2 (2004), 495–503.

44 Lines 53–56.

45 A number of critics have complicated, rightfully, a simple equation of Hardy's novels with a nostalgia for an earlier time. See especially Peter Widdowson, *Hardy in History: A Study in Literary Sociology* (London: Routledge, 1998) and George Wotton, *Thomas Hardy: Towards a Materialist Criticism* (Totowa, NJ: Barnes and Noble, 1985). I will also complicate this nostalgia, although I will use death culture for my analysis rather than other types of historical or political contexts.

46 Gray, "Elegy Written in a Country Churchyard," line 59. For a further discussion of the relationship between Gray and Hardy, see Dennis Taylor, "Thomas Hardy and Thomas Gray: The Poet's Currency," *ELH* 65.2 (1993), 451–477.

47 The tactual quality of Hardy's writing has been discussed by many. Gillian Beer calls this Hardy's seeking of the "palpable" and Marjorie Garson finds "a peculiarly intense 'skin-sense'" in *Far From the Madding Crowd*. See Beer, *Darwin's Plots*, especially page 227 and Garson, *Hardy's Fables of Integrity*, 38.

48 Other examples include another tent at the fair, the cloth of which "to the eyes of an observer on the outside, became bulged into innumerable pimples ... caused by the various human heads, backs and elbows at high pressure within" (428). A dramatic scene, between Fanny and Troy, begins with description of scenery: "its irregularities were forms without features; suggestive of anything, proclaiming nothing, and without more character than that of being a limit of something else" (130).

49 Quoted in Ian Gregor, *The Great Web: The Form of Hardy's Major Fiction* (London: Faber and Faber, 1974), 61. Gregor remarks that Hardy himself recognized this quality of leaving much unexpressed when he called his novels "a series of seemings."

50 Examples of this appear almost everywhere, such as this description of Bold-wood: "His tone ... was lowness and quiet accentuated: an emphasis of deep meanings, their form, at the same time, being scarcely expressed" (178). Here is Boldwood again: "That stillness, which struck casual observers more than anything else in his character and habit, and seemed so precisely like inan-ition" (171). Oak, not able to speak his passion, is described by these lines from *The Tempest*: "Full of sound and Fury / signifying nothing" (60).

51 For a different reading of the way that bodies in Hardy can be "read," see Tess O'Toole's exploration of genealogy as a trace written on the faces of characters. She finds that genealogical narratives often end in the corpse of a woman, using Fanny and her child as examples. *Genealogy and Fiction in Hardy: Family Lineage and Narrative Lives* (New York: St. Martin's, 1997).

52 See especially Gillian Beer, *Darwin's Plots* and Tim Armstrong, *Haunted Hardy*, who explores the influence on Hardy of Comte's theories of fetishism, in Chapter 2.

53 Hardy, *Mayor of Casterbridge* (New York: Penguin, 1997), 116.
54 Hardy, *Woodlanders* (London: Penguin, 1994), 52.
55 This helps explain why so many characters are described as "shapes," especially Fanny, who is made an object before she really becomes one in death, and Troy, who emerges from the earth, well before he goes down into it for good.
56 Armstrong, *Haunted Hardy*, 49. Armstrong discusses in particular Hardy's poem "Old Furniture," which invokes "relics of householdry / That date from the days of their mothers' mothers":

> I see the hands of the generations
>   That owned each shiny familiar thing
> In play on its knobs and indentations. (quoted in Armstrong, 49)

57 Brandon Bennett, "Hardy's Noble Melancholics," *NOVEL* 27.1 (1993), 32.
58 For a European example, see the short story "Le Chevelure" by Guy de Maupassant, where a man falls obsessively in love with an antique tress of hair, found in a hidden drawer of an old desk.
59 Something of sympathetic magic can be found in George Eliot's *Romola* (Philadelphia: Lippincott, 1902) when the title character leaves a lock of her hair for some children, "'I must go away from you now,' she said, 'but I will leave this lock of hair that it may remind you of me, because if you are ever in trouble you can think that perhaps God will send me to take care of you again'" (485).
60 Freud's theories on the sexual fetish are relevant here: a part of the body (or its clothing) are substituted for the whole. The hair jewel as a fetish is discussed extensively in Miller, "Hair Jewelry as Fetish," and Marcia Pointon, "Wearing Memory: Mourning, Jewellery and the Body."
61 *No Name* (New York: Harper and Brothers, 1893), 189.
62 Also see Thomas Henry Lister's *Granby* (London: Colvin, 1829). When the hero pores passionately and repeatedly over the glossy dark lock collected from his love, which he keeps in his pocketbook, it is "as if he were trying to conjure up the actual presence of the donor" (29).
63 *Villette* (New York: Penguin, 1979), 532. The widowed Lady Castlewood, in Thackeray's *Henry Esmond*, has a "little picture or emblem which [she] loved always to have before her eyes on waking, and in which the hair of her lord and her children was worked together." *The History of Henry Esmond* (London: Macmillan, 1905), 353. Hair trinkets abound in Thackeray.
64 A fairly common instance of the practice today is the use of copper bracelets to ward off arthritis. For the magic of gems in the Middle Ages, see Martina Bagnoli, "The Stuff of Heaven: Materials and Craftsmanship in Medieval Reliquaries," *Treasures of Heaven*, 138–139.
65 Numerous examples of talismanic jewelry can be seen at the Victoria and Albert Museum, including at least four toadstone rings. The museum also has a number of amulets containing the teeth or horns of various animals – such as wolf or deer teeth – also thought to be protective or nurturing.

66 *The Lovels of Arden* (New York: Harper, 1872), 139.

67 In his argument about how history "sits" on different gendered bodies, Jules David Law comes to a similar conclusion: "Hardy is extraordinarily sensitive to the temporal sedimentation of material culture, and to the way it expresses an archaeology of social relations" (227). "Sleeping Figures: Hardy, History, and the Gendered Body," *ELH* 65.1 (1998), 223–257. Michael Goss explores the types of time – natural and human-created – and the effects such times have on different characters in *Far From the Madding Crowd*. "Aspects of Time in *Far From the Madding Crowd*," *Thomas Hardy Journal* 6.3 (1990), 43–53.

68 Tim Armstrong calls this a "double displacement, a double absence." *Haunted Hardy*, 152.

69 Geoffrey Batchen, *Forget Me Not: Photography and Remembrance* (New York: Princeton Architectural Press, 2004), 67. He goes on, "Collapsing distinctions between being and becoming, this locket reminds us that historical identity is always a manifestation of this kind of temporal oscillation."

70 #M. 11–1972

71 Pointon, "Wearing Memory: Mourning, Jewellery and the Body," 66.

72 Barthes, *Camera Lucida*, 96.

73 Bury, in *Jewellery: 1789–1010*, discusses the scandal of replacing the beloved's hair with anonymous hair as does Pointon, "Wearing Memory: Mourning, Jewellery and the Body." For a similar occurrence in the hairwork industry in America, see Sheumaker, *Love Entwined*. Both of these books also discuss the busy traffic in human hair during the nineteenth century. The most popular hairwork instructional manual of the day, Alexanna Speight's *The Lock of Hair* (London: Goubaud and Son, 1872), has an extensive discussion on the shearing of women's hair for sale.

74 *The Family Friend* 5 (1853), 55.

75 *Cassell's Home Journal* also plays on these fears, as do all of the hairwork instructional manuals.

76 Bury (*Sentimental Jewellery*) describes the mass-production of ready-made receptacles for hair, produced so cheaply almost everyone could afford them.

77 Sheumaker, *Love Entwined*, 21.

78 The members of this set were all relic lovers. May Morris, for instance, had a "gold relic containing hair of my late father." Quoted in Bury, "Rossetti and His Jewellery," *The Burlington Magazine* 118.875 (1976), 96. This is probably the piece pictured on the cover of this book, from the Victoria and Albert Museum: a gold case containing William Morris's hair, probably made by Charles James Fox. It is inscribed: "For folk unborn this shrine doth hold / Thy silvered lock, Oh! Heart of gold / Should time's hand mar it, yet thy mind / Shall live, in deathless words enshrined."

79 This quote is from the *Life* ostensibly written by Hardy's wife Florence, but widely understood by scholars to be written by Hardy himself. Florence Emily Hardy, *The Life of Thomas Hardy* (London: Macmillan, 1962), 116.

80 Elaine Scarry explores Hardy's use of bodies to celebrate the activity of work, in "Work and the Body in Hardy," *Representations* 3 (1983), 90–123.

81 Hairwork can be linked not only to the subgenre of the sensation novel, but also to detective fiction. Other Collins novels that use hairwork as a plot device include *Basil, The Dead Secret, The Woman in White, Man and Wife, Poor Miss Finch, The Law and the Lady* (in which the Major has a hair album of his lovers' hair), *The Haunted Hotel,* and *After Dark* (in which a teacher wears three small bracelets with the hair of her three pupils worked into them). Also, see the "long tress of hair wrapped in silver paper" of Braddon's *Lady Audley's Secret.*

82 Wilkie Collins, *Hide and Seek* (New York: Oxford, 2009), 68.

83 Ibid., 118.

84 Holm ("Sentimental Cuts: Eighteenth Century Mourning Jewelry with Hair") points out that "the wearer of remembrance jewelry presents herself as a participant in a hidden intimate network, from which other viewers are excluded. Mourning jewels are exhibited secrets" (140).

85 Collins, *Hide and Seek,* 143–144.

86 In an interesting plot twist, her uncle – Matthew Grice – was scalped by "Indians" when traveling in the Amazon. Much is made of the skullcap he wears because of this and the fact that all his hair with the flesh attached to it is swinging on a pole somewhere in South America.

87 Ariès, *The Hour of Our Death,* 15.

88 Most writing on Hardy discusses this pessimism, but see especially Gillian Beer, in *Darwin's Plots,* who calls it, "a sense that the laws of life are themselves flawed" (222). We could also consider the agency Hardy gave to death as part of his much-discussed theory of an "Immanent Will," a nebulous force that he presented as malign to individuality. Yet I see it as part of a philosophy distinct from this other sort of fate. In addition, the development of this theory came well after the publication of *Far From the Madding Crowd,* so it isn't as relevant to an exploration of this earlier novel.

89 Hotz, *Literary Remains,* 100.

90 Armstrong, *Haunted Hardy,* 10.

91 Ibid., 18.

92 Beer, *Darwin's Plots,* 224. Mary Jacobus also explores Hardy's "literary post-humousness" and his temporal looping, although her conclusions bring her to a statement about "mid-Victorian gloom" and an evacuation of time, meaning, and materiality. See "Hardy's Magian Retrospect," *Essays in Criticism* 32.3 (1982), 258–279.

93 J. Hillis Miller, *Thomas Hardy: Distance and Desire* (Cambridge, MA: Harvard, 1970), 69–70.

94 Brooks, *Reading for the Plot.*

95 Martin Heidegger, *Being and Time,* trans. Joan Stambaugh (Albany: State University of New York Press, 1996), 258.

96 Ibid., 245.

97 Ibid., 244.

98 This is similar to what Beer calls Hardy's "passion for particularity." *Darwin's Plots,* 240.

Afterword

1 Oliver Wendell Holmes, "The Stereoscope and the Stereograph," *The Atlantic Monthly*, 3 (1859), 747.
2 Michael Millgate, *Testamentary Acts: Browning, Tennyson, James, Hardy* (London: Oxford University Press, 1992), 143. See also Michael Millgate, *Thomas Hardy: A Biography Revisited* (New York: Oxford University Press, 2004).
3 Millgate, *Testamentary Acts*, 145.
4 Millgate, *Thomas Hardy*, 535.
5 Millgate, *Testamentary Acts*, 146.
6 Tomalin, *Thomas Hardy*, 372.
7 See Michael Wheeler, *Death and the Future Life in Victorian Literature and Theology* (New York: Cambridge University Press, 1990) on secularization's affect on death culture. See also Elisabeth Bronfen, *Over Her Dead Body: Death, Femininity and the Aesthetic* (Manchester, UK: Manchester University Press, 1992).
8 J. Hillis Miller, *The Disappearance of God*, 7.
9 Jose Harris, *Private Lives, Public Spirit: A Social History of Britain 1870–1914* (Oxford and New York: Oxford University Press, 1993), 253.
10 Jalland, *Death in the Victorian Family*, 6. See also Audrey Linkman, *Photography and Death* (London: Reaktion, 2011), 69.
11 Ariès, *The Hour of Our Death*, 564.
12 Ibid., 373.
13 Ibid., 374. Jay Winter remarks that "those who tried to reunite the living and the dead, to retrieve their bodies and to give them a secure and identifiable resting place, faced staggering problems." *Sites of Memory, Sites of Mourning: The Great War In European Cultural History* (New York: Cambridge University Press, 1995), 28.
14 See Paul Fussell, *The Great War and Modern Memory* (New York: Oxford University Press, 1975), especially Chapter 2, and Joanna Bourke, *Dismembering the Male: Men's Bodies, Britain and the Great War* (London: Reaktion, 1996), Chapter 5.
15 Jalland, *Death in the Victorian Family*, 7.
16 Fussell, *The Great War*, 116–117.
17 Bourke, *Dismembering the Male*, 221.
18 Ibid., 223–225.
19 Ibid., 225.
20 Linkman, *Photography and Death*, 131. Linkman calls this the first photo to appear in a publication, but the photographer Anna Atkins published *British Algae*, illustrated with her own cyanotypes, in 1843.
21 Helen Groth explores the popular Victorian practice of reproducing photos of the gravestones and "homes and haunts" of celebrities in books on tourism and anthologies of poetry. See *Victorian Photography and Literary Nostalgia* (London: Oxford University Press, 2003), 40–41, 74–75, 77.

22 Linkman, *Photography and Death*, 10.

23 Stanley Burns, *Sleeping Beauty II: Grief, Bereavement and the Family in Memorial Photography, American and European Traditions* (New York: Burns Archive Press, 2002).

24 Linkman, *Photography and Death*, 20.

25 Ibid., 52.

26 Barthes, *Camera Lucida*, 80–81.

27 Ibid., 79.

28 These quotes are from the following sources: Susan Sontag, *On Photography* (New York: Farrar, Straus and Giroux, 1977), 154; Rosalind Krauss, *The Originality of the Avant-Garde and Other Modernist Myths* (Cambridge: MIT Press, 1984), 112; and Batchen, *Forget Me Not*, 74.

29 Elizabeth Barrett Browning to Mary Russell Mitford, December 7, 1843. *The Letters of Elizabeth Barrett Browning to Mary Russell Mitford 1836–1854*, ed. Meredith B. Raymond and Mary Rose Sullivan (Winfield, KS.: Armstrong Browning Library of Baylor University, The Browning Institute, Wedgestone Press, and Wellesley College, 1983), 358. For further discussions about the Victorian attitude toward photography as a memory technology, see Groth, *Victorian Photography and Literary Nostalgia* and Nancy Armstrong, *Fiction in the Age of Photography: The Legacy of British Realism* (Cambridge, MA: Harvard University Press, 2000).

30 Batchen, *Forget Me Not*, 14.

31 Ibid.

32 For pictures of such encased photo reliquaries, see Batchen, *Forget Me Not*; Burns, *Sleeping Beauty* and *Sleeping Beauty II*.

33 For examples of these, see Batchen, *Forget Me Not*, and Burns, *Sleeping Beauty II*.

34 An English example of a painted postmortem photo is in the Burns Archive, from around 1867. See plate 49, Burns, *Sleeping Beauty II*.

35 Batchen, *Forget Me Not*, 24–25. Burns, in *Sleeping Beauty II*, also explores painted and collaged photos.

36 Elizabeth Edwards and Janice Hart, *Photographs, Objects, Histories: On the Materiality of Images* (New York: Routledge, 2004), 11.

37 Batchen, *Forget Me Not*, 49.

38 Groth, *Victorian Photography and Literary Nostalgia*, 24–25. Groth describes many Victorian reactions to photography, however; this unease with it was one response among many.

39 Unless the photograph was considered an art object, like Julia Margaret Cameron's work, which meant that the material surface of the photograph mattered. But the photographs I'm referring to here are sentimental ones, made to remember the person and time period pictured.

40 However, this was complicated by the fact that Victorian photography wasn't the simple process of snapshots of today. It took a good deal of preparation, hard work, expertise, and complicated developing, thus in some ways creating its own reality.

41 Batchen, *Forget Me Not*, 48.

42 Ibid., 78.

43 Ibid., 95.

44 Fussell, *The Great War*, 3.

45 Ibid., 7.

46 Eduardo Cadava, "Words of Light: Theses on the Philosophy of History," *Diacritics*, 22, 3–4 (1992): 90.

47 Unless they are set into gravestones, an occasional practice in nineteenth-century Britain.

48 Armstrong, *Haunted Hardy*, 59. See also Chéroux, Clément, Andreas Fischer, et al., eds. *The Perfect Medium: Photography and the Occult* (New Haven, CT: Yale University Press, 2005).

49 Quoted in Douglas-Fairhurst, 1.

50 Armstrong, *Haunted Hardy*, 56. For late nineteenth- and early twentieth-century technology's linkages to death and the body, see also Pamela Thurschwell, *Literature, Technology, and Magical Thinking, 1880–1920* (New York: Cambridge University Press, 2001).

51 Jonathan Crary, *Techniques of the Observer: On Vision and Modernity in the Nineteenth Century* (Cambridge, MA: MIT Press, 1990), 10.

52 Peter Stallybrass, "Marx's Coat," *Border Fetishisms: Material Objects in Unstable Spaces*, ed. Patricia Spyer (New York: Routledge, 1998), 185.

53 Tim Armstrong, *Modernism, Technology and the Body: A Cultural Study* (Cambridge: Cambridge University Press, 1998), 78.

54 Ibid., 81.

55 Alexander Nagel argues that works of art gained a sort of relic status when relics were demoted. See "The Afterlife of the Reliquary," *Treasures of Heaven*, 214. In a similar fashion, reliquaries and what I have called "celebrity" relics increasingly entered museums, taking on another life there, one that privileged looking rather than touching.

Bibliography

Ackroyd, Peter. *Dickens*. New York: Harper Collins, 1990.

Agamben, Giorgio. *The End of the Poem: Studies in Poetics*. Stanford, CA: Stanford University Press, 1999.

Altick, Richard D. *Lives and Letters*. New York: Knopf, 1965.

Ariès, Philippe. *The Hour of Our Death*. New York: Knopf, 1981.

Images of Man and Death. Cambridge, MA: Harvard University Press, 1985.

Armstrong, Nancy. *Fiction in the Age of Photography: The Legacy of British Realism*. Cambridge, MA: Harvard University Press, 2000.

Armstrong, Tim. *Haunted Hardy: Poetry, History, Memory*. New York: Palgrave, 2000.

Modernism, Technology and the Body: A Cultural Study. Cambridge: Cambridge University Press, 1998.

August, Eugene R. "Tennyson and Teilhard: The Faith of 'In Memoriam.'" *PMLA* 84.2 (1969): 217–226.

Bachelard, Gaston. *The Poetics of Space*. Boston: Beacon Press, 1964.

Bagnoli, Martina, Holger A. Klein, C. Griffith Mann, and James Robinson, eds. *Treasures of Heaven: Saints, Relics, and Devotion in Medieval Europe*. New Haven, CT: Yale University Press, 2010.

Barker, Juliet. *The Brontës*. New York: St. Martin's, 1994.

Barnard, John. *John Keats*. Cambridge: Cambridge University Press, 1987.

Barthes, Roland. *Camera Lucida*. New York: Hill and Wang, 1981.

Bataille, Georges. *Literature and Evil: Essays*. London: Boyars, 1997.

Batchen, Geoffrey. *Forget Me Not: Photography and Remembrance*. New York: Princeton Architectural Press, 2004.

Bebbington, D. W. *Evangelicalism in Modern Britain: A History from the 1730s to the 1980s*. London: Unwin Hyman, 1989.

Becker, Edwin, and Julian Treuherz, eds. *Dante Gabriel Rossetti*. London: Thames and Hudson, 2003.

Beegel, Susan. "Bathsheba's Lovers: Male Sexuality in *Far From the Madding Crowd*." *Sexuality and Victorian Literature*. Ed. Don Richard Cox. Knoxville: University of Tennessee Press, 1984.

Beer, Gillian. *Darwin's Plots: Evolutionary Narrative in Darwin, George Eliot and Nineteenth-Century Fiction*. New York: Cambridge University Press, 2009.

Benjamin, Walter. *Illuminations.* Ed. Hannah Arendt and trans. Harry Zohn. New York: Schocken, 1968.

Bennett, Andrew. *Keats, Narrative and Audience: The Posthumous Life of Writing.* Cambridge: Cambridge University Press, 1994.

Romantic Poets and the Culture of Posterity. Cambridge: Cambridge University Press, 1999.

Bennett, Brandon. "Hardy's Noble Melancholics." *NOVEL* 27.1 (1993): 24–39.

Bersani, Leo. *A Future for Astyanax: Character and Desire in Literature.* Boston: Little Brown, 1976.

Bloch, Maurice, and Jonathan Parry. *Death and the Regeneration of Life.* Cambridge: Cambridge University Press, 1982.

"Books Bound in Human Skins." *New York Times* 25 Jan. (1886), 5.

Bourke, Joanna. *Dismembering the Male: Men's Bodies, Britain and the Great War.* London: Reaktion, 1996.

Braddon, M. E. *The Lovels of Arden.* New York: Harper, 1872.

Bradley, Ian. *The Call to Seriousness: The Evangelical Impact on the Victorians.* New York: Macmillan, 1976.

Briggs, Asa. *Victorian Things.* London: B.T. Batsford, 1988.

Bronfen, Elisabeth. *Over Her Dead Body: Death, Femininity and the Aesthetic.* Manchester, UK: Manchester University Press, 1992.

Brontë, Anne. *Tenant of Wildfell Hall.* New York: Barnes and Noble, 2006.

Brontë, Charlotte, and Emily Brontë. *The Belgian Essays.* Ed. Sue Lonoff. New Haven, CT: Yale University Press, 1996.

Brontë, Charlotte. *Villette.* New York: Penguin, 1979.

Brontë, Emily. *Wuthering Heights.* Ed. Beth Newman. Peterborough, Ontario: Broadview, 2000.

Brooks, Peter. *Reading for the Plot: Design and Intention in Narrative.* Cambridge, MA: Harvard University Press, 1984.

Broughton, Rhoda. *Cometh Up as a Flower: An Autobiography.* London: Richard Bentley and Son, 1878.

Brown, Bill. *A Sense of Things: The Object Matter of American Literature.* Chicago: University of Chicago Press, 2003.

Brown, Peter. *The Cult of Saints.* Chicago: University of Chicago Press, 1981.

Browning, Elizabeth Barrett. *The Letters of Elizabeth Barrett Browning to Mary Russell Mitford 1836–1854.* Ed. Meredith B. Raymond and Mary Rose Sullivan. Winfield, KS: Armstrong Browning Library of Baylor University, The Browning Institute, Wedgestone Press and Wellesley College, 1983.

Bruns, Gerald. *The Material of Poetry.* Athens: University of Georgia Press, 2005.

Burns, Stanley. *Sleeping Beauty: Memorial Photography in America.* Altadena, CA: Twelvetrees Press, 1990.

Sleeping Beauty II: Grief, Bereavement and the Family in Memorial Photography, American and European Traditions. New York: Burns Archive Press, 2002.

Bury, Shirley. *An Introduction to Sentimental Jewellery.* London: Owings Mills, 1985.

Jewellery, 1789–1910: The International Era. Woodbridge, UK: Antique Collectors' Club, 1991.

"Rossetti and His Jewellery." *The Burlington Magazine.* 118.875 (1976): 94–102.

Butler, John. *The Quest for Becket's Bones: The Mystery of the Relics of St. Thomas Becket of Canterbury.* New Haven, CT: Yale University Press, 1995.

Bynum, Caroline Walker. *Christian Materiality: An Essay on Religion in Late Medieval Europe.* New York: Zone, 2011.

Cadava, Eduardo. "Words of Light: Theses on the Philosophy of History." *Diacritics* 22.3–4 (1992), 84–114.

Carey, John. *The Violent Effigy: A Study of Dickens's Imagination.* London: Faber and Faber, 1973.

Cassell's Household Guide, being a complete encyclopaedia of domestic and social economy, and forming a guide to every department of practical life. 4 vols. London: Cassell, n.d.

Cecil, David. *Early Victorian Novelists; Essays in Revaluation.* Indianapolis, IN: Bobbs-Merrill, 1935.

Chéroux, Clément, Pierre Apraxine, Andreas Fischer, Denis Canguilhem, Sophie Schmit eds. *The Perfect Medium: Photography and the Occult.* New Haven, CT: Yale University Press, 2005.

Christ, Carol. "Browning's Corpses." *Victorian Poetry* 33 (1995): 391–401.

"Painting the Dead: Portraiture and Necrophilia in Victorian Art and Poetry." *Death and Representation.* Eds. Sarah Webster Goodwin and Elisabeth Bronfen. Baltimore: Johns Hopkins University Press, 1993.

Clymer, Lorna. "Cromwell's Head and Milton's Hair: Corpse Theory in Spectacular Bodies of the Interregnum." *Eighteenth Century: Theory and Interpretation* 40.2 (Summer 1999), 91–112.

Cohen, Deborah. *Household Gods: The British and Their Possessions.* New Haven, CT: Yale University Press, 2006.

Cohen, Emily Jane. "Museums of the Mind: The Gothic and the Art of Memory." *ELH* 62.4 (1995), 883–905.

Collins, Amanda J. "Forging an Afterlife: Mrs. Humphry Ward and the Relics of the Brontës." *Australasian Victorian Studies Journal* 7 (2001), 12–25.

Collins, Philip. *Dickens and Crime.* London: Macmillan, 1962.

Collins, Wilkie. *Hide and Seek.* Oxford: Oxford, 1993.

No Name. New York: Harper and Brothers, 1893.

Colvin, Howard. *Architecture and the Afterlife.* New Haven, CT: Yale University Press, 1991.

Cooper, Diana, and Norman Battershill. *Victorian Sentimental Jewellery.* London: Newton Abbot, 1972.

Cottom, Daniel. "I Think; Therefore, I Am Heathcliff." *ELH* 70.4 (2003), 1067–88.

Unhuman Culture. Philadelphia: University of Pennsylvania Press, 2006.

Cox, Margaret. *Life and Death in Spitalfields.* London: Council for British Archaeology, 1996.

Crary, Jonathan. *Techniques of the Observer: On Vision and Modernity in the Nineteenth Century.* Cambridge, MA: MIT Press, 1990.

Cruz, Joan Carroll. *Relics*. Huntington, IN: Our Sunday Visitor, 1984.

Curl, James. *The Victorian Celebration of Death*. Stroud, Gloucestershire: Sutton, 2000.

D'Arcy, Ella. "The Death Mask." *The Yellow Book* 10 (1896), 265–274.

Davey, Richard. *A History of Mourning*. London: Jay's, 1889.

Dávidházi, Péter. *The Romantic Cult of Shakespeare*. New York: Palgrave, 1998.

Davies, Stevie. *Emily Brontë: Heretic*. London: Women's Press, 1994.

De Quincey, Thomas. *On Murder Considered as One of the Fine Arts*. New York: Putnam, n.d.

DeRosa, Robin. "'To Save the Life of the Novel': Sadomasochism and Representation in 'Wuthering Heights.'" *Rocky Mountain Review of Language and Literature* 52.1 (1998): 27–43.

Dickens, Charles. *A Child's History of England*. London: Bradbury and Evans, 1854.

Dombey and Son. London: Oxford, 1974.

Great Expectations. London: Penguin, 1996.

The Letters of Charles Dickens: The Pilgrim Edition. Ed. Madeline House and Graham Storey. Vol. 1. New York: Oxford, 1981.

Martin Chuzzlewit. New York: Penguin, 2000.

The Old Curiosity Shop. New York: Penguin, 2001.

Oliver Twist. London: Penguin, 2002

Our Mutual Friend. New York: Penguin, 1998.

Pictures from Italy. New York: Penguin, 1998.

The Uncommercial Traveller. London: Chapman and Hall, 1861.

"Visit to Newgate." *Sketches by Boz*. London: Penguin, 1995.

Douglas-Fairhurst, Robert. *Victorian Afterlives: The Shaping of Influence in Nineteenth-Century Literature*. London: Oxford University Press, 2004.

Duffy, Eamon. *The Stripping of the Altars: Traditional Religion in England 1400–1580*. New Haven, CT: Yale University Press, 1992.

Duncan, Ian. *Scott's Shadow: The Novel in Romantic Edinburgh*. Princeton, NJ: Princeton University Press, 2007.

Eagleton, Terry. *Myths of Power: A Marxist Study of the Brontës*. Basingstoke: Macmillan Press, 1975.

Edgecombe, Rodney Stenning. "Violence, Death and Euphemism in *Great Expectations*." *VIJ: Victorians Institute Journal* 22 (1994): 85–98.

Edwards, Elizabeth, and Janice Hart, eds. *Photographs, Objects, Histories: On the Materiality of Images*. New York: Routledge, 2004.

Elfenbein, Andrew. *Byron and the Victorians*. Cambridge: Cambridge University Press, 1996.

Eliot, George. *The George Eliot Letters*. Ed. Gordon S. Haight. Vol. 6. New Haven, CT: Yale University Press, 1955.

Romola. Philadelphia: Lippincott, 1902.

Ende, Stuart A. *Keats and the Sublime*. New Haven, CT: Yale University Press, 1976.

Evans, Joan. *A History of Jewellery, 1100–1870*. Boston: Boston Book and Art, 1970.

The Family Friend 5 (1853).

Fay, Elizabeth. *Fashioning Faces: The Portraitive Mode in British Romanticism.* Lebanon: University of New Hampshire Press, 2010.

Fincham, Kenneth, and Nicholas Tyacke. *Altars Restored: The Changing Face of English Religious Worship, 1547–c.1700.* Oxford: Oxford University Press, 2007.

Finucane, Ronald C. *Miracles and Pilgrims: Popular Beliefs in Medieval England.* London: Dent, 1977.

Flaubert, Gustave. *Madame Bovary.* New York: Penguin, 2002.

Forster, John. *The Life of Dickens.* Philadelphia: Lippincott, 1873.

Fosso, Kurt. *Buried Communities: Wordsworth and the Bonds of Mourning.* Albany: State University of New York, 2004.

Fredeman, W. E. "The Letters of Pictor Ignotus: William Bell Scott's Correspondence with Alice Boyd 1859–1884." *Bulletin of the John Rylands Library* 58.2 (1976), 306–352.

Freedgood, Elaine. *The Ideas in Things: Fugitive Meaning in the Victorian Novel.* Chicago: University of Chicago Press, 2006.

Froude, James Anthony. *Thomas Carlyle: A History of His Life in London 1834–1881.* Vol. 1. New York: Scribner, 1884.

Fry, Paul H. *The Poet's Calling in the English Ode.* New Haven, CT: Yale University Press, 1980.

Fumerton, Patricia. *Cultural Aesthetics: Renaissance Literature and the Practice of Social Ornament.* Chicago: University of Chicago Press, 1991.

Fuss, Diana. "Corpse Poem." *Critical Inquiry* 30 (2003), 1–30.

Fussell, Paul. *The Great War and Modern Memory.* New York: Oxford University Press, 1975.

Gallagher, Catherine. *The Body Economic: Life, Death and Sensation in Political Economy and the Victorian Novel.* Princeton, NJ: Princeton University Press, 2006.

Gallagher, Catherine, and Stephen Greenblatt. *Practicing New Historicism.* Chicago: University of Chicago Press, 2000.

Gallaway-Mitchell, Lee Anne. "'Words Survive': Death and Dying in Women's Letters." Dissertation, University of Texas, Austin, 2008.

Garofalo, Daniela. "Impossible Love and Commodity Culture in Emily Brontë's *Wuthering Heights.*" *ELH* 75.4 (2008), 819–840.

Garson, Marjorie. *Hardy's Fables of Integrity: Woman, Body, Text.* New York: Oxford University Press, 1992.

Gaskell, Elizabeth. *The Life of Charlotte Brontë.* New York: Penguin, 1997.

Gates, Susan. "Poetics, Metaphysics, Genre: The Stanza Form of *In Memoriam.*" *Victorian Poetry* 37 (1999), 507–19.

Geerken, Ingrid. "'The Dead are not Annihilated': Mortal Regret in *Wuthering Heights.*" *Journal of Narrative Theory* 34 (2004), 373–406.

Gérin, Winifred. *Emily Brontë: A Biography.* Oxford: Clarendon Press, 1971.

Gibson, Ian. *The Erotomaniac: The Secret Life of Henry Spencer Ashbee.* New York: De Capo, 2001.

Gilbert, Sandra, and Susan Gubar. *The Madwoman in the Attic; The Woman Writer and the Nineteenth-Century Literary Imagination.* New Haven, CT: Yale University Press, 2000.

Gill, Stephen. *William Wordsworth: A Life*. New York: Oxford University Press, 1990.

Gilmartin, Sophie. *Ancestry and Narrative in Nineteenth-Century British Literature: Blood Relations from Edgeworth to Hardy*. Cambridge: Cambridge University Press, 1998.

Gitter, Elisabeth. "The Power of Women's Hair in the Victorian Imagination." *PMLA* 99 (1984), 936–954.

Godwin, William. *Essay on Sepulchres: Or, Proposal for Erecting Some Memorial of the Illustrious Dead*. London: W. Miller, 1809.

Goncourt, Edmond, and Jules Goncourt. *Pages from the Goncourt Journals*. Ed. Robert Baldick. New York: New York Review of Books, 2006.

Goodwin, Sarah. *Kitsch and Culture: The Dance of Death in Nineteenth-Century Literature and Graphic Arts*. London: Garland, 1988.

Gordon, Beverly. "Woman's Domestic Body: The Conceptual Conflation of Women and Interiors in the Industrial Age." *Winterthur Portfolio* 31.4 (1996), 281–301.

Gregor, Ian. *The Great Web: The Form of Hardy's Major Fiction*. London: Faber and Faber, 1974.

Griffin, Susan M. *Anti-Catholicism and Nineteenth-Century Fiction*. Cambridge: Cambridge University Press, 2004.

Grinsted, T. P. *The Last Homes of Departed Genius*. London: Routledge, 1867.

Gross, Michael. "Aspects of Time in *Far From the Madding Crowd*." *Thomas Hardy Journal* 6.3 (1990), 43–53.

Groth, Helen. *Victorian Photography and Literary Nostalgia*. London: Oxford University Press, 2003.

Hair, Donald. "Soul and Spirit in *In Memoriam*." *Victorian Poetry* 34.2 (1996): 175–191.

Hallam, Elizabeth, and Jenny Hockey. *Death, Memory and Material Culture*. Oxford: Berg, 2001.

Hardy, Florence Emily. *The Life of Thomas Hardy*. London: Macmillan, 1962.

Hardy, Thomas. *The Complete Poems of Thomas Hardy*. Ed. James Gibson. New York: Macmillan, 1976.

  Far From the Madding Crowd. London: Macmillan, 1975.

  Mayor of Casterbridge. New York: Penguin, 1997.

  The Well-Beloved. London: Macmillan, 1975.

  Woodlanders. London: Penguin, 1994.

Harris, Jose. *Private Lives, Public Spirit: A Social History of Britain 1870–1914*. New York: Oxford University Press, 1993.

Harvey, Anthony, and Richard Mortimer. *The Funeral Effigies of Westminster Abbey*. Woodbridge: Boydell, 1994.

Heidegger, Martin. *Being and Time*. Trans. Joan Stambaugh. Albany: State University of New York Press, 1996.

Herrmann, Frank. *The English as Collectors: A Documentary Chrestomathy*. New York: Norton, 1972.

Hibbert, Christopher. *Queen Victoria: A Personal History*. London: Harper Collins, 2000.

Holm, Christian. "Sentimental Cuts: Eighteenth–Century Mourning Jewelry with Hair." *Eighteenth–Century Studies* 38 (2004), 139–143.

Holmes, Oliver Wendell. "The Stereoscope and the Stereograph." *Atlantic Monthly* (1859), 747.

Holubetz, Margarete. "Death-Bed Scenes in Victorian Fiction." *English Studies* 67.1 (1986), 14–34.

Homans, Margaret. "Repression and Sublimation of Nature in *Wuthering Heights*." *PMLA* 93.1 (1978), 9–19.

Hopkins, Brooke. "Keats and the Uncanny: 'This Living Hand.'" *The Kenyon Review* 11.4 (1989), 28–40.

Hotten, John Camden. *Charles Dickens: The Story of His Life*. London: J. C. Hotten, 1872.

Hotz, Mary Elizabeth. *Literary Remains: Representations of Death and Burial in Victorian England*. Albany: State University of New York Press, 2009.

"Human Skin as Binding." *Bookworm: An Illustrated Treasury of Old-Time Literature* January 1 (1891), 148.

"Human Skin as a Binding." *Bookworm: An Illustrated Treasury of Old-Time Literature* January 1 (1893), 103.

Hutter, Albert. "The Novelist as Resurrectionist: Dickens and the Dilemma of Death." *Dickens Studies Annual* 12 (1983), 1–39.

Hutton, Laurence. "A Collection of Death Masks." *Harper's New Monthly Magazine* 85 (1892), 904–916.

Inman, Laura. " 'The Awful Event' in *Wuthering Heights*." *Brontë Studies: The Journal of the Brontë Society* 33 (2008), 192–202.

Jacobs, Joseph. "The Dying of Death." *Fortnightly Review* 72 (1899), 264–269.

Jacobus, Mary. "Hardy's Magian Retrospect." *Essays in Criticism* 32.3 (1982), 258–279.

Jalland, Patricia. *Death in the Victorian Family*. New York: Oxford University Press, 1996.

Janes, Dominic. *Victorian Reformation: The Fight Over Idolatry in the Church of England, 1840–60*. Oxford: Oxford University Press, 2009.

Johnson, Ellen Kennedy. "'The Beauty of Her Hands': The Glove and the Making of the Middle-Class Body." *Material Women, 1750–1950: Consuming Desires and Collecting Practices*. Eds. Maureen Daly Goggin and Beth Fowkes Tobin. London: Ashgate, 2009.

Jordan, Jane. *Josephine Butler*. London: John Murray, 2001.

Joseph, Gerhard. "Commodifying Tennyson: The Historical Transformation of 'Brand Loyalty.'" *Victorian Poetry* 34.2 (1996), 133–147.

Joseph, Gerhard, and Herbert Tucker. "Passing On: Death." *A Companion to Victorian Literature and Culture*. Ed. Herbert Tucker. Malden, MA: Blackwell, 1999. 110–124.

Jupp, Peter, and C. Gittings. *Death in England: An Illustrated History*. New Brunswick, NJ: Rutgers University Press, 2000.

Keats, John. *The Poetical Works and Other Writings of John Keats*. Ed. H. Buxton Forman. Vol. 8. New York: Phaeton, 1970.

   The Poems of John Keats. Ed. Jack Stillinger. Cambridge, MA: Harvard University Press, 1978.

Kincaid, James. "Forgetting to Remember: Tennyson's Happy Losses." *Victorian Poetry* 30.3/4 (1992), 197–209.

Kissane, James. "Tennyson: The Passion of the Past and the Curse of Time." *ELH* 32.1 (1965), 85–109.

Kitton, Frederic George. *Charles Dickens by Pen and Pencil*. London: F. T. Sabin, 1890.

Krauss, Rosalind. *The Originality of the Avant-Garde and Other Modernist Myths*. Cambridge, MA: MIT Press, 1984.

Kroll, Allison Adler. "Tennyson and the Metaphysics of Material Culture: The Early Poetry." *Victorian Poetry* 47.3 (2009), 461–480.

Lamb, Lady Caroline. *The Whole Disgraceful Truth: Selected Letters of Lady Caroline Lamb*. Ed. Paul Douglass. New York: Palgrave Macmillan, 2006.

Law, Jules David. "Sleeping Figures: Hardy, History, and the Gendered Body." *ELH* 65.1 (1998), 223–257.

Lee, Hermione. *Virginia Woolf's Nose: Essays on Biography*. Princeton, NJ: Princeton University Press, 2007.

Levine, George. *Dying to Know: Scientific Epistemology and Narrative in Victorian England*. Chicago: University of Chicago Press, 2002.

Linkman, Audrey. *Photography and Death*. London: Reaktion, 2011.

Lister, Thomas Henry. *Granby*. London: Colvin, 1829.

Livingstone, Justin D. "A 'Body' of Evidence: The Posthumous Presentation of David Livingstone." *Victorian Literature and Culture* 40 (2012), 1–24.

Llewellyn, Nigel. *The Art of Death: Visual Culture in the English Death Ritual c. 1500–c. 1800*. London: Reaktion, 1991.

Logan, Peter. *Victorian Fetishism: Intellectuals and Primitives*. Albany: State University of New York Press, 2009.

Logan, Thad. *The Victorian Parlour: A Cultural Study*. New York: Cambridge University Press, 2001.

Manseau, Peter. *Rag and Bone: A Journey Among the World's Holy Dead*. New York: Henry Holt, 2009.

Mansell, Darrel. "Displacing Hallam's Tomb in Tennyson's *In Memoriam*." *Victorian Poetry* 36.1 (1998), 97–111.

Marsh, Jan. *Dante Gabriel Rossetti: Painter and Poet*. London: Orion, 2006.

Martens, Britta. "Death as Spectacle: The Paris Morgue in Dickens and Browning." *Dickens Studies Annual* 39 (2008), 223–248.

Martin, Robert Bernard. *Tennyson: The Unquiet Heart*. New York: Oxford University Press, 1980.

Matthews, Samantha. *Poetical Remains: Poets' Graves, Bodies, and Books in the Nineteenth Century*. New York: Oxford University Press, 2004.

McGann, Jerome. *Dante Gabriel Rossetti and the Game That Must Be Lost*. New Haven, CT: Yale University Press, 2000.

Miller, J. Hillis. *The Disappearance of God: Five Nineteenth-Century Writers*. Cambridge, MA: Harvard University Press, 1963.

    Thomas Hardy: Distance and Desire. Cambridge, MA: Harvard University Press, 1970.

Versions of Pygmalion. Cambridge, MA: Harvard University Press, 1990.

Miller, Lucasta. *The Brontë Myth*. London: Jonathon Cape, 2001.

Miller, Pamela. "Hair Jewelry as Fetish." *Objects of Special Devotion: Fetishes and Fetishism in Popular Culture*. Ed. Ray B. Browne. Bowling Green, OH: Bowling Green University Press, n.d.

Millgate, Michael. *Testamentary Acts: Browning, Tennyson, James, Hardy*. New York: Oxford University Press, 1992.

Thomas Hardy: A Biography Revisited. New York: Oxford University Press, 2004.

Milman, H. *A History of Latin Christianity*. New York: Armstrong, 1903.

Milton, John. *The Complete Poems*. Vol. 4. New York: Collier, 1909.

Mitchell, Allan. "The Paris Morgue as a Social Institution in the Nineteenth Century." *Francia* 3 (1976), 581–596.

Moore, Carlisle. "Faith, Doubt, and Mystical Experience in 'In Memoriam.'" *Victorian Studies* 7.2 (1963), 155–169.

Morgan, Rosemarie. *Cancelled Words: Rediscovering Thomas Hardy*. London: Routledge, 1992.

Morgentaler, Goldie. "Executing Beauty: Dickens and the Aesthetics of Death" *Dickens Studies Annual* 30 (2001), 45–57.

Motion, Andrew. *Keats*. London: Faber and Faber, 1975.

Munn, Geoffrey. *The Triumph of Love: Jewelry 1530–1930*. London: Thames and Hudson, 1993.

Official Descriptive and Illustrated Catalogue of the Great Exhibition of 1851. London: Spicer Brothers, 1851.

Oppenheim, Janet. *The Other World: Spiritualism and Psychical Research in England 1850–1914*. New York: Cambridge University Press, 1985.

Ousby, Ian. *The Englishman's England: Taste, Travel, and the Rise of Tourism*. New York: Cambridge University Press, 1990.

Owen, Alex. *The Darkened Room: Women, Power, and Spiritualism*. Philadelphia: University of Pennsylvania Press, 1990.

"Painters Behind the Scenes." *The Edinburgh Review* 185 (1897), 487–506.

Parker, David. "Dickens and the Death of Mary Hogarth." *Dickens Quarterly* 13.2 (1996), 67–75.

Pascoe, Judith. *The Hummingbird Cabinet: A Rare and Curious History of Romantic Collectors*. Ithaca, NY: Cornell University Press, 2006.

Pater, Walter. *The Renaissance: Studies in Art and Poetry*. New York: Dover, 2005.

Paz, D. G. *Popular Anti-Catholicism in Mid-Victorian England*. Stanford: Stanford University Press, 1992.

Pearce, Susan. *On Collecting: An Investigation into Collecting in the European Tradition*. London: Routledge, 1995.

Peltason, Timothy. *Reading In Memoriam*. Princeton, NJ: Princeton University Press, 1985.

Plotz, John. *Portable Property: Victorian Culture on the Move*. Princeton, NJ: Princeton University Press, 2009.

Pointon, Marcia. *Brilliant Effects: A Cultural History of Gem Stones and Jewellery.* New Haven, CT: Yale University Press, 2009.

"Materializing Mourning: Hair, Jewellery and the Body." *Material Memories: Design and Evocation.* Ed. Marius Kwint, Christopher Breward, Jeremy Aynsley. New York: Oxford University Press, 1999.

"Wearing Memory: Mourning, Jewellery and the Body." *Trauer Tragen – Trauer Zeigen: Inszenierungen der Geschlechter.* Ed. Gisela Ecker. Munich: Fink, 1999.

Polhemus, Robert. *Erotic Faith: Being in Love from Jane Austen to D. H. Lawrence.* Chicago: University of Chicago Press, 1990.

Pope-Hennessy, James. *Monckton Milnes: The Years of Promise, 1809–1851.* New York: Farrar, Straus and Cudahy, 1955.

Praz, Mario. *The Romantic Agony.* New York: Oxford, 1978.

Puckle, Bertram. *Funeral Customs: Their Origin and Development.* London: T. Werner Laurie, 1926.

Richardson, Ruth. *Death, Dissection, and the Destitute.* Chicago: University of Chicago Press, 2000.

Ricks, Christopher. *Tennyson.* New York: Macmillan, 1972.

Ritchie, Carson I. A. *The British Dog: Its History from Earliest Times.* London: Robert Hale, 1981.

Robertson, Oliver. "Bound for Glory: The Macabre Practice of Book Bindings Made of Human Skin." *Rare Book Review* 33 (2006), 29–31.

Robson, Catherine. "'Where Heaves the Turf': Thomas Hardy and the Boundaries of the Earth." *Victorian Literature and Culture* 32.2 (2004), 495–503.

Rosenberg, John. "Stopping for Death: Tennyson's 'In Memoriam.' " *Victorian Poetry* 30.3/4 (1992), 291–330.

Rossetti, Dante Gabriel. *Collected Poetry and Prose.* Ed. Jerome McGann. New Haven, CT: Yale University Press, 2003.

The Correspondence of Dante Gabriel Rossetti. Ed. William Fredeman. Vol. 4. Cambridge: Brewer, 2002.

Poems. Ed. Oswald Doughty. London: Dent, 1957.

Sacks, Peter. *The English Elegy: Studies in the Genre from Spenser to Yeats.* Baltimore: Johns Hopkins University Press, 1985.

Sanchez-Eppler, Karen. "Decomposing: Wordsworth's Poetry of Epitaph and English Burial Reform." *Nineteenth-Century Literature* 42.4 (1988), 415–431.

Sanders, Andrew. *Charles Dickens: Resurrectionist.* London: Macmillan, 1982.

Scarisbrick, Diana. "The Aberdeen Jewel." *Burlington Magazine* 130 (1988), 427–428.

Ancestral Jewels. London: Deutsch, 1989.

Scarry, Elaine. "Work and the Body in Hardy." *Representations* 3 (1983), 90–123.

Schaffer, Talia. *Novel Craft: Victorian Domestic Handicraft and Nineteenth-Century Fiction.* New York: Oxford University Press, 2011.

Sheumaker, Helen. *Love Entwined: The Curious History of Hairwork in America.* Philadelphia: University of Pennsylvania Press, 2007.

Schiefelbein, Michael. "Little Nell, Catholicism, and Dickens's Investigation of Death." *Dickens Quarterly* 9.3 (1992), 115–125.

Schor, Esther. *Bearing the Dead: the British Culture of Mourning from the Enlightenment to Victoria.* Princeton, NJ: Princeton University Press, 1994.

Scott, Patrick. "Tennyson, Lincolnshire, and Provinciality: The Topographical Narrative of *In Memoriam.*" *Victorian Poetry* 34.1 (1996), 39–51.

Semmel, Stuart. "Reading the Tangible Past: British Tourism, Collecting, and Memory After Waterloo." *Representations* 69 (2000), 9–37.

Sendry, Joseph. "*In Memoriam* and *Lycidas.*" *PMLA* 82.5 (1967), 437–443.

Sharp, William. *Dante Gabriel Rossetti: A Record and a Study.* London: Macmillan, 1882.

Shaw, W. David. "Tennyson's Late Elegies." *Victorian Poetry* 12.1 (1974), 1–12.

Shelley, Percy Bysshe. *The Complete Poems of Percy Bysshe Shelley.* New York: Modern Library, 1994.

   The Complete Works of Percy Bysshe Shelley. Ed. Roger Ingpen and Walter E. Peck. Vol. 7. London: Ernest Benn, 1965.

Shonfield, Zuzanna. *The Precariously Privileged: A Professional Family in Victorian London.* Oxford: Oxford University Press, 1987.

Sinfield, Alan. *Alfred Tennyson.* New York: Oxford, 1986.

Slater, Michael. *Charles Dickens.* New York: Yale University Press, 2009.

Sontag, Susan. *On Photography.* New York: Farrar, Straus and Giroux, 1977.

Sox, David. *Relics and Shrines.* London: Allen and Unwin, 1985.

Speight, Alexanna. *The Lock of Hair.* London: Goubaud and Son, 1872.

Spencer, Herbert. *Principles of Sociology.* Vol. 1. New York: Appleton, 1898.

Stallybrass, Peter. "Marx's Coat." *Border Fetishisms: Material Objects in Unstable Spaces.* Ed. Patricia Spyer. New York: Routledge, 1998.

   "Worn Worlds: Clothes, Mourning, and the Life of Things." *Cultural Memory and the Construction of Identity.* Eds. Dan Ben-Amos and Liliane Weissberg. Detroit, MI: Wayne State University Press, 1999. 27–44.

Stewart, Garrett. *Death Sentences: Styles of Dying in British Fiction.* Cambridge, MA: Harvard University Press, 1984.

Stewart, Susan. *On Longing: Narratives of the Miniature, the Gigantic, the Souvenir, the Collection.* Durham, NC: Duke University Press, 1993.

Stone, Harry. *The Night Side of Dickens: Cannibalism, Passion, Necessity.* Columbus: The Ohio State University Press, 1994.

Strachey, Lytton. *Queen Victoria.* London: Chatto and Windus, 1921.

Strange, Julie-Marie. *Death, Grief and Poverty in Britain, 1870–1914.* Cambridge: Cambridge University Press, 2005.

Taylor, Dennis. "Thomas Hardy and Thomas Gray: The Poet's Currency." *ELH* 65.2 (1993), 451–477.

Taylor, Lou. *Mourning Dress: A Costume and Social History.* London: Allen and Unwin, 1983.

Tennyson, Alfred. *The Poems of Tennyson.* Ed. Christopher Ricks. 2nd ed. London: Longman, 1987.

Thackeray, William Makepeace. *The History of Henry Esmond.* London: Macmillan, 1905.

Thurschwell, Pamela. *Literature, Technology and Magical Thinking, 1880–1920.* New York: Cambridge University Press, 2001.

Tick, Stanley. "Cruncher on Resurrection: A Tale of Charles Dickens." *Renascence* 33 (1981), 86–98.

Tillotson, Kathleen. "'Haworth Churchyard': The Making of Arnold's Elegy." *Brontë Society Transactions* 15 (1967), 105–122.

Tomalin, Claire. *Thomas Hardy.* New York: Penguin, 2006.

Tomko, Michael. "Varieties of Geological Experience: Religion, Body, and Spirit in Tennyson's *In Memoriam* and Lyell's *Principles of Geology.*" *Victorian Poetry* 42.2 (2004), 113–134.

Trelawny, Edward. *Records of Shelley, Byron, and the Author.* New York: New York Review of Books, 2000.

Tromp, Marlene. *Altered States: Sex, Nation, Drugs, and Self-Transformation in Victorian Spiritualism.* Albany: State University of New York Press, 2006.

Vine, Steven. *Emily Brontë.* New York: Twayne, 1998.

Ward, Mrs. Humphry. *The History of David Grieve.* London: Macmillan, 1891.

Watson, Nicola. *The Literary Tourist: Readers and Places in Romantic and Victorian Britain.* New York: Palgrave Macmillan, 2006.

Weiner, Annette. *Inalienable Possessions: The Paradox of Keeping-While-Giving.* Berkeley: University of California Press, 1992.

Wesley, Charles. "Hymn XXII: On the Corpse of a Believer." *Hymns on the great festivals, and other occasions.* Music by John Frederick Lampe. London: Cooper, 1746.

Westover, Paul. *Necromanticism: Traveling to Meet the Dead, 1750–1860.* New York: Palgrave Macmillan, 2012.

Wheeler, Michael. *Death and the Future Life in Victorian Literature and Theology.* New York: Cambridge University Press, 1990.

Widdowson, Peter. *Hardy in History: A Study in Literary Sociology.* London: Routledge, 1998.

Winter, Jay. *Sites of Memory, Sites of Mourning: The Great War in European Cultural History.* New York: Cambridge University Press, 1995.

Wolffe, John. *Great Deaths: Grieving, Religion, and Nationhood in Victorian and Edwardian Britain.* Oxford: Oxford University Press, 2000.

Wordsworth, William. *The Letters of William and Dorothy Wordsworth.* Ed. Alan G. Hill. Vol. 6. 2nd ed. Oxford: Clarendon, 1982.

   The Poetical Works of William Wordsworth. Ed. E. De Selincourt. Oxford: Clarendon, 1940.

Wotton, George. *Thomas Hardy: Towards a Materialist Criticism.* Totowa, NJ: Barnes and Noble, 1985.

Young, G. M. *Victorian England: Portrait of an Age.* London: Oxford University Press, 1936.

Index

Figures in italics indicate captions.

middle classes
  distancing living from dead, 170*n*15
  and photography, 159
Millais, Sir John Everett, 46, 190*n*3
  Dickens's death mask, 74
  Christ in the House of His Parents, 46
  Lorenzo and Isabella, 44
  Ophelia, 47
Miller, J. Hillis, 59, 72, 73, 85, 98, 152, 157,
    200–1*n*28
Millgate, Michael, 155–6
Milliken, Richard Nicholls, 160
Milnes, Richard Monckton, 43–4
Milton, John, 24, 41, 132
  "Lycidas," 120–1
mind
  as a mansion with many rooms, 111–12
  memory of the lost one located in, 112
miniatures, 7
miracles
  blood, 19
  false, 27
  healing, 19, 55
mirrors, covering, 58, 184*n*37
modernity, 51
  inauthenticity of, 150
  looming doubts of, 124, 154
  scientific, 153
  secular, 153
monasteries
  dissolution of, 22
  removal of relics from, 22
Monck, General, Duke of Albemarle, 195*n*63
Montrose, Duke of, 173*n*19
Montrose, James, Marquis of, 173*n*19
monumentum, 113
More, Sir Thomas, 22
morgue, Victorian visits to, 83, 93–4, 194*n*45
Morris, May, 211*n*78
Morris, William, 46, 147, 148, 211*n*78
mortality
  gothic approach to the body and mortality,
    30
  literary ideas about, 3
  thoughts of, 35
Mortlake Cemetery, London, *110*
Motion, Andrew, 36, 179*n*97
mourning culture, 183*n*24
  elaborate and ritualistic, 57
  hairwork, 134
mourning jewelry, 89, 148, 176*n*60, 191*n*18,
    195*n*70, 212*n*84
Moyse's Hall Museum, Bury St. Edmunds,
    Suffolk, *93*, 98
Munro, Alex, 75

Musée Carnavalet, Paris, 200*n*17
museums, 31

Naples, Cardinal of, 19
Napoleon Bonaparte
  and Byron, 25
  relics of, 25, 55, 175*n*50, 182*n*11
Natalia, St., 199*n*11
National Gallery, London, 31
National Gallery of British Art. *See* Tate Britain
National Maritime Museum, London, 175*n*50
National Portrait Gallery, London, 31, 191*n*12,
    191*n*14
nationalism, 25, 30
Natural History Museum, London, 31
natural supernaturalism, 33, 50
"necro-tourism," 107
Nelson, Admiral Lord Horatio, relics of, 55, 56,
    131, 132, 175–6*n*50, 189*n*80
Nevers, central France, 55
Neville, Lady, 131
New belle assemblée, 132
Newgate Prison, London, 91
Newman, John Henry, 65
Nile, Battle of the (1798), 189*n*80

objecthood, 2, 71, 83, 137, 162
Oppenheim, Janet, 124
organ-replacement, 168
other, the
  death of, 36
  emerging philosophies of, 29
  and the self, 10, 29–30, 33, 38, 41
  and subjectivity, 10
otherness, 3, 4
ottava rima, 40
Otto III, Holy Roman Emperor, 205*n*12
Ousby, Ian, 34
Owen, Alex, 123
Oxford movement, 65–6

paganism, 70, 141
Pains Hill, Surrey, 109
paintings, 7
  of beautiful corpses or deaths, 46, 181*n*132
  painted photographs, 163
Palmer, Dorothea, 134
Palmer, Emily, 135
Parker, Richard, 196*n*79
Parnell, Thomas, 34
Parry, Jonathan, 188*n*70
Pascoe, Judith, 30, 31–2, 56, 131
Pater, Walter, 47
Patman (Bateman), Mary, 198*n*104
Patricia, St., 19

CAMBRIDGE STUDIES IN NINETEENTH-CENTURY LITERATURE AND CULTURE

GENERAL EDITOR: Gillian Beer, *University of Cambridge*

Titles published